LOVE & WAR

Enjoy. I think this is a good book for you to Read. Thought about in the Navy.

Hugs.

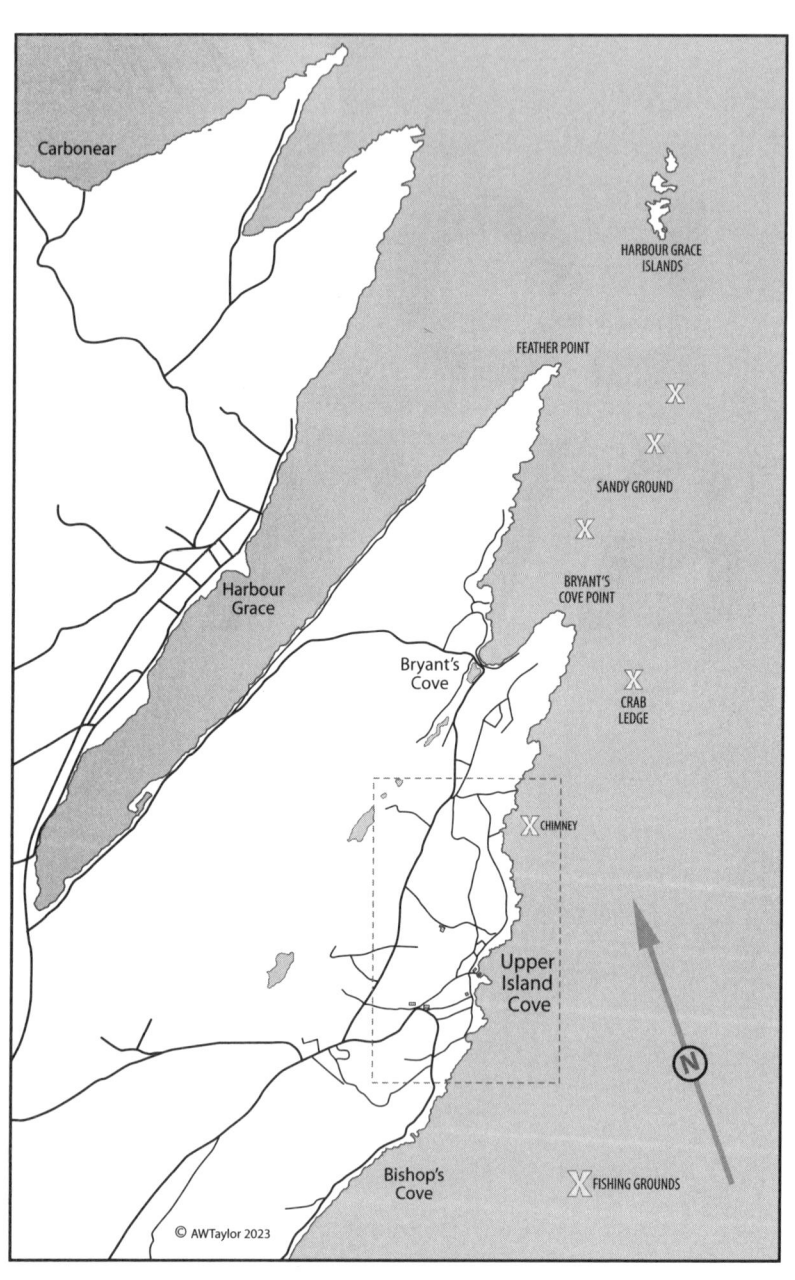

LOVE & WAR
THE TRUE STORY OF WILLIAM AND EDITH LUNDRIGAN

ROBERT W. LUNDRIGAN

FLANKER PRESS LIMITED
ST. JOHN'S

Library and Archives Canada Cataloguing in Publication

Title: Love and war : the true story of William and Edith Lundrigan / Robert W. Lundrigan.
Names: Lundrigan, Robert W., author.
Description: Includes bibliographical references and index.
Identifiers: Canadiana (print) 20230505295 | Canadiana (ebook) 20230509819 | ISBN 9781774571620 (softcover) | ISBN 9781774571637 (EPUB) | ISBN 9781774571644 (PDF)
Subjects: LCSH: Lundrigan, William. | LCSH: Lundrigan, Edith. | LCSH: World War, 1939-1945—Personal narratives, Canadian. | LCSH: Upper Island Cove (N.L.)—Biography. | LCGFT: Personal narratives. | LCGFT: Biographies.
Classification: LCC FC2199.U67 Z48 2023 | DDC 971.8—dc23

© 2023 by Robert W. Lundrigan

ALL RIGHTS RESERVED. No part of the work covered by the copyright hereon may be reproduced or used in any form or by any means—graphic, electronic or mechanical—without the written permission of the publisher. Any request for photocopying, recording, taping, or information storage and retrieval systems of any part of this book shall be directed to Access Copyright, The Canadian Copyright Licensing Agency, 1 Yonge Street, Suite 800, Toronto, ON M5E 1E5. This applies to classroom use as well. For an Access Copyright licence, visit www.accesscopyright.ca or call toll-free to 1-800-893-5777.

PRINTED IN CANADA

This paper has been certified to meet the environmental and social standards of the Forest Stewardship Council® (FSC®) and comes from responsibly managed forests, and verified recycled sources.

Cover Design by Graham Blair

FLANKER PRESS LTD.
1243 KENMOUNT ROAD
PARADISE, NL
A1L 0V8

TELEPHONE: (709) 739-4477   FAX: (709) 739-4420   TOLL-FREE: 1-866-739-4420
WWW.FLANKERPRESS.COM

9 8 7 6 5 4 3 2 1

We acknowledge the [financial] support of the Government of Canada. *Nous reconnaissons l'appui [financier] du gouvernement du Canada.* We acknowledge the support of the Canada Council for the Arts, which last year invested $153 million to bring the arts to Canadians throughout the country. *Nous remercions le Conseil des arts du Canada de son soutien. L'an dernier, le Conseil a investi 153 millions de dollars pour mettre de l'art dans la vie des Canadiennes et des Canadiens de tout le pays.* We acknowledge the financial support of the Government of Newfoundland and Labrador, Department of Tourism, Culture, Arts and Recreation for our publishing activities.

Contents

Introduction xi

1 — Willie 1
That Terrible Day, November 3, 1940
300 Miles Northwest of Bloody Foreland, Ireland

2 — Willie 8
Becoming an Adult, November 1935 – September 1939

3 — Willie 19
Time to Decide, September 3, 1939

4 — Edie 22
Childhood Memories, 1923–1939

5 — Willie 28
The Early Days, October 25, 1939 – August 1940

6 — Willie 36
I Too Thought of My Mother, November 3, 1940

7 — Edie 45
Boyfriends and Bombings, 1940–1941

8 — Willie 50
Scapa Flow, August 1, 1941 – September 28, 1941

9 — Willie 57
The Convoy and the Caribou
November 1941 – November 1942

10 — Edie 62
Will My Brother Come Home? Spring 1942

11 — Willie 66
After Asbury Park, Winter 1943 – Fall 1943

12 — Willie 78
Loaned to America, January – March 1944

13 — Willie 84
The Real Fight for Freedom, June 6, 1944

14 — Edie 90
Tying a Knot in Hell, November 1944 – June 1945

15 — Willie 98
No Longer Needed, January 19, 1946

16 — Edie 106
Can I Ever Forgive? September 1945

17 — Willie 110
Upper Island Cove is Calling, April 1949

18 — Edie 117
My First Ocean Voyage, April 5–11, 1949

19 — Edie 124
Meeting Aunt Sis, April 1949

20 — Edie 130
Going Back in Time, 1949–1960

21 — Willie 147
'Tis All Right . . . But 'Tis No Good, 1949–1961

22 — Willie 152
Comrades, 1957–1963

23 — Willie 156
Five-Point Apples, 1963–1972

24 — Willie 170
A Lighter Load, 1964–1972

25 — Willie 178
Life is a Roller Coaster, 1964–1972

26 — Willie 186
Ocean Therapy, 1972–1992

27 — Willie 206
Trials and Tribulations, 1994–2004

28 — Edie 215
Digging Deeper, 1994–2004

29 — Edie 220
All Roads Lead Home, 2005

30 — Robert 233
The Last Post, 2006

31 — Edie 239
Life After Bill, 2006–2016

32 — Edie 247
Can I Finally Forgive? 2012–2016

Conclusion — Robert 253
Forever England, 2016

Acknowledgements 265
Index 271

INSPIRED BY:

My wife, Bernice Lundrigan, who through unfathomable love and selfless generosity has given me life;
our daughters, Jennifer Lundrigan and Stephanie (Lundrigan) Andrews, for whom I am thankful every day to be a dad.
And our two wonderful grandchildren,
Fiona Elizabeth Lundrigan Hagerty
and
Benjamin Robert Hagerty.

DEDICATED TO:

Edith "Edie" Ellen Emily (England) Lundrigan and William "Willie" Lundrigan, for the incredible love and the unquenchable determination to always want the best for their children, regardless of the challenge before them. They have always motivated me to keep looking forward. Their lifetime appetite for knowledge, especially through reading, made them both true lifelong learners.
And siblings,
Jean (Lundrigan) Eveleigh and Philip Andrew Lundrigan,
both gone way too soon but so lovingly remembered.

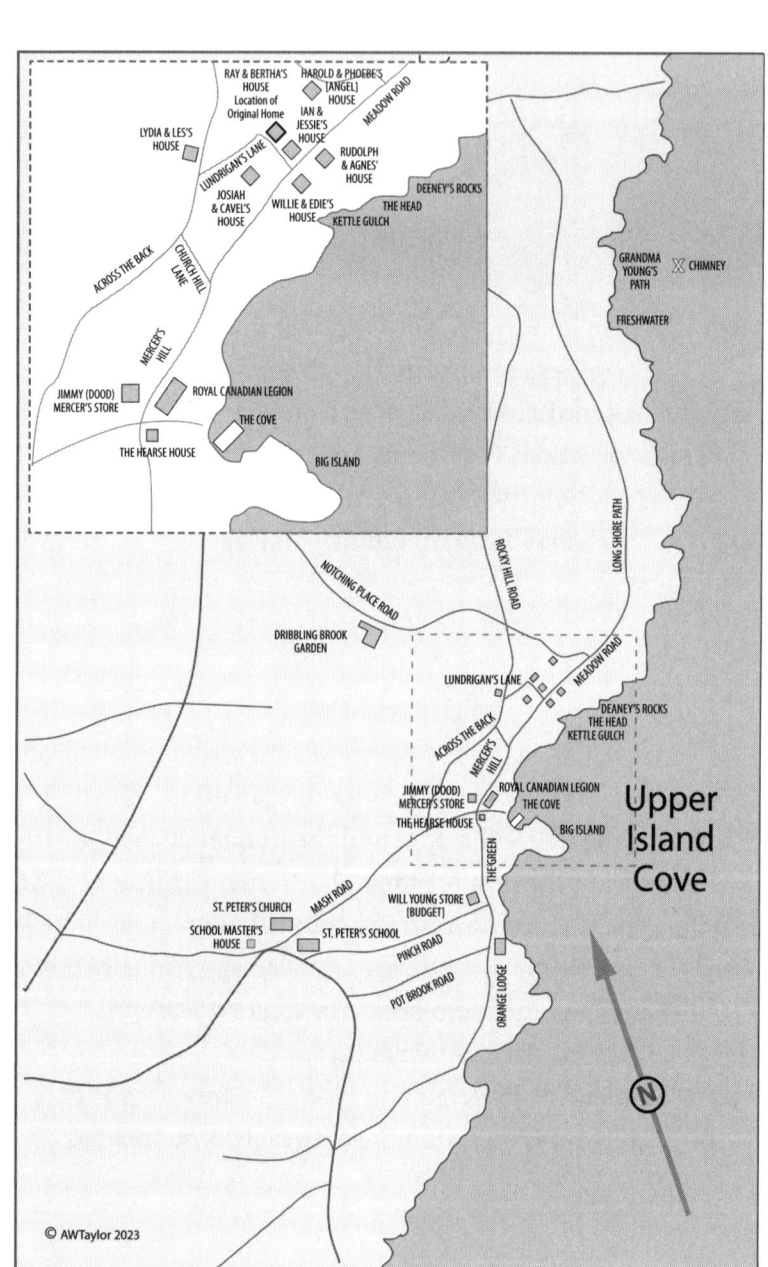

Introduction

Willie and his buddy Joe stood on the step outside the general store in Upper Island Cove, Newfoundland, and listened. Edie sat between her mother and father at their home in Essex, England, and listened. They both heard:

> "The task will be hard. There may be dark days ahead, and war can no longer be confined to the battlefield, but we can only do the right as we see the right, and reverently commit our cause to God. If one and all we keep resolutely faithful to it, ready for whatever service or sacrifice it may demand, then with God's help, we shall prevail."
>
> — King George VI, Speech to the Commonwealth, September 3, 1939

Little did this eighteen-year-old boy from Newfoundland and the barely sixteen-year-old girl from England realize the importance of this speech in shaping the rest of their long lives together.

I don't know how I imagined men and women fought, struggled, and suffered during the battles of World War II. But through conversations and the various writings of their stories, such understandings, as well as the stories of their lives together, were gradually revealed. In very different ways, each of my parents experienced what my siblings and I, even now, cannot quite imagine or fully comprehend.

William and Edith Lundrigan, always referred to casually as Willie and Edie, were both quiet, humble, and unassuming people who had lived most of their adult lives in a small bungalow at the edge of the ocean in the picturesque and close-knit community of Upper Island Cove in Newfoundland and Labrador.

As a boy, Willie grew up in a world in Newfoundland where time must have seemed to stand still. His world, during the 1920s and 1930s, was one of survival, with little hope for a brighter future, in the oldest British colony, Newfoundland. Like many, he had experienced wrenching poverty, limited schooling, and a sense of hopelessness. By age eighteen, he had already experienced the death of his father and an older sister, and it was then he made a life-altering decision.

In part to escape these conditions, Willie decided to enlist in the war effort. When he left Upper Island Cove, what he saw and experienced must have been a complete shock. He had never even been to St. John's before, but now he promptly boarded a ship, steamed to England, and subsequently served in active theatres of war throughout Europe until the war ended in 1945. There, the rest of his life would be carved out in a way that he could never have imagined.

Throughout his adult life, Willie had always tended to keep to himself, say little, and express less. I often wondered why that was. It seems to me he had a strong and vibrant spirit, although you could see and feel that something wasn't quite right. He didn't act irrationally, or have limited ability, or refuse to let you in. It was more that—the culmination of a whole series of events that were completely outside his control, but imposed upon him, had led to a complex personality that, even today, I'm not sure I fully understand.

Edie, strong of character, determined, and protective always, was much more of an open book, except, that is, when it came to sharing her deepest feelings. She did, however, soften remarkably as the years passed. Their six children lived their lives being loved by two parents, who tended not to openly show or express that love, either to their children or publicly toward each other. Yet as children, through the actions of their parents, the children knew and felt the unbreakable bond of love.

Even with the likelihood of the impending war, Edie, the British-born mother, could never have imagined what her life would be like. She grew up in a working-class family and enjoyed a good life. She began working in 1939, at age sixteen, and was required to stay there for the next six years, all the while anxiously awaiting news from her brother who was a prisoner of war. Edie quickly came to understand the evil of the Nazis and the power of the Luftwaffe's constant bombing. She understood the almost constant danger and the need to take cover, in the backyard air-raid shelters on many occasions. But there was so much that she, just like Willie, could not have anticipated.

In this book, you will also experience and learn how, in the middle of the war, this young Newfoundland sailor and younger English lady, from two completely different backgrounds, met and fell in love. It might not have been love at first sight, or was it? After all, they spent the evening dancing and didn't part, ever again, until Willie's death sixty-two years later.

It was really after the war that their journey together would begin in earnest. It would take them from the cobblestone streets of England to the rugged hills and barren lands of Newfoundland, to Willie's hometown of Upper Island Cove. There they built a home and were settled into a new life when, as a young man, it was determined that Willie could no longer work. This, combined with the continuing impact of World War II, played a big role in Willie's life. The significant cultural change, coupled with the pain of a life of separation of Edie from her family and homeland, as well as the horrific death of her brother, were incredible challenges for her.

Under these very challenging circumstances, their spirits were tested but never broken. And importantly, it was the small, close-knit, and proud community of Upper Island Cove and its people that became so instrumental in nurturing the very survival of this war veteran and his transplanted war bride.

Readers should note that the stories contained in this book are the stories of Edie and Willie Lundrigan, written or told by them. The author has attempted to keep their voices heard throughout the book. The opinions expressed, as well as the timing, sequence, and recall of events, are theirs and may not be 100% historically accurate. As an author, it was my role, extrapolating only minimally, to bring all the pieces together.

I hope you enjoy their story.

1 — Willie

THAT TERRIBLE DAY

November 3, 1940
300 Miles Northwest of Bloody Foreland, Ireland

We got the raft ready, tied a long rope on it, and lowered it over the side. I was thinking about what I had to do next and expecting any minute for a second torpedo to hit. At that instant I realized that my lifebelt was not inflated. I hadn't blown any air into it. After getting my lifebelt inflated, I felt a bit more confident, and I was hoping that when I hit the water I would float.

Hesitant still to jump, I looked around this large tilted ship and realized that the water was now coming in over the port side. By that time the ship was nearly turned over. I looked down in the water and could just see the Carley float, and to make matters worse, I couldn't swim!

I just closed my eyes and jumped.

It seemed like a long time before I hit the water. I didn't know how far I went down, but I never thought I would come back to the surface anymore. It was during that desperate time, when the cold water seemed to shock me into a state of calmness and reflection, that, as they say, my whole life flashed before me.

I thought, *How in the devil did I get here?*

The image of my father, sitting in the fishing boat, lay before me . . .

Five years earlier—Friday, November 15, 1935

I was already awake when I heard the floorboards creak as someone approached the door of the bedroom I shared with my younger brothers Ray and Ian. Then came *tap, tap, tap,* followed by Father's gruff voice, saying, "Come on, Willie, it's time to get up."

There was not much subtle about Mark Lundrigan. I slowly opened my eyes as I stretched out with an audible yawn. I listened as a gusty wind whistled through the old storm sash in the window on the west end of the house. The rain dancing on the roof seemed to drive from west to east. Even though we went fishing every day of the week during the fishing season, except Sunday, Father drew the line on fishing during stormy weather. Hearing the wind and rain abuse the house, I almost believed that Father wouldn't tap on the door this November morning, or if he did tap on the door, he would simply say the weather wasn't civil enough to go.

But, "On my way, Father," I replied. I sat on the side of the bed for a moment, noting to myself that because it was now the middle of November, we should haul up the boat for the winter soon.

Of course, deep down, I fully realized that Father's definition of bad weather was not mine, and so the weather would have to be nothing short of a hurricane before he would not have wanted to go fishing down alongshore. There, as usual, after a thirty-to-forty-minute row in our small boat, we would return to the rich but jagged-bottomed fishing grounds of the Old Chimney and Freshwater Rock before we rowed southeast to Crab Ledge and finally on to Sandy Ground.

This morning was different, though. Father was quieter and slower to get ready than usual. Also noticeable was a small drop of blood on the handkerchief that dangled out of the back pocket of his old trousers, even though there was no visible sign of any cut or injury to his hands or face. It was strange to me when Father said, "My son, get a bit of lunch ready for us, will you?" Father hadn't asked me to do this at any time before now, but I dutifully and without questioning him proceeded to concoct the usual lunch of homemade bread, coated in molasses, and then placed it in the small, well-worn canvas satchel we used for this purpose. Father blew out the lamp as we left the house to a dark, damp, and cold morning. Daylight was still more than an hour from breaking in the eastern sky.

At fourteen years of age, I was not especially interested in going fishing on a cold, wet, and windy morning in late fall, so I was encouraged somewhat when I also noticed the rain had let up quite a bit. The moderate wind, which sometimes got stronger with the rising sun, had also begun to subside somewhat. As usual, I rowed the boat down the bay to the fishing ground because the southwest wind was at the stern. Otherwise, Father would not have allowed it. Even though a pretty good oarsmen for my age, I hoped that the wind didn't drop out too much. If it did, the spanker, a small sail placed just inside the transom of the boat, which helped us steer, would serve as nothing more than a tidily wrapped brin bag. A light wind at our back was our friend, since without any wind it would have been harder to row the boat all the way to the fishing grounds.

After about an hour, the southwest wind, which had lightened earlier, had now increased somewhat and caused the salt spray to dampen Father's face. The small trickle of blood congealed near his nose was still visible. I was apprehensive about this situation.

Just after daylight on a damp November 15, 1935, I asked, "Father, are you feeling better now?" I asked this because I had just witnessed him retch over the gunwale, wincing in pain as he tried to sit back up in the bow of the boat as we neared the fishing shoal called Crab Ledge.

Father replied, "Yes, I'm all right, my son. Probably just a little seasickness, I suppose."

He paused and wiped his mouth with his handkerchief, then said, "Now, don't be telling your mother about this. You know she's a real worrier and will get all concerned over nothing."

I was about to remind Father this was not the first time the bleeding had happened, when he put an abrupt end to any further discussion.

As I felt his eyes burn through me, he said, "Now, you listen to me, Willie. You heard what I said. You are not to speak to anyone about this, most of all your mother."

I nodded in affirmation, turned around, and continued to row the small boat.

But then, surprisingly, Father said, "But 'tis not a really good morning down here, so maybe we will go back in now and wait till later on."

Seizing the opportunity, I immediately turned the boat toward home and directly into a thick southwest wind. I tried sculling our boat, but in this wind, and for the distance I had to go, I quickly realized the futility of my labours. I began rowing, and as I did so, my thoughts were of the previous times I had seen Father fall ill like this. The blood frightened me because I didn't know where it was coming from and, I realized, nor did he. I didn't for a minute believe that Father had fallen ill to seasickness. Father, who was fifty-two years old, had fished all his life. I'd been fishing with him for five years, and I hadn't seen him sick before. I never heard tell of it from any of his brothers or fishing buddies, either.

Now that I come to think of it, some bleeding had occurred earlier in June in perfectly calm waters off Freshwater Beach, where I was helping Father cast and load the boat with capelin. Most recently, I had seen a spot of blood on the ground where Father had been bending down and coughing while we were picking blueberries behind the Old

Tilt Hill, not far from Bryant's Cove. I also knew that my mother had witnessed Father having a bad stomach, but had she seen the blood?

I glanced over my shoulder and saw that Father had slipped sideways and was lying awkwardly on the cuddy. I was rowing the boat as hard as I could while also looking, from time to time, to see if there was any sign that Father was moving, even breathing. There was no movement in his crumpled body, and as I rounded the point of land known as the Head, just east of the Lundrigan stage, I was anxious to see if there was anyone nearby.

My elder brothers, John and Edward, seven and five years older than me, were away and still engaged in the fall fishery out of the Battery in St. John's, with Uncle Walter Baggs, who was married to Father's only sister, Rosanah. God, if only they were here now!

I was desperately hoping that one of my friends would be down on the stage catching tomcods. I knew in my heart, though, that this wasn't likely, because who in their right minds would be on the stage on a cold and wet November morning, catching tomcods? It was more likely that my friends, who were no longer in school, would be busy with their own families carrying fish from the stage, so that it could be transported to the schooner in Harbour Grace, or feeding the cattle or fetching water from the well for the day.

I was rowing really hard and afraid to stop for fear the boat would go sideways with the lop and possibly capsize. As the boat came around the Head, where the wind was blowing off the land and not as strong, I glanced over my shoulder at Father and shouted out in desperation, "Damn it, damn it, what am I going to do?"

Immediately as I said these words, and maybe because I said them so desperately and so loudly, Father started to move slightly in the boat. When that happened, I dropped the two oars into the boat and jumped from the middle thwart to the one near the cuddy, where Father was silently slouched.

"Father, are you okay? Can you hear me?"

With that, Father slowly opened his eyes and, gradually, with my help, struggled to sit up in the boat. With him facing me and then the landscape as the boat rolled with the sea swell before him, Father seemed to be desperately trying to make sense of his surroundings.

He asked, "Where are we, my son? What happened?"

But even as Father was whispering these words, he slowly slid back down on the cuddy and closed his eyes, saying, "I'm very tired, Willie. Take me home."

I said, "Here, Father, take my coat. I'm warm and sweating from rowing and don't need it."

I placed it over him and returned to the middle thwart, gritted my teeth, and pulled the oars with whatever strength was in me. We had drifted a good bit while I was attending to Father and were now perilously close to the breaking rocks near the Dog Gulch. Fortunately, it was only a matter of a few minutes before I was able to manoeuvre us out of harm's way and toward the Lundrigan stagehead.

My friend Wilbur Osbourne was looking at the boat from up in the garden, where he and Joe Crane had seen our boat come around the Head. This was much earlier in the day than expected, which made them especially curious. They had seen me rowing as fast as I ever had, while someone lay lifeless across the cuddy. When I got within feet from the stagehead, Wilbur and Joe became concerned, especially when they could look directly down and see a large dark red area near where Father's head was resting on a coil of rope.

As I reached the fishing stage, I ran to the bow of the boat and held it from banging on the rough wooden framing. Then I quickly tied the painter to the stage and turned my attention to my father.

Father's body still lay motionless, with his eyes half open and a trickle of blood running from his mouth and down the side of his face. I felt sick! A huge knot seemed to grip my stomach, and just for a minute, I think I cried. Then, thinking that my tears were of no value, I quickly wiped my eyes in my sleeve, climbed up over the stage, and ran as fast as I could up the stage path, searching for an adult to help me.

In addition to Wilbur and Joe, I eventually found Uncle Lije (Elijah) Mercer. I don't remember a lot about what happened next, but Uncle Lije and a couple of men from farther down the Meadow were able to lift Father out of the boat and up the approximately seven-foot distance to the top of the stage. Luckily, the tide was almost top high, though, since at low tide you could add on another four or five feet of lift.

I felt that all of this was entirely my fault. Even though Father made me promise to keep his secret, I regretted so much not telling my mother or one of my sisters about what had happened out in the boat earlier when my father spat up blood. Father could die now, and it was my fault. I became so distracted with self-pity that I didn't realize what was going on around me, until I saw that the men had Father on the hand-cart and were carrying him up the stage path to our house up in the garden.

In my desperate attempt to make sense of what was happening, it seemed that hours had passed as I sat in the stage at the top of the Kettle Gulch. My father's health was in a very precarious state, and it seemed there was nothing his family could do to help.

2 — Willie

BECOMING AN ADULT

November 1935 – September 1939

In the days that followed the incident where Father became so terribly ill in the boat with me, he gradually became more alert and was able to get around, although still somewhat weak. Despite the frightening experience in the boat that morning, I was starting to believe he would be okay.

One morning about two weeks after the incident in the boat, as was his custom, Father got up before anyone else and went downstairs to light the fire in the only stove in the house. My siblings John, Edward, and Mabel were working in St. John's, while the rest of us, including Myra, Lydia, Ray, and Ian, along with me, were still sleeping. Mother was also ready to get up, but it was still dark, so she just lay back for a few minutes until the fire started to warm the house. On this particular morning, however, after a few minutes, Mother realized that she wasn't hearing the usual sounds coming from downstairs. She didn't hear the floorboards squeak as Father walked from the porch to the kitchen stove. She didn't hear the usual iron damper rattling sounds as Father removed it to light the fire. There was no sound of water pouring into the wash basin.

Concerned now, Mother moved quickly, got up, and went directly downstairs to check on Father. There was no sign of her husband and partner of almost twenty-four years. She looked in the kitchen, and the stove was not lit. Mother saw the porch door open. She went to see if Father was there. When she reached the porch, she was startled to see Father slumped across the woodbox. Mother went immediately to him and spoke. He didn't answer, and holding her cheek close to his face, she could tell he wasn't breathing.

My mother seemed like she was always calm under pressure, but suddenly I heard her scream out, "Willie! Willie! Come quickly to the porch."

This scream caught me sleeping. As I scrambled out of bed, I knew something was terribly wrong. I called back, "Coming, Mother," but before I could get to the stairs, Myra was ahead of me and going over the stairs two steps at a time. She went to the porch and saw Father now lying on the porch floor. She gasped and was about to cry when Mother, now in more control of her emotions, said, "Myra, run out next door and tell John I need him here right away. Now, go!" Myra did as she was instructed, and while she was gone, Mother and I kept checking to see if Father was breathing. He wasn't. By the time Father's brother John arrived minutes later, he could only confirm that it was too late for my father. At the age of fifty-two, my father passed away at home, down in the Mcadow, early that morning of November 29, 1935.

The death of my father was a tremendous blow to our family, especially to Mother and the younger children, including Lydia, Ray, and Ian, who were twelve, ten, and six years old respectively. It seemed that, as time passed, I not only mourned his loss, but deep within, I couldn't help but feel a strong sense that I could have done more to help Father. I repeatedly asked myself why I hadn't shared my father's plight with my sisters or with Mother, or with anyone, for that matter.

I never did know what caused Father's death. What I suspected, but was not sure of until some years later, was that someone else did know about Father's bouts of spitting up blood. Not surprisingly, it turned out that my mother knew. As I got older, it became more obvious to me that she would have been very aware of any signs of him being or seeming unwell. She would also have detected even the slightest bloodstain on his body, clothing, or bedding.

As a fourteen-year-old, I didn't really think this through. It was not until several years later, when Mother and I had a conversation about Father's death, that clarity prevailed. At that time, Mother, flabbergasted that, as she put it, I had "needlessly placed so much blame" on myself for Father's untimely death, revealed that, of course, she did know about the bleeding episodes. She too was worried about him those many years ago and tried to persuade Father to see a doctor. But being a mother, wishing to shield her children from all that could inflict harm, she felt it important to try to protect her children, including me, from what she saw as "worry and torment." She thought it best to not talk about it with us.

I had very much enjoyed time spent with Father. Unfortunately, by the time I got to the age where I could learn from him, his time with us was over. He could have taught us so much—his carpentry skills, his knowledge of the sea and of fishing, and so much about how to live, interact, and function in this world as an adult. And Mother, a bright and independent woman, always putting the well-being of others over her own, was now so consumed with keeping us all fed and warm, she rarely smiled as she once had. My life, indeed the lives of my whole family, had irreversibly changed.

Mother was also incredibly good at taking care of as much of the hard manual labour as possible, but as I got older, I began to accept more and more responsibility within my family. And while I made every effort to do my best, I couldn't help but think I should have been better able to help my family, who had so little. If it weren't for our eldest sibling, John, I expect one of the younger children could have starved, as others did in the community during this time. He worked away and often came home with extra food and clothing, especially cloth and wool, that Mother used to make or repair garments for people in the community. My second-eldest brother, Edward, helped as well, but less so with material things. He was the happy-go-lucky type and always spent time with us, where his strength was making us laugh and feel loved with both his jokes and his antics. He generally kept everyone's spirits up, no matter the obstacles facing us.

The spring after Father died, Mother was concerned that we would have to sell our small Newfoundland pony, Tiny, because we had little to feed her. The scraps of potatoes, cabbage, and turnip only went so far, and we had little hay by the end of February. By spring, Tiny had lost a good bit of weight.

John and Edward did so much work when they were home, but that was becoming less and less a factor as they spent more time fishing in the Battery with our Uncle Walter Baggs. As the eldest boy in the family, still at home, I took it upon myself to make sure we were better off. Early in the spring, with the help of my sisters Myra and Lydia I took Tiny in over Rocky Hill to the Dribbling Brook Garden to plow up the ground. Mother still did most of the work, and Ray came with us sometimes, but Mother wasn't keen on that because he was only ten years old. The work of plowing the ground, picking out the endless rocks, then drilling it all up in preparation for setting potatoes, was hard. Before we came out of the garden, Mother or I cut so much hay so that next morning we could turn it in order for it to dry. In the evenings, after Tiny was fed and watered for the night, I used to cut the hay down under the bank near where Father had had the stage.

During that summer, Lydia, Myra and I spent little time with our friends because we had to make this work. We had to have food, and we had to be able to keep Tiny. Losing our horse would be the end of any sense of independence for us. Tiny was needed to help with plowing, bringing home firewood, bringing capelin up off the beach, and so many more tasks.

"Willie, come on in, now. That's enough for today," Mother would often say around eight o'clock in the evening,

"Yes, I'll be right there, Mother," I responded, and then continued as long as there was light in the sky. That was the routine day after day in order to get as much for ourselves as possible. In between these responsibilities, I also had to fulfill my obligations to whoever allowed me to fish with them for at least a part of the summer.

In the fall, the task of harvesting the garden and drying the fish was very hard work, especially when the weather started to get cold and wet. By the time we had it pretty much finished up near the end of October, it was obvious that the fruit of our labour was not so plentiful. We managed another winter to make ends meet just so that we could start the cycle all over again the next spring.

Times were tough for every family, not just ours, but the death of my father stands out as a point at which my easygoing youth changed overnight to the demands and responsibilities of an adult. During what had now become endless work hours, I often reflected on happier times of my youth. One incident always brought a smile to my face as I worked away. It was about our town constable.

On one cold, clear, and starlit winter night, we went for a ride on our slides. Joe Crane and Wilbur came by, and Joe yelled, "Hey, Willie, wanna go sliding?"

Mother was upstairs, and Father was napping on the daybed.

"Yes, Joe," I replied. "Let me get dressed, and I'll meet you at the top of the Little Hill."

Generally starting on the higher ground of the Rocky Hill cart path and sometimes even in as far as the Notching Place, we came out past our house, then down past the old Anglican graveyard, there taking a sharp left turn down the Church Hill, now going at a blistering speed on our slides. We navigated a sharp right turn down Mercer's

Hill, through the Cove, and if the going was good, we often ended up over as far as the bottom of the Pinch Road.

One winter's cold and blustery night, there were about six of us on four slides. The snow was so hard-packed that it was more like ice than snow. We were going full speed, when we had to make the turn at the bottom of the Church Hill onto Mercer's Hill. As soon as we straightened up, we could see the small hand-held lantern swinging in the dark about 200 yards ahead, at the bottom of Mercer's Hill, near the Husseys'. We often tied our slides together, and when we tumbled, we all became willing victims at the same time. That night, we had four of our slides tied together, one after the other, with an old piece of fishing rope, and we were going quite fast as we struggled to stay upright on the harrowingly sharp turn.

Wilbur and I were on the lead slide, and both of us knew the plan as soon as we saw the faint light from the lantern. With a shared grin, but without a word between us, we headed for the lantern. When we got mere feet from the light, both of us dug our left foot into the hard-packed snow. Over we turned, sharply sideways, taking the other three slides and their occupants in the same jolting direction. We all crashed to the ground and were flailing wildly over the hard-packed snow.

The result was as planned—over the top of us, tumbling unceremoniously, was the helpless constable. Before the good police officer could gather his scattered wits, his pride, and his now shattered lantern, we had pulled the slides together and were running through the Cove, past the Hearse House and over the Green, at a clip that was not even thinkable for the heavy-set constable.

The impact on the family of the death of Father, and the subsequent tough financial circumstances we were experiencing, were only heightened with the illness, in 1937, of my eighteen-year-old sister, Mabel.

I remember the day that Mabel went off to work in St. John's. Mother didn't want her to go, but many of her friends had already gone or were going, so she was adamant about going, too.

Mother said, "Mabel, my dear, why don't you stay here with us? There's always lots to do, and you are only sixteen. There's lots of time for you to go off to work."

But just like some of her friends, Mabel was determined to go.

"Mom, we have talked about this a lot, and I really want to go and see the world, and I want to make money. The girls tell me the shops in St. John's have everything, and if I get to work with the right family, I will have money to buy nice clothes as well as a bit to send home to you."

It was obvious that the exuberance and strong will of Mabel won the day, and Mother agreed for her to go. She found work as a domestic servant with a merchant family who lived just off Water Street. She used to write to Mother and sometimes to Myra. She was happy and doing well. Occasionally she would get home for a short break. On one visit, she seemed to have a bad cold and did a lot of coughing, but she assured Mother she was fine. She got a ride on the horse and cart belonging to someone farther down in the Meadow, which took her to the train station in Riverhead, then back to St. John's. That was the last time I saw Mabel alive. After that, Mother continued to get the occasional letter, but Mabel was not well.

Mabel spent close to three years working in St. John's. Work could be hard and demanding, but at least she had a roof over her head and was well-fed. She would try to save anything she could to send home to Mother. This was especially important to her after Father died and the family struggled even more. But Mabel's cough continued to get worse, and eventually she was diagnosed with the dreaded tuberculosis (TB).

Not long after her diagnosis, Mabel was placed in the Sanitarium (San) on Topsail Road in St. John's. This was a hospital specifically designed for TB patients. There were separate rooms for isolating patients, and many of the rooms had access to an outside veranda, since it was believed that a good form of therapy was fresh air.

Unfortunately, like so many, Mabel's condition continued to deteriorate, and just a couple of months shy of her nineteenth birthday, she died on July 29, 1937. Our family members, especially Mother, really struggled to come to terms with this horrible loss, which occurred just two years after the loss of Father. There was a lot to process, and these were all thoughts that were going through my mind as I turned eighteen in June of 1939.

Instead of showing signs of improvement during the 1930s, the economy seemed to go from bad to worse. Most people needed help from government to survive, and the "dole," as that support was known, amounted to the cash equivalent of six cents a day. This consisted of a ration note (not cash) for food, which was the amount of food considered appropriate for one person for a month.

We didn't have a choice on what we could get to eat. We just took a ration note to an authorized store in the community, the larger of which were that of Uncle Jimmy Dood in the Cove and the store belonging to Uncle John and Aunt Bertha Young in the Mash.

One day, seemingly out of no where, Mother said, "That Lodge man is going to be the death of me." At first I was puzzled by this statement, but eventually I began to piece it all together. As it turned out, my mother felt that the local Commission of Government relief inspector, or dole officer, as we knew him, did not treat many families properly, including hers. She was convinced that this dole officer, a person not from or living in Upper Island Cove, did not provide some families in the community with the support that their personal situations reflected. The word in the small towns was that, throughout Newfoundland, the tighter the dole officer ran the financial assistance program, the more favour he found with the British-appointed government commissioners.

Add to that, there had always been a big Loyal Orange Order (Lodge) presence in the whole Conception Bay North area, and Upper Island Cove and Bishop's Cove were a big part of that. My father, Mark, had initially been a member of the Lodge in Bishop's Cove, joining in the late 1890s. He joined there because it would be three more years before there was a Lodge in Upper Island Cove. According to local Lodge officers, once the Lodge in Upper Island Cove was built over in the Pot Brook area, all the members in the Bishop's Cove Lodge, who resided in Upper Island Cove, were transferred to the Upper Island Cove Lodge.

A sectarian-based organization, the Lodge was at that time an integral part of the largely Anglican community of Upper Island Cove. Many people will speak to its rich history of supporting the church and of supporting many individuals in need through their outreach programs. But that might not be the way my mother felt.

One day, not long after my father died, Mother said, "Willie, I want you to go over to the Lodge and tell them you want your father's gun and anything else there that belongs to him. Tell them I sent you, and when you get it, bring whatever is there directly home to me."

"Mother, why is Father's hunting rifle at the Lodge?" I asked.

"I don't know, my son, but I'm told they keep all the guns belonging to members there," replied my mother, in an annoyed and frustrated tone.

Apparently, Mother seemed to feel that, at the time of Father's death, the Lodge had not provided the family support that all Orange Lodges pledged to their members through the Orange Benefit Fund. Bringing insult to injury for Mother was that, at that time, this already disdained dole officer was a member of the Upper Island Cove Loyal Orange Lodge

And in July 1939, there was about to be a fuss.

The Orange Lodge generally paraded in the community twice each year. One time was at Christmastime (usually Boxing Day), and the other of course was often on July 1, when for some reason they paraded to recognize Orangemen's Day, which was July 12. In Upper Island Cove, one of the people who regularly participated in the parade was the dole officer. My mother was not a fan of the actions of the Lodge of the day. She felt even the Lodge that she had a dispute with had inflicted further insult on itself. After all, it had allowed this individual, who she felt had failed to provide some residents with necessary food and clothing supports, to walk with them in the parade. She further felt these actions were inconsistent with such a church-associated organization, and therefore he should be barred from being a part of their Lodge, and especially the parade.

Lodge members, complete with sashes and marching brass band, led by a man on a large horse who was imitating King William of Orange, always paraded from the Lodge building to St. Peter's Church. After a church service, they paraded out the Mash Road, across what we called the Back, then downhill through Lundrigan's Lane, to the Meadow Road. This time, however, the privately owned Lundrigan's Lane became the hill on which Mother decided to stand. I'm sure that others may have told her that her assertions were not accurate, but for this mite of a woman, trying to feed and clothe a family of small children and feeling alone and ill done by, no one was going to change her mind.

She was finally done with what she saw as the insufferable actions of the Commission's dole officer, as well as the way she felt the Lodge leaders of the day embraced the dole officer and had also failed to provide benefits due her after the death of my father. As a show of protest and defiance, my tiny mother, probably one of the quietest women in the community, put up the stiles and stood in front of them. There she waited in the middle of Lundrigan's Lane as the parade approached, led by a man dressed in a colourful mantle on a large, white, intimidating horse. She was accompanied by my thirteen-year-old brother, Ray, who on Mother's instructions was carrying my dead father's muzzleloader, which I had earlier retrieved from the Lodge.

It was a bold thing for her to do, but after four years trying to care for her family, my mother had reached a breaking point. Her husband was dead, and there was no money and very little food for her children.

As they approached, with the brass band blaring out some hymn she by now was too nervous to hear, she shouted, "Turn around and go back. Ye will not be passing here today."

King William raised his arm, and the band fell silent. "What is your issue, Mrs. Lundrigan?"

"You know my issue, and that man over there"—pointing to the Dole Officer—"knows my issue. Ye have failed to uphold your obligation, and you will not pass here today."

After a few minutes, where there was a brief but muffled discussion among some of the members, King William pulled on the reins of the horse and turned without a word. The parading members did likewise, and within minutes the band could be heard again as they went down the Church Hill Lane to the Cove.

I'm not sure if my young brother Ray, who stood by Mother, really understood why she was so mad, but she was clearly not to be deterred in her decision. Staring them down, the widow and the boy with the muzzleloader turned back both the King of Orange and the Commission's dole officer that day.

This was the only time I was aware of that Mother did anything of this nature. Because I left Upper Island Cove within several months, I really didn't know what happened after that incident. One thing was sure—now that I had left, the burden of having enough food to go around had lessened. As far as I knew, Mother continued to feel ill done by in those desperate days. Other than what she had done, there was no other means of encouraging or facilitating change or correcting a wrong.

3 — Willie

TIME TO DECIDE

September 3, 1939

Despite our challenges, Mother kept us all together and we got along well, but the summer of 1939 was no less difficult for our family than it had been for the last several years. After Father's death, our own stage and fishing gear had fallen into disrepair and were no longer usable. Additionally, when I turned eighteen, the local dole officer cut the dole to a lower amount because, as he said, "Willie is off the books." I was now considered old enough to be financially independent of the family.

One day in late summer, my friend Joe and I were walking across the Hearse House area, on our way back from picking up some kerosene oil from Uncle Will "Budget" Young. My mother gave me the last of her money she had tucked away to get the oil for the kitchen lamp. As we approached the store of Uncle Jimmy Dood, we saw that a small crowd had gathered. Joe asked someone what was going on, and he was told, in a hushed voice while someone was beginning to speak on the radio, "It's the King. They say there will be another war."

It was not unusual to see a few people outside Uncle Jimmy's place, especially in the warmer weather, since this was one of two places in Upper Island Cove where there was a radio. Instead of walking by that day, we stopped with the crowd and listened to what King George VI of England was saying on the radio.

It was September 3, 1939, and according to the King, Britain had just declared war on Germany. In the days and weeks that followed that speech, the war and related news (or rumour) was the constant topic of discussion throughout the community. For the most part, people felt that they were so far away from Europe and protected by the giant Atlantic Ocean that it would have little if any impact locally.

On the other hand, many older people remembered well the previous war, which everyone had said was the war to end all wars. They remembered the young men from Upper Island Cove who travelled by boat to fight for Britain, and they remembered that some of them had not returned. They also remembered that some of those who did return seemed to be quite different from the young men who went off to war.

None of us knew about the early persecution by the Nazis or the invasion of Poland or the compromising position taken by Britain's Neville Chamberlain in his attempt to appease an aggressive German Nazi leader, Adolph Hitler. People still felt close to Britain, and many wanted to help.

Over the weeks that followed the King's speech, a number of the boys my age in Upper Island Cove, including me, chatted about whether or not going to war would be something any of us wanted to do. As it turned out, a number of my friends did choose to do that. I guess hearing the speech and listening to what my friends were saying also caused a small stir of patriotism within me. But in my small world, I had never even been to St. John's, so my view of the international scene would have been limited at best. For me, taking a burden off my mother, escaping this hopelessness, and seeking adventure were what mattered most in my decision to join the navy.

I used to wonder about life and what the world outside of Upper Island Cove and the few neighbouring communities looked like. Surely there had to be more. We heard stories about what life was like in the big cities—about all the houses crowded together, the fancy cars, and the cobblestone walkways and roads. There was little education, crude and slow communication, a very poor transportation network, and frankly little need to travel very far. I had never been on a train or in a car. What did places like Britain, the United States, and Europe really look like? At that point, I was finally ready to find out. I made my decision, and I soon found out in ways that I could never have imagined!

4 — Edie

CHILDHOOD MEMORIES

1923–1939

My early years growing up in England were quite pleasant. My parents were caring but strict. I remember growing up in a very comfortable middle-class home, where there was always plenty to eat and nice, warm, and stylish clothes to wear. We were certainly not rich, but we wanted for very little. My father worked in a management position with a coal production company, and my mother looked after us and the day-to-day affairs of the house. My three brothers—Alfred, Harry, and Sid—my sister Lil, and I lived a happy childhood, where going to school, attending dance classes, taking piano lessons, going to picture shows, and going on vacations at the beach were a regular part of life. Sid was my closest sibling in age, but even he was eight years older than me. From time to time, he would take me for a drive in his small sports car. Sometimes we would go to a picture show, and sometimes he would take me for Rossi Ice Cream at Southend-on-Sea. I also remember distinctly watching my elder brother, Harry, who was an owner and racer of pigeons. He was quite skilled at training the birds and won a number of awards for wining various races. It was interesting to see how pigeons were used during the war by the British military to send various communications.

As a part of my childhood, I always remember visiting my grandparents each Sunday, especially if I had new clothes to wear. There were apple trees and cherry trees in Gran and Grandfather's garden, and I was always allowed to go in and pick some of the fruit in the summertime to take home with me.

I had the benefit of attending a well-established school system in England. As a child, I usually walked from my home on Charlton Street, in West Thurrock, Essex, up a roadway called "The Chase," across London Road and up Mill Lane. There, as a young child, I attended Mill Lane Primary School for Girls, and, in my later years, Mill Lane Secondary School for Girls.

West Thurrock was located close to an industrial area near the Thames River Estuary in East Essex, about thirty kilometres east of London, England. I was born on August 28, 1923, the youngest child of Alfred and Annie Louisa (Steel) England. I was one of a twin. Sadly, my fraternal brother, Wally, was stillborn.

Even having a good childhood and having no real hardship, I was brought up believing that you had to be strong and resolute to survive in the world. When I was a teenager, I was in the middle of a war. That made being able to remain strong and determined even more important, especially when we saw the examples set by our leaders like Churchill and King George VI. On September 3, 1939, King George VI was making a speech over the BBC. Mom, Dad, and I sat in the front room listening as he spoke to the nation, telling us that we were going to war with Germany. None of us

Edie England, 1941, age eighteen

knew exactly what we were in for, but with the strength of the Nazi air force and their improved navy, we knew it would mean a very difficult time for our small island, which was so close to the rest of Europe. I remember Dad saying that our leaders will do all they can, but winning this war will depend on each and every one of us playing our part. "We must remain strong," he said. One night, in the fall of 1940, the bombing was loud and getting louder all the time. Mum was clearly worried and kept peeking out through the closed curtain. Dad was sitting in his usual spot reading the newspaper as though this was a regular evening at home. After some time, Mum turned to him and said, "Alf, do you think we should make our way to the air-raid shelter?"

Dad responded, without moving his eyes from the newspaper page, "Not right now. I believe the bombing will move farther up the Thames soon. There is not much here that the Germans want to waste their bombs on."

Fortunately for us that day, the bombings did seem to eventually fade off in the distance, and we settled in for a more restful night. There were bombings on so many, many nights with so much destruction, including a massive number of injuries and lives lost. We had no choice but to go through it, but to survive all this, you had to believe in yourself and your country and never let yourself get down emotionally.

Of course, as teenagers we were all concerned about not being able to live life as we were used to, but we were also very much aware of the dangers and carnage of war on a regular basis. Many people realized that, if not for the collective strength of Britain's wartime leader, Winston Churchill, and the people of the British Isles, Britain would very likely have succumbed to the Nazi tyranny.

Owning this characteristic of strength in a time of danger does not mean that a person would care less or be unfeeling. It means, rather, that the British people always approach life straight on, with the ability and intestinal fortitude to fight tirelessly through the darkest days and the most difficult challenges.

Mum felt that the struggles and difficult challenges during the two World Wars, as well as the choices that had to be made, would also ultimately mould the way people lived the rest of their lives. Mum and many other mums had to be strong, since there was little choice during a war.

My mother always had a stern look about her. She was the one who made the rules, and I dared not disobey them. When I wanted to do something special or go somewhere different, I usually went to my father for permission. My father was easier to talk to, but when I went to him, he would often say to me, "And what did your mum say?" That question, when answered by me, would often be followed with, "Well, I think you should talk to your mum about that."

My dad was the second-youngest of six children (four girls and two boys) of George and Ruth (Chiddicks) England, who grew up in North Stifford, Essex, England, some thirty-five kilometres from London. His family lived in a small thatched-roof cottage at the bottom of Dog & Partridge Hill and on a sweeping right curve on Sifford Street (later known as High Street). This was located just east of the historic Dog & Partridge Pub and a short distance from St. Mary's Church, where, later, Bill and I were married.

With regard to the thatched-roof cottage, I remember reading something about it one day that talked about how old they were and that they had been owned by the England family for several generations. They were built in the seventeenth century from lathe, plaster, timber, thatch, and tile.

Dad was a quiet, competent, and respected man. His unassuming demeanour was a considerable asset in his work and life generally when dealing with difficult people and circumstances. He had a tendency for, and rather enjoyed, spending time alone and maintaining the quieter voice, even in a crowd. It would be inaccurate to suggest or interpret this behaviour as a lack of ability or interest. Quite the contrary, my father appeared to have an understanding of both his immediate surroundings as well as the impending gravity associated with deteriorating world affairs, as any mid-level diplomat might reasonably be expected to have.

He worked at Wouldam's Cement Factory in South Stifford for most of his early work life. Eventually he seized an opportunity to advance his career, as well as his family's income, by leaving the cement business and working, up until his retirement in 1942, as a union shop steward in a coal processing and sales facility operated by William Corey and Son Ltd. in Purfleet.

The work associated with coal loading and unloading was dirty at the best of times. Dad, however, went to work each time a new shipment of coal arrived, punctually clocking in daily at the same twenty minutes early, dressed in a clean but modest black jacket and pants and wearing a blue closed-neck shirt. Whenever he was to attend a more formal work or a social function, he characteristically wore a black, single-breasted suit and matching vest. His shirt was white, well-starched, and ironed with a perfectly aligned and neatly tied black necktie.

Out of his shirt pocket hung a glistening gold pocket watch, attached to the inside of his necktie clip, which looked as though it was more a part of his appendage than of his apparel. His shoes, which always seemed a size too long for his feet, were gloss black, impeccably polished triple-E Oxfords. The shoes weren't always new, but given his part-time job as a highly skilled cobbler, they always looked as though they were.

Interestingly, my father worked in an environment where some of the coal porters with whom he regularly interacted with were big, burly, and able men who were able to win any longshoreman's battle. Dad, though, did not present an imposing physical presence. His five foot, nine inch frame weighed in at a modest eleven stone, yet unlike many of his maybe less refined colleagues, my father commanded respect by his very presence. I remember my elder brother, Alf, telling the story of a tiff between one of the workers and a plant manager. The worker, Paddy Flynn, was a tall man who enjoyed a large presence among the coal workers. One day, one of the plant managers got upset with him over his boisterous and loud behaviour in the lunchroom. The manager confronted Paddy, and in the wink of an eye, Paddy had the much smaller manager pinned up by the wall by grabbing him with one hand around the neck. Another worker came running to Dad and said, "Alf, you're needed over here, because Paddy is ready to hurt someone." According to Alf, Dad got up from his desk, buttoned his suit coat, and walked over to where Paddy had the manager pinned to the wall. Dad observed the situation for a moment and said, "Paddy, you are going to have to put him down." To which Paddy simply replied, "Okay, Mr. England. Shall I follow you?"

My father was a rather conservative man but enjoyed his routines, especially time at the local pub. Late on almost every regular Friday afternoon, he would walk out of the Dog & Partridge Pub after consuming his usual two ales. There was something wonderfully comforting to him about the Dog & Partridge Pub. Maybe it was the longevity of the building, which still displayed, with honour, the clock housing from the former "Clockhouse" building that was torn down and replaced by the current building more than 300 years ago. Maybe it was the reassurance of the same friendly faces, sitting on the same stools, drinking the same ales, telling the same stories week after week and year after year. Dad always sat alone but never felt lonely there. He never deviated from his routine of leaving work on Friday and going to the same pub at the same time and drinking the same brand of ale before walking the three miles to his Charlton Street home, where my mother, Annie Louisa, had prepared supper and waited as patiently as was her limited capacity to do.

5 — Willie

THE EARLY DAYS

October 25, 1939 – August 1941

". . . For the sake of all that we ourselves hold dear and of the world order and peace it is unthinkable that we should refuse to meet the challenge. It is to this high purpose that I now call my people at home and my people across the seas who will make my call their own. I ask them to stand calm and firm and united in this time of trial. The tasks will be hard. There may be dark days ahead and war is no longer confined to the battlefield but we can only do the right as we see the right and reverently command our cause to God. If one and all be resolutely faithful today, ready for whatever service or sacrifice it may demand, with God's help we shall prevail. May He bless and keep us all."
— King George VI Speech, September 3, 1939

In late October 1939, exhausted with the burden of poverty and a sense of hopelessness, my journey into the bowels of the war in Europe was about to begin. A few of my friends, including Fred Mercer next door and a couple of others, went in the first or second contingent. I didn't talk to many people about it, and only when I was almost ready to go, did I tell my sisters and Mother. Both Myra and Lydia especially were upset and tried to persuade me not to go. Before I left, my whole family pleaded with me not to go, but I knew they understood more than anyone else why I felt I needed to.

On November 25, 1939, at the age of eighteen and a half years, I went to see Dr. McGrath in Harbour Grace to have my medical for military service completed. Dr. McGrath told me that the result of the examination was graded as First Class or Grade A.

Sometime in early December 1939, I went to see Captain Jack Dowling of Bishop's Cove. Captain Dowling, born in Britain, was by now retired from the British Army. He was a highly respected man to the locals, having seen action in both the Boer War as well as in World War I. He later served out of the garrison in Halifax and had married a woman from Bishop's Cove. In this period, many young women had gone to work as domestic servants, some locally, some in St. John's, and some farther away. A number of local women actually went to Halifax to find such work, and it was in that capacity that Jemima Smith met and eventually married Captain Dowling. In 1937, the couple moved to Bishop's Cove, where they lived after his military service.

Willie Lundrigan, January 1940

I went to see the captain because I was required to have my application for serving with the British Royal Navy signed by him before it went to St. John's. I had the application completed and forwarded to the proper authorities. Later that month, I was given instructions to be in St. John's to travel overseas early in the new year.

Then on January 3, 1940, in company with George Drover and Dick Coombs, I left Upper Island Cove by horse and slide to go to Riverhead, Harbour Grace. There we boarded a train to take us to St. John's. We arrived in St. John's late that same day and had to stay at the CLB Armoury for several days while waiting to board the ship to Liverpool in England. Our whole group was going off to fight in a war that we knew virtually nothing about. None of us had ever even been to St. John's before.

When we got to St. John's, we had to wait at the Armoury until the ship was ready to take us all to England. I remember how terrified we were that we would get lost in St. John's. When we went out for a look around, one of us would walk up to the next intersection and signal the okay to the others. For instance, we wanted to go to see the ships in the harbour, so I went east on Harvey Road and stopped at Garrison Hill. Dick and George came up to where I was, and then George waited there while Dick and I went down Garrison Hill to Queens Road. Dick stayed there, and I went west on Queens Road as far as Queen Street. That's when Dick signalled to George, who came all the way from the top of Garrison Hill to meet me at Queen Street. We carried on that way, remembering our landmarks until we were on the waterfront and knew exactly how to get back to the CLB Armoury.

The ship we sailed on was the RMS (Royal Mail Service) *Newfoundland*. On January 7, 1940, all 175 of us new recruits, some from St. John's and many who came to St. Johns from small communities throughout the island, left the CLB Armoury and paraded down to Water Street and onto the harbour apron, where a small crowd had gathered to cheer us on. The crowd consisted mostly of military officials, a few VIPs, as well as the families of the fellows with us who lived in or near St. John's.

We all came to this place as young boys, and yet we now stepped on board the RMS *Newfoundland* as members of the third contingent of Newfoundlanders to enlist and travel overseas for service in World War II. We were now members of the British Royal Navy.

We thought we would be going directly to Britain, but because of U-boat activity in the North Atlantic, the standard procedure by the British Admiralty by January 1940 was to have several ships travel together in convoys. That way we were under the protection of at least one, but often several, large destroyers, each of which had a significant military arsenal to be used on any unwanted intruder. While the RMS *Newfoundland* travelled to Halifax alone, it would likely have never gotten far, heading east alone, before being targeted by German air or, more likely, sea power.

After making the short diversion to Halifax, my new comrades and I realized we were now on a ship that was but one of approximately twenty ships leaving together at that time, all heading to Liverpool, England, under at least some protection by destroyers of the Royal Navy.

We proceeded by train to Devonport Barracks, near Plymouth, England. While there, we were each given a uniform and provided with some basic training in seamanship. This training included such basic tasks as splicing a rope, tying various knots, along with generally using and steering a ship with a compass.

I was only there for a couple of weeks when I became sick and was taken to Stonehouse Military Hospital, where I was found to have pneumonia and an ear and throat infection. I was kept there at the hospital from February 6 to April 27, 1940, a period of just over eleven weeks.

Once released from hospital, I returned to Devonport Barracks and was looking forward to seeing George Drover and Dick Coombs, as I didn't know anyone else. Of course, Dick and George were long gone from the barracks, and I never did see them again during the wartime service, except once when I saw Dick Coombs around September 1940 at Liverpool Station.

A person who was classified as a "rating" in the Royal Navy was one of a landsman, a regular seaman, an able seaman, or a petty officer. I was first a regular seaman but later designated as an able seaman. As a rating, there was no protocol for someone like me to know the strategy and reasoning behind why I was assigned or moved from one posting to another during World War II.

Less than three weeks after being released from hospital, on May 14, 1940, I, along with some fifty more sailors, was taken from the barracks with our kit bags and hammocks and piled into the back of four navy trucks. We were then taken to the railway station, where we boarded a train for the village of Thurso in the north of Scotland.

The group then crossed the Irish Sea by ferry to Belfast in Northern Ireland. Shortly after we arrived in Belfast, we were taken, again by truck, to our own ship, HMS *Laurentic*.

The ship was an armed merchant cruiser, and when I saw her, I thought this ship was beautiful. It was the biggest ship I had ever seen in my life. It took me a while to find my way around the ship. She was 18,724 tons. The mast was high, and there was a barrel seventy feet up that mast. The sailors called the barrel the crow's nest. While we were at sea, we had to take turns climbing up the metal ladder to get in that barrel and then stay there an hour, keeping watch and reporting anything and everything we saw to the bridge below.

On one occasion when it was my turn to do watch duty from the crow's nest, the wind was blowing quite strongly, causing the ship to roll from side to side. As I approached the barrel, well above the deck, my feet slipped. As a result, I ended up swinging from the ladder by my arms as the ship tipped from one side to the other. With the roll of the ship, I was actually hanging by my hands only, over the water on one side of the ship and then the other. I was frantically trying to get my feet back on the ladder, and after several wild swings from one side to the other, fortunately I managed to plant my feet firmly on the ladder again. It was not a minute too early, since I was losing strength in my hands.

Being of slim build was not always an advantage to me, but being nimble was. One day I was ordered to help a fellow sailor from a predicament created, in part, by his big stomach. The way up to this high lookout was to initially climb an open ladder and then twist and position your body to get up through the small hatch in the floor of the barrel-shaped lookout above. The sailor who was next on watch one day had a big belly, and he somehow became stuck trying to get up through the hatch in the bottom of the lookout barrel. The officer in charge ordered me to climb up to help him get himself clear. In order to do this, I had to go all the way up to where the sailor was stuck and then somehow get past the stuck sailor and climb over the outside of the enclosed barrel. I managed to do this and then got down into the barrel and had to find a way to loosen the sailor and help him go back down. I managed to get him free, and then I did that shift for the poor frazzled fellow that evening.

HMS *Laurentic* was docked in Belfast for about ten days while crew members were taking on enough fuel and provisions to last a month. It seemed strange to me that one of the things they packed into the ship was a large number of empty forty-five-gallon oil drums. But as it turned out, this was a strategy by the navy to slow down the possible sinking of a vessel that might be hit by enemy firepower. The idea was to save lives and make the enemy's job that much harder by creating extra buoyancy with the empty barrels.

When we completed loading the barrels and had taken on enough fuel and provisions, we left Belfast, Northern Ireland, for the Northern Patrol, which operated in the Denmark Strait between Iceland and Greenland. The purpose of this patrol was to find and sink any German ships and U-boats coming through the North Sea and the Denmark Strait from German-held territory. We also had orders to search for what the military referred to as contraband. This contraband included any cargo or supplies that the British Admiralty saw as potentially dangerous to Britain and the Allies.

The Admiralty was expecting the German battleship *Bismarck* to come through the Denmark Strait to get into the Atlantic Ocean. Fortunately (for us), we didn't meet her. Many of the seamen on our ship were apprehensive about the possibility of coming upon the *Bismarck*, because the word was that she was unsinkable.

For logistical reasons, including giving the sailors some rest time, the Admiralty had arranged for each crew to engage in these patrols for rotations of about a month at a time. During these patrols, HMS *Laurentic* captured three German warships and took them into Iceland, where the crews were taken as prisoners of war. There the German ships were given another crew and used as British warships. We stayed in the Denmark Straits for the whole of the summer of 1940.

The home base for HMS *Laurentic* was Liverpool, England, and that is where, after approximately a month at sea, it docked for fuel and provisions. I had relatives of my mother living in Liverpool, and while in port, I often visited them.

I enjoyed being there, because after a month at sea I liked relaxing there. I actually was able to visit my mother's relative Mrs. E. E. Smith. This was my grandfather Smith's brother's wife, Auntie, as she was affectionately called. I thought that she was such an absolutely lovely person. When I visited there, I felt it was like being at home. Auntie often asked me questions about what it was like living in Newfoundland, including what the fishery was like. It seemed that she had at least some understanding of the fishery in Newfoundland. While I never asked how she knew, I concluded that she must have heard her husband talk about the Labrador fishery.

I visited her home every month for about eight months, from April 1940 through October 1940. In the course of these visits, the war was still raging, and at one point I had a close encounter. Of course, there was no light at night because of the complete blackout. Every night during that period, the Germans would drop bombs and use machine-gun fire on the city of Liverpool and elsewhere. One night, probably in August or September 1940, there was a heavy air raid by the Germans, and Liverpool was bombed continually from about 8:00 p.m. until 8:00 a.m. Many houses were destroyed or badly damaged. I was sleeping in Auntie's house that night.

Auntie and her granddaughter Flo were out in the air-raid shelter, but I didn't bother to go. They came in to encourage me to come out with them, but I again said no. Shortly after that, we heard the planes some distance away. At about 2:00 a.m., I woke with a start as a bomb fell close to the house, and the whole house shook violently. The windows and glass came in across the kitchen, the chimney broke, and the blast caused the roof to collapse. I had a hard time trying to get out of the house.

Then about 3:00 a.m., Flo and I took Auntie from the air-raid shelter and carried her about a half-mile to her daughter Mary's house. The only light we had was from the burning buildings and the explosions of the bombs. It was a trying time for the old lady. I heard it was the worst air raid Liverpool experienced during the war.

After that night, I stayed there with Flo's mother and father, but after a couple of days, I went back to my ship. Auntie lived with her daughter after that night. I did visit her there a couple of times after the bombing, but I felt it wasn't the same anymore. There was a big family at Mary's house, and that changed the whole feeling I had about visiting there.

I returned to HMS *Laurentic*, and the unfolding war had other plans for me.

6 — Willie

I TOO THOUGHT OF MY MOTHER

November 3, 1940

Although the British Royal Navy had a reputation as one of the world's most formidable naval forces on earth, the sheer magnitude of this war, including the many resources of Germany, had already placed a massive strain on the naval fleet. There were a number of large and well-equipped British ships and destroyers as well as other classes of naval ships already deployed there, but it was not enough if the Allies were to be able to turn back German aggression on the seas.

As a result of a shortage of vessels, the Admiralty had taken possession of a number of privately owned civilian ships to help in the war effort. One of those vessels was the ship that I was initially assigned to as an able seaman. HMS *Laurentic* (formerly the SS *Laurentic*) had been a luxury liner engaged in the transatlantic passenger route from Liverpool to Montreal and Quebec City. This ship was actually a coal-burning ship and was the second ship with the same name to have been converted for war use by the British Royal Navy. The first HMS *Laurentic*, built in 1908, was an ocean liner serving the Europe-to-Canada route. This ship was sunk in 1917 just outside the port of Lough Swilly, County Donegal, Ireland, after striking German mines.

The year 1940 was still relatively early in the war, and the United

States of America, although supportive, had not yet officially entered the conflict. The Land Lease Agreement, signed by both Britain and the USA and which saw a dramatic increase in British sea power, had not even taken place. Throughout most of 1940, HMS *Laurentic* had seen some success in intercepting enemy ships, but that certainly wasn't due to either its firepower or its stealth manoeuvrability.

The *Laurentic* was big by any measure and had a top speed of around sixteen knots. Its guns consisted only of two four-inch guns installed in the bow and stern. It had also been refitted to carry and launch a small number of depth charges. We all knew these armaments were very little to repel the might of a large German battleship such as the *Bismarck*. With much more sheer determination than it had machinery, however, the British Admiralty used every possible resource it had available.

After a stormy but otherwise uneventful day in November 1940, things were about to change abruptly for the captain and crew of HMS *Laurentic*. The night was dark, and there was a big swell running. The wind had been blowing hard all day, but it had moderated by evening. I was not on duty that night, but at about 2200 hours, the action station bells suddenly rang out, and everybody jumped out of his hammock and proceeded up toward his action station. My responsibility was to be at the number two gun station, near the bow on the port side. We seemed to be in the midst of organized chaos, with several of us running to get to our assigned locations. On the way to mine, I was suddenly thrown off my feet by an explosion of what I quickly realized was a torpedo.

The German Otto Kretschmer, known to friend and foe alike as "Silent Otto," for never using radio communication while closing in on torpedoing a ship, was about to solidify his place as a remarkable German U-boat captain. Prior to being torpedoed, our ship had moved from the Denmark Strait farther west between Iceland and Ireland. We were on our way back to Liverpool when the dreaded event occurred.

When we got to our action stations, the ship had about a forty-degree list to starboard and seemed to me to be in danger of turning over. One of our gunners fired a star shell, which lit up the area, allowing us to see all around, including, to everyone's surprise, the submarine that was attacking us. When we realized the submarine had now surfaced, three of our guns fired and almost hit it.

HMS *Laurentic*, 1927 to November 4, 1940

Unfortunately, the submarine dived before damage could be inflicted. In the meantime, our ship was listing more all the time and taking on a lot of water. As a result, we were ordered by our captain to abandon ship. Fortunately, our ship's wireless operator had gotten off a SOS signal before we had completely lost our power. The SOS was picked up by a British destroyer that we had met at around 1300 hours that afternoon but was steaming in the opposite direction.

When the U-boat torpedoed us, we were positioned about 300 miles off a land area in Ireland known as Bloody Foreland. The area takes its name from the way the setting sun highlights the natural red of the granite cliffs near Gweedore in Northwest Ireland.[1]

---

1 Ireland's West Coast unofficial website dedicated to Ireland's Wild Atlantic Way

During this ordeal, I met up with Churchill Parsons, a fellow sailor who hailed from Jeffrey's on the west coast of Newfoundland. He and I were looking around for some way to get off the ship when the second torpedo hit HMS *Laurentic* at 2230 hours. There was a lot of smoke and a strong smell of cordite from the ammunition exploding. At that time, many people had been injured or killed, and many had been forced into the water, where conditions were dreadful. I remember so well the sounds of the groaning and creaking of the sinking ship, but most of all I remember the sounds of the men in the water. There was a lot of screaming and crying, and men who before this were going about their daily routines on the ship now desperately crying for their mothers.

As the U-boat continued to circle us, like a shark circling its prey for the kill, I noticed that two of our ship's lifeboats had been destroyed by the explosion of the U-boat's second torpedo. As a result, the lifeboat that I was assigned to was already taken by other sailors who, seeing their own lifeboat destroyed, simply took the next one available to them. This action by other sailors resulted in us having nowhere to go and limited options for any chance of survival.

As it turned out, while the people in that lifeboat were in the process of being rescued by HMS *Patroclus*, a torpedo from *U-boat 99* hit pretty much under that lifeboat, killing many on the ship, as well as all the HMS *Laurentic* sailors who were on the lifeboat.

Most everybody had gotten off the ship by now, and while we were looking for some kind of raft, the captain came along and ordered us to get off the ship right away. It was then that we discovered a Carley float (a small raft named after the inventor, Horace Carley) tied to the side of the ship near where we were.

Churchill Parsons and I got the raft ready, and we tied a long rope on it and lowered it over the side. While I was thinking about what I had to do next, and expecting any minute for a third torpedo to hit, I realized that my lifebelt was not inflated. I hadn't blown any air into it. The belt worked like an inner tube, except that the air could be blown into it manually. After getting my lifebelt working, I felt a bit more confident, and I was hoping that when I hit the water I would float.

Hesitant still to jump, I looked around the tilted ship and realized that the water was now coming in over the port side. By that time the ship was nearly turned over. I looked down in the water and could just see the Carley float, and to make matters worse, I couldn't swim!

I just closed my eyes and jumped.

It seemed like a long time before I hit the water. I didn't know how far I went down, but I never thought I would come back to the surface anymore. Then, suddenly, I surfaced and got my breath back. I started to get my bearings, and while looking around, I saw many people in the water. Some were calling out and crying. I think there were about 150 sailors in the water in the area where I was that night. Some of them were on Carley floats, some on rafts, and others clinging to wreckage, barrels, or whatever would keep one afloat. My friend Churchill had also jumped from the ship, and we both managed to get to the Carley float we had thrown over the side.

The Carley float was intended for no more than ten people. Within a few hours, however, there were ten to twelve and sometimes more like thirteen to fifteen people gathered on it. Of course, with all the weight, the float was partially submerged in the water so that all on the float were up to their waist in chillingly cold water for what would be all night, from around 2230 hours until about 1100 hours, the next morning.

It was a night fighting for survival, and it was not uneventful. Probably around 0300 or 0400 hours on November 4, 1940, the German *U-boat 99* surfaced again and came close to our raft. We all jumped off the raft and scattered, since we all had lifebelts on. We had been told that the Germans might take some of us prisoners, and there was always the fear that they would open fire on us. Instead, the submarine just passed on by us. After the Germans left, we all climbed back onto the raft and continued to hope for a rescue vessel to show up.

I know that during the night there were some who became numb with the cold and just fell off the raft and disappeared into the darkness. As soon as one would fall off, there were others waiting to take his place. It really was the survival of the fittest.

In the dark and in the distance, we could hear people talking to each other; some praying, some calling out to their families, some to their mothers or fathers or children. Maybe the darkness was a blessing! Maybe we wouldn't want to see what was going on around us.

I thought about Upper Island Cove—about how safe it was, about how I knew everyone and everyone knew me. I thought of the pranks we played on each other, and for some reason I felt very badly about the tricks we played on the town constable. I hoped I would live to see him and apologize. I also hoped that I would live to come home. If I did, I was sure I would never leave Upper Island Cove again.

I always had a close relationship with Mother and my family. I remember Lydia being so upset when Dick and I walked down the lane that cold January morning in 1940. Myra, equally upset, chose to stay in the house. When I looked back through the kitchen window, her face was wrapped in Mother's apron, as Mother too displayed a look of sadness that almost made me change my mind about leaving. I regularly received a number of letters from my younger sister, Lydia, along with Myra. Each of them being the next-eldest and the next-youngest sibling no doubt accounted for me being especially close to both of them. I thought of them and my other siblings and friends during the night.

At about 1000 or 1100 hours the next morning, a larger lifeboat floated near us, and all of us got in it. This was better than the Carley float, but there was a leak in the lifeboat, and because my legs were numb, I was not able to stand, so I sat in the cold water again. I didn't realize both my legs were so numb as to feel paralyzed. I had to be lifted up and put into the lifeboat. About three hours later, we saw a British destroyer coming, and everybody started waving his hands and saying help was on the way. But it took a long time before that ship reached us, because she was actually hunting for the U-boat, which was believed to be in the area.

I always wondered if the captains of HMS *Laurentic* and HMS *Patroclus* might have made a critical and deadly error in picking up survivors, but one very much based on compassion for the sailors in the water. The clear orders of the British Admiralty were that the protocol when encountering another ship being attacked was to first, engage the enemy, and only when the enemy vessel had been silenced or had escaped from attack should there be any effort to recover potential survivors.

In our case, the captain of HMS *Laurentic* likely placed us in harm's way when he chose to pick up survivors of the smaller SS *Casanare*. When HMS *Laurentic* was hit, the captain of HMS *Patroclus* came to the rescue of the crew of the torpedoed, but still afloat, HMS *Laurentic*. Both ships were torpedoed, likely as a consequence of their distracted actions, which allowed the U-boat to continue its carnage.

When the destroyer HMS *Achates* came alongside sometime early afternoon, they had their scrambling nets down over the side so that the survivors could climb aboard. Everybody managed to get on board the rescue vessel except me and two other sailors. We just couldn't walk.

While this was going on, the captain of the rescue ship called on the radio to say that he had to leave as he had a report that the U-boat was in the area. At that point, someone from the ship got down in the lifeboat and took hold of my sweater, and that's how I was lifted on board. Those rescued were put into the engine room, and some of us were put on the warm grates. There I was looked after and fed while lying on an old mattress until I was well enough to go on deck, first with assistance, and then on my own.

When life came back into my legs, the pain almost drove me crazy. There were approximately fifty or more of my comrades lost that night. It should be noted that our ship, as well as HMS *Patroclus*, were both rather stubborn to sink. This caused the U-boat much valuable time and ammunition.

Despite our ship's major tilt to starboard, and although we could not see everything going on because of our low vantage point on the raft in choppy seas, we realized that we (as well as HMS *Patroclus*) were hit as many as five times by torpedoes without sinking. Our ship did not sink until almost 0400 hours on November 4, when the U-boat fired a final torpedo at very close range.

Thinking back to when we were in Northern Ireland, I remembered we had loaded the drums into the lowest areas of the ship, where cargo or supplies would not ordinarily be placed. When hit by the torpedoes, though suffering significant damage, the ship kept floating to a stubborn and frustrating degree from the perspective of the U-boat captain.

Many of these drums could be seen floating in the hours after we abandoned the ship. Some sailors clung onto these barrels during the night, which helped keep them alive to be rescued the next day. The U-boat captain, used to firing one or at most two torpedoes in most cases, spent many hours and much ammunition trying to sink these two ships. He used about nine torpedoes, thereby more quickly depleting his munitions stocks. This was a great tactic used by the Admiralty.

No one really knew, but the word among sailors was that the captain of the *Patroclus* felt responsible for the men he lost. The captain did not survive that night, and it was said that, knowing he had deliberately ignored orders, the captain might have chosen that fate rather than face the consequences of his actions if rescued. Also, during the same night, another ship, the merchant cruiser SS *Casanare*, was torpedoed by *U-99* and sank.

Silent Otto Kretschmer had destroyed three British ships in one night, resulting in the loss of many lives as well as destroying hundreds of tons of essential supplies and vessels needed by Britain. There were a number of Newfoundlanders on each of these ships, including but not limited to the following;

HMS *Patroclus*: 76 dead, including:

Bertram Leslie Moore of Dildo (3rd Contingent).

There were 230 survivors, including the following Newfoundlanders:

James H. Paddock, Bonavista (3rd Contingent)
Albert Froude, Burgoyne's Cove (3rd Contingent)
Joe Clarke, Dunfield, Trinity Bay (3rd Contingent)
William Mouland, Bonavista (3rd Contingent)
George Sheppard, Lark Harbour (4th Contingent)
Robert Greene, St. John's (7th Contingent)
Fred Gullage of Corner Brook (4th Contingent) was wounded and died in hospital in Scotland on January 1, 1941.

The ship's captain, William Wynter, was also lost.

HMS *Laurentic*: 47 dead, including:

Roy McLeod, Bay Roberts (3rd Contingent)
Francis J. Roche, Placentia (5th Contingent)

The following Newfoundlanders survived the sinking of the *Laurentic*:

Leonard Nash, Branch (1st Contingent)
John Power, Branch (3rd Contingent)
William Lundrigan, Upper Island Cove (3rd Contingent)
Churchill Parsons, Jeffrey's
Angus Crowley, Holyrood (3rd Contingent)
Patrick Gushue, Conception Harbour (3rd Contingent)
Percy Morris, Jeffrey's (3rd Contingent)
James Whelan, Buchans (3rd Contingent)[2]

---

2   © Christopher Paddock & NL GenWeb, NL Military History, The Sinking of HMS *Patroclus* and HMS *Laurentic*

7 — Edie

BOYFRIENDS AND BOMBINGS

1940–1941

Growing up in England, I was fortunate to have a fair amount of education for the late 1930s. I finished school at the age of fifteen, which was the average age most children finished school, unless one wished to enter college. Doing this, however, was an expensive proposition.

From secondary school I went to work in a small village post office, which was combined with a candy store and newspaper stand. I stayed there for a few months until the summer of 1939. I was then excited to join some of my friends and work in a margarine factory named Van den Berg and Jergens.

My mother wanted me to take a course in hairdressing, but my friends weren't into that, so that wasn't for me. I worked in the factory for six years and enjoyed it. A short while after I started working at the factory, the Second World War started. It was September 3, 1939, just a week after my sixteenth birthday. The war was about to change the whole way of life for all of us. It really felt as though we were fading from light and into darkness and were bound there for, at that point, an indeterminate amount of time.

Even if I hadn't just finished school, there would be no more casual walks through the Chase or skipping up Mill Lane. There were some limited recreation activities we could take part in, but with so much danger, combined with such an oppressive feeling everywhere, it took a lot of getting used to.

I began to see a boy who was visiting a friend who lived not far from my home. I didn't know him well, but he seemed kind and considerate. He had a great smile and was clearly interested in me. My friend Dot Humphries, who was slightly older than me, was also seeing a boy, but neither of us would dare tell our mothers. One night the four of us went walking together, and before long, Dot and the boy she was with took off, leaving me alone with my "boyfriend," so to speak. I don't know if the boys planned the separation or if it just happened. When it did, it seemed to expose a side of the boy I was with that I had never seen or anticipated. He was quick to try to take advantage of me and pushed me against the wall of a building. I squirmed but could not free myself from his grip. The only weapon I had was my small purse. Once I got my left arm free for an instant, I immediately hit him in the face with my purse. He released his grip, and I twisted myself free. Just as I started to step away, he lunged after me, hitting my shoulder. I tumbled into the cobblestone street headfirst, hitting the left side of my head, hard on the ground. I did not lose consciousness but was dazed and lost time in my effort to escape. He was coming toward me again, but fortunately for me, a man and a woman stumbled out of a nearby pub. They saw me on the ground with this boy standing threateningly above me. They both ran toward me, and my assailant ran away into the dark alley. I never saw him again.

The couple, obviously somewhat inebriated, helped me up and asked if I was okay. My face was bleeding a bit, and I had a strong ringing in my left ear, but I was embarrassed and scared, so I assured them I was fine. I managed to get home and to my bedroom without Mum or Dad seeing me. Sometime later, Mum saw the mark on my face, and I told her I had fallen and bumped my head. That is all she ever knew, and that's all I ever said about it. She did know that I had a loss of hearing in my left ear, which the doctor said was likely related to the harsh bang on my head. Neither Mum nor Dad were ever aware that I had been attacked that night. Maybe I should have told my parents, but it all seemed so insignificant when, in the following days, the Germans began their assault of Britain, with a rain of bombs falling on us daily.

The war with Germany, especially the period of the Blitz, which lasted from September 1940 to about May 1941, entailed lots of emotional trauma. Everyone, including adults and children, was literally one bomb away from serious injury or death, and everyone felt the burden of the situation. People quickly came to dread the air raids, knowing that avoiding falling bombs was totally outside our control. Families were spending nights sleeping in the cold, damp, and cramped air-raid shelter, and of course we never knew if we were going to survive. It was always so difficult seeing friends and neighbours get killed or maimed. There were some nights I came home from work to find all the windows in the house broken from the blasts of the bombs. It was not unusual to come home to find my parents being cared for by neighbours in the Anderson air-raid shelter built in our back garden. Dad had it installed according to the instructions, which required that it be covered on both sides and the top with thirty inches of gravel. He also had a barrier of dirt about three feet in front of the door so that we entered from the side and then went through the small door. It was pretty dreary, but we did have some blankets, food, and water there in case we had to stay for a lengthy period.

In addition to the emotional toll, that period entailed an awful lot of hard work. All the routines of daily life had been replaced with this new and fluid way of living. There was no real planning for regular sleep, regular meals, or regular grocery or food shopping. There was simply nothing regular or stable about our lives. People were often forced into eating when they could. Food was all rationed, and clothing was a scarcity, so making do with old, worn, and tattered clothing was often the best there was. Then there were the constant repairs to our house and property from flying debris from bombs, or the soot and the smoke from fires due to the bombing. This was one of the things that forced people to become tough and resilient.

One night we had a difficult time at work as all production was interrupted on several occasions because of German bombings, which forced us into the air-raid shelter a couple of times. It was scary, but we made the most of it by telling cheerful stories about what we wanted life to look like after the war. It was nearing daylight by the time my shift was over. The bombings had pretty much stopped, except for the occasional rumble of a bomb nearby as the planes headed from London back across the English Channel. There was some damage at the factory, but when we walked home, we could see the massive destruction to buildings everywhere. Unfortunately, many homes nearby were hit that night, resulting in a high loss of life.

As I approached our street, I could see the property next to Mum and Dad's had been pretty well destroyed. As I got closer, I could see that the front door of our house was blown out, as were some of the windows. I ran into the house and called out to my parents, but there was no one there. I then headed for the backyard, where during a bombing they often retreated to the Anderson air-raid shelter. As I went through the back door, I could see the shape of a person lying on the ground. When I got closer, I could see that it was Dad.

I knelt down and could see that he was alive and just beginning to move. He was full of glass and had some cuts on his hands but seemed otherwise okay. I helped him to sit and then to stand. He was a bit wobbly, but we were able to get to the shelter, where after getting Mum's attention I was able to help him inside. Apparently, when the air-raid siren went off, they didn't move out of the house as quickly as they should have. The bomb hit the house next door, and Dad told Mum to go and, whatever she did, not to leave the shelter until all bombing had ceased. As Dad closed the door to the house, the blast of the bomb that hit next door damaged our house, and the blast wave blew him off the step. Thankfully, neither of them were seriously hurt. As we sat in the air-raid shelter, I thought about what was happening to us and to the world.

Tonight, we were safe, but what about tomorrow night?

The shelter had likely saved Mum and Dad more than once, and we were thankful the government had supplied one for our use. It was cold and damp, but it protected us, at least from a direct hit.

We also had government-issued gas masks there in case the Germans dropped some kind of chemicals. The wife of my eldest brother was pregnant during the war. I remember well that, one night during some intense bombing, her water broke while they were in the air-raid shelter. There was nowhere to go and no way to get any help. My nephew David was born in the shelter as the bombs rained down nearby. Both the mom and the child were none the worse for the experience.

I recall that, although these years were very dangerous and scary, there were times when we could enjoy ourselves. Some of the local hotels that remained open would have dances and picture shows. We could still buy some clothes, but like everything else, they were rationed, and coupons had to be given for each article being purchased. All food items were rationed, and fresh fruit was a luxury. Fortunately for us, some of the local farmers had orchards, so we were able to get fruit from there.

My friends and I wanted to leave the factory and join the Auxiliary Territorial Service (ATS), but we were not permitted to leave the margarine factory, since this work had been deemed essential by the authorities. We operated under government orders. Our factory was bombed twice, and fifty of the girls, myself included, had to relocate to an ice cream factory. There we made and packaged margarine until the old factory was put back in running order.

8 — Willie

SCAPA FLOW

August 1, 1941 – September 28, 1941

"Everybody was armed except Nathan and me. There were no more rifles left, and as the captain inspected the landing party, he asked me why I wasn't armed. Before I spoke, the captain was informed that there were no more arms. The captain told the officer in charge to check again to make sure, and when he came back, all he could find were two swords."
— Willie Lundrigan

Those who survived the sinking of HMS *Laurentic* in November 1940 were obviously elated to have been rescued, but some of us were yet still subdued by the intense physical ordeal we had experienced. When we docked in Scotland on November 5, 1940, we arrived to a wonderful welcome and were given warm clothes and hot drinks. We stayed there all that night, and the next morning we boarded a train for the long ride to Devonport Barracks, located in the southwest of England, and arrived there the following morning, November 7, 1940.

At the barracks, everyone was given a thorough physical exam, and the group was on the move again. Some of the survivors were injured worse than others, with some of them being admitted to hospital immediately. All of those well enough to do so were given new clothes, boots, and shaving gear, plus a new gas mask and lifebelt. Then they were ready to go.

Unfortunately, one of the sailors who was not ready to go anywhere was me. It took me a month or more before I could walk, which I attributed to being "chilled to the bone." I was placed in hospital with a diagnosis of pneumonia for the second time in a year and remained there for several weeks. Overall, this took me out of active service for about three months. Not happy with being penned up in barracks, and after a lot of me badgering my superiors, the doctor told me that I could go back into service if there was a doctor on any ship that I was assigned to.

Except for those killed or seriously injured, the war did not end for us with the sinking of HMS *Laurentic*. On February 27, 1941, the day after I was released from hospital, a number of sailors who were hospitalized, including me, were told to get our kit bags and hammocks and put them on board a truck, which took us to the railway station. We were on the train all that day, and sometime during the night, the train stopped. As was not unusual, we were told to get our kit bags and hammocks and put them in another truck, which took us to a dock. There, two days after being released from hospital, the group was put on a small boat that took us out to a supply ship called HMS *Maidstone*. Interestingly, this ship, which was anchored in the harbour of Scapa Flow in the north of Scotland, had three doctors on board.

Strategically located at the very northern tip of Scotland, this ship supplied the British Navy fleet with everything including ammunition, medical supplies, food, and all sorts of other items used by seagoing navy ships and submarines. There was an enormous stock of explosives on board HMS *Maidstone*, from torpedoes to ammunition for battleships, to depth charges for destroyers.

I did not see many people I knew from Newfoundland through my war years. Yet, by coincidence, when I got released from hospital and was getting ready for active service after the sinking of HMS *Laurentic* the previous November, I met Nathan Mercer, an old acquaintance from back home in neighbouring Spaniard's Bay, Newfoundland. I knew Nathan before the war, since he used to come down from Spaniard's Bay to Upper Island Cove with the Loyal Orange Lodge band.

Nathan told me that he had entered the British Royal Navy through a process known as the draft. He said that it meant he knew he was going to serve somewhere, but for security reasons, he wouldn't know where until he got *there*.

As soon as I arrived on board this ship, however, I knew that I didn't want to be there, because I realized that ship wasn't going anywhere, and I wasn't used to that. I wanted to be on a ship that was going places, but we were anchored there permanently. We were on this ship until early March 1941. On March 4, 1941, we were transferred to another depot ship, HMS *Tyne*.

We were there for about a month, and Nathan Mercer and I got restless as we both wanted to go to sea. Nathan was with me in Scapa Flow when I got my only tattoo on my right arm. I didn't intend to get a tattoo, but as we were walking down the street, Nathan said, "Look, over there, there's a tattoo parlour. I have always wanted a tattoo." I had no interest, but at Nathan's insistence, we went in the store to have a look around. There were two sailors there getting a tattoo, which we watched from a distance. While I was looking at the different tattoo sample pictures, I spotted one that intrigued me. It was called "Heart and Sword." I was surprised by my own spontaneous action and had the tattoo placed on my right forearm when I left the store. Nathan also got a tattoo that day.

I also remember one night Nathan and I were dying for a smoke. Of course, smoking was not allowed outside at night because of the blackout regulations, which required all sources of light (even from a cigarette) be covered so as not to alert the enemy. Nathan and I tucked ourselves away underneath a big tarpaulin to have our puff.

We were carrying on and joking, and both of us would occasionally burst out laughing, and then there'd be hush when we thought someone might be coming. Not surprisingly, we got caught by one of the ship's officers. Nathan was caught first, and for some reason he got a more serious punishment than I did. Nathan had to do a week of deck scrubbing and lost his daily ration of rum for a week as well. I got away with only losing my rum ration, but no deck scrubbing for me.

While we were there, Allied destroyers would come into Scapa Flow in order for a depot ship to supply it with arms or equipment. Sometimes they would be in need of two or three seamen. Often the sailors deployed on these destroyers and battleships were the most likely ones to be injured or killed in action or washed overboard. One day a destroyer came alongside HMS *Tyne* for fuel and ammunition. When they tied up alongside our ship, Nathan and I got talking to one of the seamen. After some time, we saw two sailors leaving the ship.

The sailors we talked to told us that the two who were leaving the ship were from New Zealand and were leaving the ship to go to gunnery school for a three-month course. So, Nathan and I asked the officer if we could take their places. Our request was turned down flat. Then we heard that the ship was staying there all night, so we asked to see the captain in the morning.

The captain asked, "Why do you want to go on a destroyer?"

I told him, "I want to be on a boat that is going to sea."

The captain asked me, "Have you been on a seagoing ship before?"

I told him, "Yes, I was on board an armed merchant cruiser that had been patrolling in the Denmark Strait for ten months."

He asked, "Why did you leave that ship?"

I told him, "We didn't leave the ship. Rather, the ship left us." I then told him that HMS *Laurentic* got torpedoed and sank while we were on our way back to Liverpool for supplies.

At about 1100 hours on August 12, 1941, the captain told us that we could come aboard the destroyer as replacements for the two New Zealanders while they were at gunnery school. At about 1400 hours, HMS *Escapade*, with us as crew members, left Scapa Flow for Iceland, where we arrived late the next night. There we met Britain's newest battleship, HMS *Prince of Wales*, with the British prime minister, Sir Winston Churchill, on board. This was the final leg of the journey for him after he had been meeting in Argentia, Newfoundland, with President Roosevelt of the USA, August 10–12, 1941.

The prime minister went ashore in Iceland to inspect the British and Commonwealth troops stationed there. Then, on August 17, 1941, in company with the other British destroyer, we escorted the *Prince of Wales* back to Scapa Flow, Scotland. On August 18, 1941, the prime minister boarded the train for London.

We then left Scapa Flow later in the day on August 17, 1941. After getting out to sea, we found out that the convoy we were part of was going to Murmansk in Northern Russia. It was terribly cold and stormy all the way to our destination. It took us a long time to get there because the seas were so rough. The German planes bombed the convoy at least once a day, and their big ships and submarines were a constant threat.

Accompanying the convoy was a battleship that could also take care of any ship the Germans might send out to interfere with us. Our ship was the escort ship, which meant it was our job to go ahead and use ASDIC (anti-submarine detection, an early British version of sonar) to track down any submarine that may attack the convoy. Some of the Allied planes operating out of Iceland drove the submarines away, and the German Navy didn't bother the convoy too much.

During the trip, we received a coded message from the Admiralty to leave the convoy we were with and to proceed in another direction to meet yet another convoy. Three days later, we met the convoy, and only then did we know that we were going to Spitsbergen, an island owned by Norway, which was around 650 miles south of the North Pole. Our orders were to take possession of the island, as it was believed there was a possibility the Germans had taken the island, occupied it, and were using its weather station as well as its coal mines.

We didn't know it at the time, but the Germans were not in possession of that island, but a German reconnaissance plane was following our convoy. The mines, as well as the weather station, had previously been strategically destroyed by the Canadian Navy, and all the equipment from the weather station had been removed. The convoy that our ship, HMS *Escapade*, was part of had an aircraft carrier accompanying us, and one of their planes from that carrier flew over the island and reported that they couldn't see anyone on the island of Spitsbergen.

HMS *Escapade* and another destroyer were to enter the harbour with orders to destroy any German ships that might be there. The harbour was frozen solid when we got there in late August, early September 1941. Before we entered the harbour, we had to wait for a tanker to go ahead of us and break the ice.

On the ship, before we entered the harbour, we were formed into a landing party. This included all the crew of HMS *Escapade* and the other destroyer, all except the crew manning the guns. However, before we entered the harbour, we were all armed with some kind of weapon, mostly rifles, machine guns, revolvers, and hand grenades.

Everybody was armed except Nathan and me, as there were no more rifles left. As the captain inspected the landing party, he looked to me and asked, "Why aren't you armed?" Before I spoke, the captain was informed that there were no more arms. The captain told the officer in charge to, "Check again to make sure!" When he came back, all he found were two swords.

He strapped one sword on Nathan and one on me. I told the captain, "This is the first sword I have ever seen." The captain replied, "At least you are armed." Nathan Mercer was a short man, and when he strapped on the sword, it dragged awkwardly on the ground. As soon as our ship went alongside the landing, we all jumped ashore and proceeded toward the weather station. We had a signal operator and a wireless operator with us, and the wireless operator was in constant contact with our ship.

When we arrived back at the ship, we all had to check in our arms. Nathan and I had to check in our swords. Fortunately, we didn't get a chance to use them. Our ship stayed in the harbour for seven or eight days. Most of the crew went ashore on the island while we were waiting for a convoy of British troops that was under way to permanently occupy the island of Spitsbergen, also known as the Land of the Midnight Sun.

At that point, our time on HMS *Escapade* was about to end, so on September 28, 1941, Nathan and I had to go back on board HMS *Tyne*.

Nathan and I were together for some tough times, but we also had fun. We were on the *Tyne* for a few more weeks and were sent back to Devonport Barracks on October 14, 1941, and attended gunnery school for a few weeks.

9 — Willie

THE CONVOY AND THE *CARIBOU*

November 1941 – November 1942

From Devonport we went to Liverpool, where on November 4, 1941, a year to the day that we were rescued from the torpedoed HMS *Laurentic*, I joined another destroyer, HMS *Reading*. HMS *Reading* was originally an American ship previously known as the USS *Bailey*. When I joined her crew, she was escorting convoys from Liverpool in Britain to St. John's, Newfoundland. As a result of this deployment, I was able to get home to Upper Island Cove for a couple of days on the first trip the ship made to Newfoundland. Unfortunately, the destroyer did not turn out to be an especially reliable ship for Britain.

Our convoy was varied, and at one point the route changed so that we were steaming from St. John's to Londonderry, Ireland, and then back to St. John's. We were going to and from St. John's and Ireland all that winter. On one occasion after making a trip to Newfoundland, our engines gave us a lot of trouble. We left St. John's to escort a convoy to Londonderry, but shortly after we got under way, one of our engines stopped. After another hour, the other one started to give trouble. We returned to St. John's on one engine, and the engineers from the St. John's dockyard worked on the engines for two days. After having engineers come in from Halifax, they finally got the engines going again. We then left St. John's alone, having to catch up with the convoy.

We were going about twenty-four hours when both our engines broke down and we were left drifting freely about 600 miles from St. John's. During this time sitting there, our engineers were doing all they could to get our engines going.

While HMS *Reading* was stopped in the middle of the North Atlantic Ocean, our ASDIC picked up the sound of a ship approaching. When the ship came into sight, HMS *Reading* sent a recognition signal to the approaching ship, but that ship did not reply to the signal. The captain and crew were in a quandary now, and for that short while, we were very concerned, since we did not know what nationality the ship was.

We could not recognize their signal, and this ship was approaching fast, so our captain ordered everyone to action stations. Our ship had eight torpedo tubes and four guns, and they were all loaded and ready to fire. My action station was on the four-inch gun up on the forecastle, and there were six of us in the crew, including my friend Walt Lester and another young fellow from St. John's.

This was the young fellow's first time on a warship. By now it was pitch dark, and our ship's captain called our gun captain and told us to stand by to fire a star shell. My friend Walt and I had been together a long time. We knew that the young fellow didn't know what was going on. When the gun captain started to set the fuse on the star shell so that it would explode at the required height, the young fellow said to Walt, "What is buddy doing with that shell?"

Walt said, "After the fuse is set, that shell will explode in fifteen seconds." The young man turned as white as snow.

Then he turned to me and said, "Hold this shell for me, buddy. I got to go to the bathroom."

The role of this same young man during combat was for him to pass me a loaded shell, then take a spent or used shell case back when I had fired it. The routine was that the spent shell was always tossed overboard.

I recalled that on one occasion, instead of throwing a spent shell overboard, this young fellow must have gotten confused or scared during rapid firing of the ship's guns and threw a loaded shell overboard. This could have been a dangerous situation because of the possibility of the shell exploding close to the ship. Fortunately, it didn't explode and the gun crew did not mention the incident, out of concern that the young fellow would have gotten into big trouble.

It also turned out that the ship approaching us was an American ship. The reason they did not recognize our signal was that the signal changed every four hours, and there was a three-and-a-half-hour difference in the times being followed by each ship. The American ship towed us for three days while we were in rough seas. Then the tow rope broke and we were left alone again. It was now the middle of May 1942, and the engineers got the engines going again, so we crippled to Londonderry, but the engineers there could not repair the engines. As a result, we steamed on to London, England, through the English Channel, where, after about a month, the engineers at the London dock also reported there was nothing that could be done to repair the engines.

On June 6, 1942, the entire crew of HMS *Reading* were sent back to their barracks. Just as we had arrived in Devonport, 500 sailors, including me, were rounded up to do some specialized training at a training camp in a place called Glen Holt. It turned out that the training did not actually happen. We learned later that the reason for the planned training might have been preparation for a possible assignment for Dieppe.

We were then enrolled in a gunnery course, and after six to eight weeks, when partly through the course, we were sent back to barracks and told to get our kit bags and hammocks ready. Then in early October 1942 we travelled by train to Thurso, Scotland. From there about sixty of us boarded a large former ocean liner headed for North Sydney, Nova Scotia. I was told that I had two weeks leave in Newfoundland. The plan was that I would proceed to the USA to join a new ship, but that did not happen.

In recalling the trip, I remember that for safety reasons during wartime, ships rarely took a direct route. They would often take a sort of zigzag pattern to help avoid detection by German U-boats. Partially as a result of this zigzag routing, the ocean liner actually arrived in North Sydney, after the long trip, later than anticipated. That made it too late for me and others to make the connections with the SS *Caribou*, which was the regular ferry designated to cross the Cabot Strait to Newfoundland.

I estimated we missed that connection with the *Caribou* by about an hour or so. I often said luck must have been with us, because on that trip from North Sydney to Port aux Basques, the SS *Caribou* was torpedoed. The date was October 14, 1942, but because of the nature of news and communication in wartime, it was a couple of days before we heard about the SS *Caribou*'s sinking and loss of life.

Since we missed the crossing and because the ferry service to Newfoundland was suspended for safety reasons for about three weeks, about fifty Newfoundlanders were sent to the Canadian Naval Barracks at Strathcona to await further instructions on transportation home to Newfoundland. We were told that, while there, we would have to abide by the Canadian military rules. That entailed getting up at 0530 hours and being back in the barracks by midnight. We all disagreed with these requirements, because as far as we were concerned, we had been assigned, under British orders, to travel to the USA in order to join a ship being taken over by the Royal Navy from the Americans. That meant we were under the Royal Navy rules and not Canadian rules.

After a couple of days, we were sent instead to the YMCA on Barrington Street in Halifax, with all expenses paid. We waited there for two weeks. One day, another sailor, Ernest Simms from Twillingate, and I decided to walk down to the wharf to see how many ships were there. While we were there on the wharf looking around, somebody called out to me, saying, "What are you doing, Lundrigan?" I turned to the sound of the voice and immediately realized who the young man was.

It was Clarence Pynn from Harbour Grace. Of course, he wanted to know what we were doing in Halifax. When we told him the story of how we were trying to get home, he said that he was a crew member on a south coast schooner that was leaving Halifax that night at 2130 hours. He said he would go and ask Captain Heber Keeping of Grand Bank if he would take us to St. John's.

The captain told us he would love to take my friend and me because he was two men short. He said we would have to get permission from the Canadian Naval authorities in Halifax. As a result, my friend and I immediately went to see the commanding officer and told him the story. Unfortunately, he turned us down flat.

Then the captain of the Newfoundland schooner went to see the navy commanding officer. When the captain came back, he told us to get our kit bags and hammocks and come aboard the schooner. We finally left Halifax at 2130 hours that night with a load of supplies for the south coast of Newfoundland. It took us nine days to get to St. John's, and I arrived home in Upper Island Cove the following day. In my mind, nine days on a schooner was a minor change in plans compared to being on the SS *Caribou* to Newfoundland the night she was torpedoed.

Once we got to St. John's, I went to Spaniard's Bay by train. Then I walked down through Bishop's Cove until I came to a house where I heard singing and music playing. Someone took me by the arm and pulled me into the house and sat me down at the table.

Then another person said, "There's going to be a wedding here tonight."

I was already half-drunk before I got to Bishop's Cove, but then I had another few drinks. Then, after we had a meal, we all went down to the Bishop's Cove church for the wedding ceremony. I don't remember very much about the service as I was asleep most of the time. I remember leaving the church and walking down to Upper Island Cove. After a couple of drinks at a friend's house, I left and went up to the old Lundrigan house.

10 — Edie

WILL MY BROTHER COME HOME?

Spring 1942

"The young man was gone, and so too was any colour in my father's face. I have never forgotten the look of such anguish he carried. To me he seemed to have aged twenty years in the short time since he stepped outside, closing the front door behind him. As he walked slowly toward me, he said in an almost trembling voice, 'Go upstairs and tell your mother to come down, please.'"

— Edie England

In our home at Upper Island Cove, there was a rich history of Britain and of the Second World War. Many stories, some sad, some hilarious, were told by Bill and me over the years. There was one story that, though I found the strength to tell it, distressed me deeply every time I spoke of it. I had to tell my children about it.

Early in the war, my family and friends often had to watch helplessly while sons and brothers were going off to war, away from us and overseas to fight for Britain and the Allies, some never to return. Among those who went were my three brothers—Sid, Harry, and Alf.

I remember in February of 1942, my father told me of reading in the newspaper about the island of Singapore being seized by the Japanese. As a result, tens of thousands of soldiers were captured and were now being held as prisoners of a brutal regime and under intolerable treatment.

My brother Sid was the next-eldest in age to me, and we shared many memories together. Sid was a member of the Sixteenth Division of the Suffolk Regiment of the British Army. His division had been deployed to Southeast Asia, so the news shared by my father about troops being captured by the Japanese was worrisome, since we didn't know exactly his location. We did know that many of these soldiers had been killed, while the rumour locally was that a large number had been used as slave labour. As time went by, Mum sent letters and packages to Sid, but she did not receive any response from him.

I remember one day Mum being especially upset. She said to Dad, "Alf, I don't know what's wrong with Sid. I keep writing him and sending him packages and he used to answer, but lately I have not received any reply. He must know we are worried about him."

Dad, having heard about the increased hostilities in the Far East, simply said, "Annie, I'm sure those young fellows don't have access to the mail on a regular basis like we do here. I'm sure we will hear from him soon." Of course, they never did, and indeed, bad news was on the way before long.

One day in late spring 1942, a letter arrived at my parents' home from the War Office. My father read the letter and said to me, "Let me know when your mother comes home."

Mum was downtown shopping at the time.

When Mum arrived, Dad told her, "Annie, I have some news about Sid. I understand from the military that he is missing and believed to be a prisoner of war. Assuming he is a POW, he is part of a group of others in his unit who have been moved to Burma, where there are better facilities to house them." They were both upset. Mum cried and I cried, but Dad tried to be cheerful and said, "I'm sure we will hear from him soon."

Sidney John Thomas England

Mum responded, "You mark my words, we will never see Sid again." We did not know about his treatment or his death until September 1945, two years after he had died such a horrible death. Indeed, at the time of his imprisonment, he was among the tens of thousands of POWs who were being forced to work under brutal conditions during the building of a railway between Burma (now Myanmar) and Thailand. This railway was ultimately known as the "Death Railway." The railway was planned and ordered to be built by the Imperial General Headquarters (IGHQ) in 1942, "and from the official orders issued in June [1942] it was clear that it would be built immediately regardless of costs in money and human life."[3]

In fact, the railway was built by not only prisoners of war but with many thousands of local people from Thailand and Burma. The area that my brother was located in was on the Thanbyuzayat section, where an older section of the railway had been built in 1921.[4]

What none of us could really understand was that there were laws, specifically those of the Geneva Convention, by which warring countries had agreed to treat other human beings.

"Oh, how these laws were so ignored by the Japanese!" Mum used to lament.

---

3   *The Thailand to Burma Railway: An Illustrated History* by Geoffrey Pharaoh Adams, p2.
4   *The Thailand to Burma Railway: An Illustrated History* by Geoffrey Pharaoh Adams, p2.

The Japanese deliberately chose not to become a signatory to the Geneva Convention. That is, they would not agree to the basic human rights conditions of war as agreed to by the international community.

While my family didn't know too much during the war about what exactly Sid was being subjected to, what we did come to learn and understand was the truth about the brutal way Sid and others were treated. This was a lifelong nightmare that never ended for my parents or for me.

The evidence available, including the words of a former POW who served in the railway camps, suggests that it was all but certain that Sid had died a violent and brutal death at the hands of his Japanese Army captors. In essence, Sid had been a POW and died long before the Japanese formally surrendered on September 2, 1945.

In that same month of September 1945, my family found out that Sid had succumbed to the dreadful and inhumane treatment and conditions he had endured two years prior to that, on October 16, 1943. Our lives were shattered, and I became very bitter about how a people could treat other human beings in such a manner!

Where, I have often wondered, does forgiveness live?

11 — Willie

AFTER ASBURY PARK

Winter 1943 – Fall 1943

After the nine-day trip along the south coast by schooner, I was home for two weeks, after which it was time for me to begin the second leg of this trip since leaving Devonport, England.

Sometime in November 1942, I went back to St. John's and then crossed Newfoundland to Port aux Basques by train. I took the ferry across the gulf and then went, again by train, to Asbury Park in the United States. There were about sixty of us, and we all stayed at the Monterey Hotel while we waited for a new ship. The ship, built at Bethlehem-Fairfield Co., Baltimore, Maryland, was called an LST, which were code letters for "tank-landing ship."[5]

These ships were used to transport army tanks, trucks, ammunition, and troops to and from various battle zones throughout Europe. The ship was designed with a flat bottom and with two large doors at the bow, which opened to allow the loading and unloading of various vehicles and supplies. This was accomplished by running the ship, bow first, onto various beachheads in Europe, at which point the large bow doors were opened and the ramp dropped on the beach, allowing for troops and equipment to quickly disembark.

---

5   NavSource Online: Amphibious Photo Archive, LST-408

The ship's landing time was usually coordinated (as much as possible) with the tide charts. It was preferred that the tide's height would allow time to unload, and then, with the help of the bow anchors, the ship would be pulled back off the beach. Of course, the needs of the navy to transport soldiers and supplies did not always coincide with the tide table. From time to time, an LST became stranded on a beach for several hours until the rise of the next tide. Even with this operational flaw, however, LSTs would become an essential asset during the invasions of Italy and France as the war progressed.

The ship that my fellow crew members and I would be acquiring, like most other ships of this class, was never given an actual name. Instead, they were just a number. Our ship was built originally for the US Navy and called the USS *LST 408*. It would soon be commissioned as HMS *LST 408* before leaving the United States for active war service.

HMS *LST 408*, which Willie served on 1943–45

During this time waiting in New Jersey for modifications to be done on the ship, invitations for the sailors arrived from citizens along the Eastern Seaboard for the crew members to spend Christmas of 1942 in their homes. Along with a fellow from Scotland who I knew simply by the name of Mackenzie, I was invited to the home of a British sea captain and his wife, who were living about four or five hours away in Boston. My friend and I went there for several days, and from my point of view, we were treated just like one of the family. I recall that there were wonderful meals, and the family made us very welcome in their home.

Finally, on December 23, 1942, the ship that we went there for was ready for the Royal Navy to board and take possession of. At first there were only a few seamen, the captain, and four or five engine room ratings (sailors who worked in the engine room). About a week after that, more seamen came on board. Then, the following week the ship was commissioned, and the British flag, the White Ensign, was hoisted, making it a Royal Navy ship. HMS *LST 408*, with me on board, left Norfolk Navy Yard the following week and then on to Chesapeake Bay to do weeks and weeks of sea trials. Early on April 6, 1943, we left the USA for North Africa with a load of tank oil for the Allied armies fighting there. We were in a convoy of sixty or seventy ships when we ran into a storm some 200 miles before we reached Bermuda. After battling the storm for two days, the cargo of oil in our ship shifted and squatted together, all on the starboard side. This caused our ship to become badly listed and unmanageable to navigate. The oil was in five-gallon drums, and the damage caused our ship to list to starboard forty degrees.

At that point, the commander of the convoy dispatched a destroyer to stay with us until the storm abated. We were headed into the wind, but because of our damaged cargo and the high wind, we had to stay there thirty-six hours. Then, finally, we headed toward Bermuda, only doing a quarter speed. After three days we arrived in Bermuda

Harbour. There we had to get the dockyard workers aboard and secure the oil cans.

While we were in Bermuda having our cargo secured, there was another storm, which was more intense than the one that we were in originally. The wind was so strong in Bermuda Harbour that two of the lifeboats that were used for bringing sailors to shore quickly swamped, and four sailors were drowned. We were in Bermuda for ten days, and it was there in the warm ocean water that I learned to swim. We had little to do, and we were in the water swimming every day. After having our cargo adjusted, we were ready to go again.

The next land we saw was the Azores. The next port of call was Gibraltar, at the mouth of the Mediterranean Sea, where we spent four days. After that we sailed on to Algiers and then on to the island of Malta. After a week we were on our way to Tripoli in Libya, where we unloaded the cargo of oil. We then took some supplies up the coast for the army, as they were badly in need of them.

Then we docked in Algiers. We were there for six weeks, as we had an engine part broken. We had to send to the USA for a part that had to be flown to North Africa. At about this time, mid-1943, the chief of combined operations, Lord Louis Mountbatten, arrived in Algeria to set up his headquarters. Since our ship was immobile and would be for a month, there were twelve sailors from our ship, me included, selected to go ashore as guards to protect his headquarters. In all there were about 500 soldiers and fifty commandos plus ten army tanks and fifteen fighter planes. We sailors really enjoyed ourselves, as it was a change from being on a ship all the time.

After six weeks, the part for the engine arrived. Then we moved farther up the coast with supplies for the Allied armies to places in Algeria as well as Sfax and Sousse, in Tunisia. The crew worked hard loading supplies both night and day on both July 8 and 9, 1943. Then we loaded twenty army tanks, provisions for the army, plus twenty-five army trucks on the top deck.

As the ship left Tripoli, we joined in company with hundreds of other ships and landing craft, carrying among them thousands of men, along with several hundred tanks, guns, and other vehicles. On July 10, 1943, this vast armada descended on Sicily, and our ship, along with a couple hundred others, landed at Augusta and Catania as part of Operation Husky.

As we approached Sicily, it was daylight and we were going full speed toward the beach. We were all apprehensive. Our ship had to sail through a double line of battleships, which were firing the big guns over our heads at targets twenty-five miles inland. As we got close to shore, the noise of the battleship guns, of 300 of our aircraft dropping bombs, as well as the rockets being fired at the German shore was deafening. When we hit the beach, some of the German tanks broke through our defences. We had it rough for a while. The enemy shelling was constant, causing us to be unable to approach the beach because of the carnage of ships, already burning, that lay before us. Eventually there was a break in the shelling, and our captain was able to manoeuvre our ship around the sunken and burnt-out ships and make it to the beach. We immediately opened the massive loading doors, and as we did, the ramp was lowered onto the beach in shallow water. Once the tanks we were carrying were able to get ashore and become organized, things quietened down.

As soon as we had unloaded our twenty tanks and twenty big trucks loaded with fuel and provisions, we left the area with our escort to go across the Mediterranean to Tripoli for another load of tanks, then back again to Sicily. We kept going bringing tanks and fuel and food until the island of Sicily was captured.

In thirty-eight days, the island of Sicily was in Allied hands. In that time, our ship made twelve crossings from Tripoli in Africa with tanks and supplies. We then went back to Sicily, where we had to clean the ship after having so many troops on board, and some of them had been seasick.

After Sicily was captured, the ship's crew had a break for a few days to rest. Then we heard rumours that there was something else big about to happen. On August 6, 1943, the ship was ordered to go to Tripoli to be loaded with tanks, guns, and ammunition. Once loaded, we were ordered to anchor in the harbour and wait for further orders. On September 3, 1943, the captain received his orders, and our ship, along with many others, began the invasion of Salerno.

The invasion was the biggest and toughest one so far because the Italians had given up, resulting in the Germans taking their places. The Germans were desperate. We headed to the beaches of Salerno to deliver supplies to the ships stationed there. Starting about ten miles from the beach, we were being shelled by the Germans all the way in. A couple of our ships got hit, and the shells were landing in the water all around us. It was amazing that we got into the beach at all.

We finally made it to shore, and as soon as we hit the beaches, we came under heavy crossfire from German guns. The troops we landed had to fight their way to shore. The sound of the blasts and the sounds of shells heading toward us was so loud it was maddening. Our ship received direct hits from ten eighty-eight-millimetre shells, eight of which passed right through the ship's hull. The midship portion of our ship received fifteen or sixteen shell holes in the port side, plus there were five shells that passed completely through the bow of the ship but failed to explode. That area of the ship was where we stored most of our provisions, and most of them were spoiled with the shelling impacts. Fortunately, the shell holes were above the waterline.

Then something happened that remained a precious memory for me. The ship's flag, the White Ensign, was also torn to pieces.

About a month before this, I asked the captain, "When the time comes to replace the flag, I wonder if I could have it."

He said, "Yes, Able Seaman Lundrigan, when it is taken down, and if both of us are still here, you can have it."

True to his word, when it was taken down, he gave it to me. It is torn and battle-scarred, but it is priceless.

While we were on the beach being shelled, we had some 200 soldiers on board waiting to go ashore. Of these, there were three who were wounded. All of the troops we had on board were members of the Fifty-First Highland Division of the British Army. I was so struck by the fact that, even in all the confusion and despite the shelling, the soldiers on board marched off the ship to the bagpipes playing the tune "Will Ye No Come Back Again?" I couldn't believe how they marched off the boat as calm as if they were on the parade ground. I will always remember that day.

One soldier standing near me had his thumb blown off by a piece of shrapnel. He also had his rifle broken in half. I helped to carry him to the first-aid post, and the medic gave him a shot of morphine and then dressed his hand. A little while after, when the morphine had started to wear off, the soldier jumped up and took one of the ship's rifles. He ran off our ship, looking for his comrades. We never saw him again, but his action was a wonderful display of courage.

As soon as the tide came in, sufficiently to float our ship, with our crew of about sixty sailors, we left the beach. We were on our way to Tripoli with a load of approximately 200 prisoners, both German and Italian. These prisoners were captured by the Allied forces when our forces broke through the enemy defences about a mile from the beach. Some of them were injured, and they were well looked after as usual. We always had two doctors on board all the time. It took about fifteen hours for our convoy of about fifty ships to get back to Tripoli.

As soon as the *LST 408* got back, there were a lot of tanks and guns waiting for us to pick up. The crew unloaded the prisoners, then loaded the tanks and guns. The *LST 408* was once again on the way to the Salerno beach. The ship was a bit late this time because we had to wait for an escort.

After delivering the cargo, and once our ship got back into the water, we had to go to Malta for a day to have steel plates welded on both sides of the ship. While there, we filled up with a supply of fresh water. As we approached the shore of Malta, a wonderful sight greeted us. The Italian fleet had capitulated to the Allied cause and come over to Malta, much to the chagrin of the Germans!

At this time, we had on board a British-born Italian who was a tremendous help in translating what the Italians were saying to us. I remember him using words *Uma Memento*, *Kapeesh*, and others. Also, during this trip, we had on board a political prisoner who was supposed to have been searched when he boarded the ship. I was one of the men responsible for bringing him food and water. On one occasion when I had taken water to him, he reached into one of his boots and took out a small revolver that was still loaded. He handed it to me and said, "Please give this to your captain." I was really shocked by this, as he could have easily shot me or anyone else. I guess even the enemy had decent people in their midst.

Then the *LST 408* was on its way again to Tripoli in North Africa, to get another load of tanks and ammunition to transport back to Salerno. In all, HMS *LST 408* made fifteen round trips to Salerno, carrying a total of over 300 tanks plus ammunition, fuel, and food. On each trip the ship made to the beaches with supplies, the crew took back a load of prisoners or a load of wounded.

On one such trip, we brought back some badly wounded Canadians. Some of them required special care while being transported. I remember one Canadian officer who had lost one of his arms. We were always there to do whatever we could to make them comfortable. When we arrived back in North Africa and were about to carry them ashore, one of the Canadian officers called to me. When I went to see what he wanted, he gave me a nine-millimetre pistol.

I hesitated, since only officers were allowed to wear a sidearm.

He said, "You and your friends have been good to me. I want you to have this, since I won't be using it anymore."

I accepted it and always carried it, night and day. I had it stuck in my belt, and it was always loaded with the safety catch on. I really wasn't allowed to have it, but the captain didn't know that I was in possession of the gun until I left the ship in 1945. I thought about keeping the pistol when I turned in my uniform and other military items. We were told, however, in the strongest fashion that we were not permitted to keep such items, and if we did and got caught, there would be serious consequences. I knew of others who took the chance and were successful, but after thinking about it, I decided it was not worth the risk.

After the Salerno battlefield front had sufficient supplies and things settled down, the *LST 408* and fourteen other LSTs were again sent to Ferryville, in North Africa. I certainly thought it was a beautiful harbour. The entrance was partially blocked by sunken ships, but all the LSTs got through into the harbour. During our stay there, we had to again clean up the ship.

The crew also painted the ship on the outside, especially the bow, where the shell holes had been welded over, since the shells had gone in on one side and come out the other. It was at that time I was assigned to repaint the inside of the water tank. I took what I thought was the right paint and painted the tank as I was told. When we refilled the tank and were at sea, everyone was complaining of the taste of the water. Apparently I had used the wrong paint and had painted the tank with oil paint instead of the water paint that should have been used.

We were in Ferryville for three weeks. Then we went back to Salerno, but this time it was a lot quieter. We had a lot of supplies, consisting of mostly food and fuel, as well as many medical supplies. Additionally, we also took a load of wounded soldiers to Tripoli in Africa.

For the next four months we took food, tanks, oil, and ammunition to Italy until the Salerno beachhead was completely secure. One time the ship was transporting a load of army Jeeps from North Africa to Italy. Unlike the tanks and trucks, for which there were designated drivers, a contingent of the crew, including me, were selected to off-load the Jeeps. Of course, I had never driven a vehicle before, but that didn't seem to matter. Ten of us would drive Jeeps off the ship to a place a little way inland, and then we would all pile into two Jeeps and return to the ship to repeat with another ten Jeeps, until they were all unloaded.

In December 1943, we were told that we were going back to England, and of course we were pleased with that news. There were over fifty LSTs operating in the area, and all of them were ordered to go to Naples in Italy. The ships arrived there in early December 1943, and of course their crews were all hoping to get back to England for Christmas. But such was not to be for all of us.

On the day we were supposed to leave, we watched the other LSTs steaming out of the harbour in the direction of Gibraltar. They all left except for fifteen ships, and the *LST 408* was one of that fifteen. The ship and crew ended up spending Christmas in Boyar, Italy. When we arrived there, we docked alongside another LST. When we had secured our ship, I saw a sailor with a Newfoundland shoulder tag on his uniform.

I went over to see him and asked, "What part of Newfoundland are you from?"

"I'm from the west coast," he said.

"Is there anyone else on the ship from Newfoundland?" I asked.

He said, "Yes, there's a fellow Mercer from Upper Island Cove."

I said, "When you go back on the ship, ask Mercer to come up on deck, would you?" When he arrived, it was Jim Mercer, nicknamed "Jim Hann." Jim and I spent a couple of weeks together and had a great time.

While both ships were docked there, Jim and I went to Naples a few times on the train, as the station wasn't very far from our ship. We would see each other every other day. One night we went into a store that had been bombed out and decided to take a case of wine. We finished off the case and headed back to our individual ships. When we got there, however, Jim's ship was tied up right alongside the dock, but mine was a fair distance off with a rope stretched out to the ship. I was supposed to have been back much earlier, and now I had no way of getting back on board. Being a slight bit intoxicated, I probably didn't have my wits about me when I made the next decision.

I had to find a way to get aboard our ship, so I decided that I would climb the rope across the water to get to the ship. I started out going hand-over-hand until my arms got tired, then I pulled my feet up and used them as well. When I was about halfway across the rope, I looked at the ship and saw the captain on deck. I know he saw me, but he left the deck—I assumed so that I wouldn't get a fright and drop into the water! Anyway, I kept going and finally made it across and got on board.

The captain didn't have anything to say for a couple of days. When I started to think he might not have seen me that night, he called me to his quarters and let me know that he had indeed seen me. He gave me a stern lecture, to which I hardly knew how to respond. When he was finished, I left his cabin vowing never to do such a thing again, and I never did!

From the time that I left Upper Island Cove with Dick Coombs and George Drover, I had been able to get back home and see my family on a few occasions. The only one I did not get to see was my elder brother. That was because later in 1940, Edward had also joined the Royal Navy and went overseas in the eleventh volunteer naval contingent from Newfoundland. I hoped he was well and that maybe we would cross paths.

Seeing him was important to me. I looked up to Edward and my eldest brother, John, both of whom had been fishing with Uncle Walter Baggs in St. John's before the war broke out. They had both been a very positive influence on my life, and, especially after Father died, were instrumental in keeping the rest of our family fed and clothed. In addition to that, now that both Edward and I had joined the Royal Navy, this had given us something else to share stories about. Every time I was at port and there were other British sailors around, I always kept a keen eye out, but in that period of almost four years I had not been fortunate enough to see him. I often wondered what parts of the war theatre he may have been in. Was he okay? Did he get taken as a prisoner of war?

One of my assigned tasks when we were in port was to pilot a small powerboat used to transport personnel, mail, and small supplies, and in particular to hand-deliver war communications from the Admiralty or from one vessel to another. Military superiors did not want to use radio communications for fear of the Germans picking up information.

During our time in one harbour, and while we were anchored outside, we were spending quite a bit of time going from one ship to another with mail and various officers. After making our rounds, we returned to our own ship.

I happened to say to my friend, "You know, I have been keeping an eye out for my brother, who I thought I might have seen at some point."

When I named the ship I thought he was serving on, my friend said, "Willie, that ship was just in the harbour today."

He then told me where it was anchored, and my immediate thought was to get in the small powerboat and visit the ship. Unfortunately, before I had a chance to do anything, my friend pointed to the ship, presumably with my brother Edward on board. It was just slipping out of the harbour.

12 — Willie

LOANED TO AMERICA

January – March 1944

The *LST 408* next went to Naples, and the crew reloaded the ship. First when we arrived there, the ship anchored out in the stream for a week and then eventually moved in alongside the loading dock, where we took on water, fuel, and food. The captain went ashore and met for three days with a group he called the Strategic Planning Committee. The crew members heard a rumour there was a big invasion planned, but there were no other details. We all wondered when and where.

The following day, the ship took on twenty tanks, twenty army trucks, and fuel, along with three doctors and some first-aid personnel. Then, when our ship moved away from the dock, the captain called all the ship's company together and told us we were going to make another invasion in Italy. This time it would be farther up the coast near Rome at a place called Anzio. The crew members were also told that the fifteen LSTs, including ours, had been loaned to the US Army and that General Mark Clark of the US Fifth Army was in charge of the operation.

We were also told this particular landing could be an easy operation since the Italians had already capitulated. On the other hand, it could be the hardest invasion we had been involved in so far, since it was only twenty miles from Rome. With the Italians having already surrendered, the Germans would put up a desperate fight. The sense we were getting was that the Germans realized that if they lost Rome, the chances of them winning the war were getting slimmer every day. Their backs were against the wall.

On January 20, 1944, the ships including our *LST 408* had moved farther out into the harbour in preparation for the trip to Anzio. By that afternoon, the convoy was well out to sea, covered from enemy attack by our aircraft. Both the weather and the tide were well suited for the convoy of ships to land successfully on the beach of Anzio.

Then on January 22, 1944, the convoy arrived off the coast of Anzio's beachhead. It was still dark, and from what could be seen, it didn't look very good. There were shells pitching around the convoy everywhere. Then the LSTs, including the *LST 408*, were ordered to make for the beach at full speed. When the ships got about half a mile from the beach, the ship ahead of ours got hit. We had to make a sharp turn to starboard to get around the ship that got hit. It was a close call, but we made it and then hit the beach at full speed. We unloaded the tanks and troops. As soon as we were off the beach itself, the soldiers and equipment we had just unloaded ran into the German tanks. For the next couple of hours, there was a savage tank battle right alongside the beached LSTs.

At about the same time, an Italian one-man submarine headed for the *LST 408*. However, he came too close to the beach and became grounded. The person operating the small vessel was one of the Italians who had chosen to stay and fight alongside the Germans. The strategy of the submarine operator was to head toward its target, and then he would jump out and swim to shore while the submarine inflicted damage or sank its target.

The mini-submarine was known as a "pig" because of the difficulty controlling it. In this case the operator got the submarine stuck and was sighted by the Americans who were there as part of the Allied operation. They captured the submarine operator and took both him and the submarine away. The submarine was later dismantled, and it was placed on their ship, along with the pilot, to be taken back to England for inspection and further studies.

As soon as the soldiers and tanks were unloaded, we tried to get off the beach and finally made it off with the help of our stern anchor. We left right away for Naples for another load of tanks, as they were badly needed at Anzio. Sometime earlier, our captain had said that the landings at Anzio could be the easiest one of the three—Sicily, Salerno, and Anzio—but the reality of it was that it was one of the hardest.

We always landed on the beach at high tide, and when we unloaded with the help of our stern anchor, we would back out into the water. On the next trip to Anzio, we went into the beach at full speed and unfortunately were there about four hours. In that period the tide had fallen quite a lot, and when it was time for us to get off the beach, we couldn't. Due to the gentle slope of the beach from the shoreline, the water had fallen and was about sixty feet behind the stern of our ship.

My friend and I decided to go for a walk along the beach and the road adjacent to it. We walked about half a mile when the Germans suddenly began to shell the road, and the shells kept coming closer to us.

My buddy said, "Lets go back to the ship," but then there were a couple of shells that came much closer. In an attempt to avoid being hit, my friend and I crawled under a truck for safety.

When the shells eventually stopped falling, we crawled back out from under the truck none the worse for crawling in there. As we walked away from the truck, two Americans came along.

One fellow asked, "Hey, man, what were you guys doing under our truck?"

My buddy said, "We crawled in there for safety from the shelling."

The two Americans laughed for about five minutes. When one of them could catch his breath, he said, "That truck is loaded with ammunition. That's why we ran away from it when the shelling started."

Glad that the shells hadn't hit the truck, we were a little embarrassed to realize what we had done.

On the way back to the ship, my buddy said, "Of course, if one of those shells hit that truck, I doubt if we would ever be able to tell anyone about this story."

As a result of the rising tide, at about 0400 hours the next morning, our ship was afloat again, and in company with about twenty-five other ships, we went back to Naples.

Even after the success we had achieved so far, one night not long after this, the Germans broke through the Allied defence lines and almost recaptured Anzio. There was a lot of fighting, and our LST was stuck on the beach again. On that night, a strange thing happened at Anzio.

About a year before this, a friend of mine from Wales, who we simply called Foley, said to me, "I have a brother in the army, but I haven't seen him since he joined up. I have always wondered where he was."

Then that night, on our third trip to Anzio, after we unloaded the tanks and were about to leave, someone saw a soldier staggering around the beach.

At first, fellows said he was drunk. Some of the sailors on the *LST 408* found the soldier and brought him on board the ship. Two doctors said he wasn't drunk at all but rather was shell-shocked. To everyone's surprise, he turned out to be my friend's brother who he hadn't seen in three years. When our ship got back to Naples, the soldier was sent back to England for treatment. My friend, the brother of the so-called shell-shocked soldier, took the news so badly that, shortly after this incident, he had to be sent home as well.

The crew of the *LST 408* by now was into a bit of a routine. We continued to carry troops, tanks, guns, food, and fuel to Anzio. Each time we unloaded, we would reload with a load of wounded and sometimes a load of German prisoners of war to be taken back to Naples.

One time when we were assigned to patrol the Mediterranean, inspecting ships for contraband destined for the enemy, we intercepted a schooner and found out it was destined for a home port in Newfoundland. The captain was from Twillingate. He and his crew had been waiting for three weeks for the wind to rise. We didn't find any contraband, and the schooner's captain was allowed to continue on his journey.

One day after landing tanks, soldiers, and supplies, we were again waiting for the tide to rise to allow the ship to move offshore. At that point things had settled, and we were no longer under extensive gunfire.

I was alone, walking through a cemetery near the beach not far from our ship, when suddenly a German plane flew over and dropped its payload. There was no shelter nearby, so I hit the ground headfirst, with both hands going deep into the soil. As I did, my hand hit something. When the bombing was over and as I was about to get up, I realized that what my hand had hit was some kind of medal. Quite a few years after the war, I found out that the medal was one awarded to an Italian military person during the Italian-Ethiopian war of 1935–1939.

I also recall that, on one occasion when our ship was on the Anzio beach, we had about 200 prisoners on board. My friend and I were assigned to give the prisoners water. We were always ordered to treat the prisoners in a humanitarian way and always according to the rules that had been laid down by the Geneva Convention.

We were delayed from moving from the beach because we had to wait for the tide to rise. There was a further delay because we had to wait for an escort to accompany the *LST 408* back to North Africa. In view of these circumstances, we had the prisoners aboard almost three days before we could get them back to Tripoli.

One particular prisoner kept asking for water, and I would always give him some. He looked sickly and frail, and just before we arrived at Tripoli, this prisoner asked me for more water. As I went toward him with some water, he put something in my hand. It was a gold ring, and he said that he wanted me to have it. I didn't know what to say. Of course, when our ship's crew got to know about it, they all wanted to see the ring. It was a souvenir of the German Afrika Korps. Today that ring belongs to, and is occasionally but proudly worn by, my eldest son.

Finally, on March 18, 1944, HMS *LST 408* left the Mediterranean. The next stop was Gibraltar. One of the most significant memories for me was that of the courage and resilience of the people of the island of Malta, which is located in the central Mediterranean Sea.

During World War II, Malta was a colony of Britain. Its location was of strategic value to both the Allies and the Axis powers. Churchill referred to it as "our only unsinkable aircraft carrier."[6] For two and a half years, the Germans and the Italians tried to beat the Maltese and invade the island. They bombed the island day and night for that two-and-a-half-year period, but the people of Malta and British and Commonwealth troops would rather die defending the island than live under a dictatorship. It was said that Malta was the most heavily bombed land on earth. In 1942, King George VI awarded Malta the George Cross Medal to bear witness to the heroism and devotion of the people of Malta. As I recall, it was also awarded as well to all of those who were "defenders" of Malta.

As a member of the British Royal Navy serving in the Mediterranean Sea, from the spring of 1943 until the spring of 1944, I was incredibly proud that I could support the people of Malta during these turbulent times. Some years after the war, I qualified for and became a member of the George Cross Society. In 1992, the Government of Malta issued the George Cross Fiftieth Anniversary Medal, which was awarded to members of eligible groups who served Malta during the period June 10, 1940, to September 8, 1943. One of these groups was the Allied Armed Forces who helped defend Malta during that period, a group of which I was a member. I have always been proud to say of the people of Malta that their sacrifice will always inspire democracy to continue forever.

---

6   Nora Boustany, "The Consummate Diplomat Wants Malta on the Map," the *New York Post*, July 13, 2001.

13 — Willie

THE REAL FIGHT FOR FREEDOM

June 6, 1944

"... When we got about one-half mile from the shore, my friend and I had to go up forward on the bow of the ship. We were ready to open the bow doors. It was a very dangerous place to be, because if there were any mines on the beach, that part of the ship would be the first place that would be hit ..."

In March 1944, after the Anzio beachhead was secured and the campaign in Anzio was still not over, the *LST 408* finally went back to England. We arrived in Devonport, England, my old barracks, and we stayed there about three weeks. We then did more training at Plymouth, England, the port that most LSTs were to leave from, for the beaches that, to them, were not yet named.

Realistically, though, we knew they were somewhere in France. The crew members of the *LST 408* were then all given two weeks' leave, and I spent my time in London. All the sailors had been in the toughest of fighting zones for many months by now, and yet we knew that the biggest battle was likely just ahead of us. To let off some pent-up energy and anxiety, many of the sailors who were given leave went to London to "let loose," so to speak.

While on leave that spring, I stayed at the Union Jack Club in London. There I became acquainted with a man from Glenwood, Newfoundland, by the name of Peddle. Both of us liked to have a drink, and having some spare money, we made good use of it. One night we were in our room, which was about eight to ten floors up, and we heard the train going past the building below. Being in the mood for some fun, we had the brilliant idea to take the chamber pot from under the bed and throw it out the window onto a moving train.

You should have seen that pot smash into thousands of little bits! We thought this was great fun, and we went to other rooms and took those chamber pots as well. We finally were reported and were told in no uncertain terms that, if it continued, we would have to leave the building. So, unfortunately, our fun came to an abrupt stop.

After we went back to the ship from leave, we were told that all LST crews had to do more intensive training, as there was something very big coming up.

So, for all of April and May 1944, we went on training sessions nearly all night long. We would take a load of tanks after dark and get perhaps a couple of miles up the coast and then unload and go back for another load. We developed the art of loading twenty tanks, twenty trucks, food, guns, and troops in one hour and eight minutes, and that was in the dark, since we did all our training at night. We had an army officer on board checking on how fast we could load and then unload. We had no problem being the top of the class, since we had a lot of practice previously in Africa and Italy.

We heard rumours of a cross-channel invasion. In fact, the military was doing everything it could to make the Germans believe an invasion would be across the Dover Strait to Dunkirk or Calais, which is about twenty-five miles across. This of course did not happen, and by the time the Germans realized their mistake, it was too late.

When it got to May 20, 1944, we were not allowed to go ashore. We were confined to our ship, and as D-Day approached, the tension mounted. By now we all realized this was going to be the biggest invasion in history. We did have confidence in the outcome, since by 1944 the Allies had three times as many planes and guns as the enemy. We still realized, of course, that the Germans would fight tenaciously for every yard of beachhead, but their courage alone could not make up for the Allies' air and sea power.

Most of the LSTs were at Plymouth. We were there for four days when the captain called all the ship's crew together and told us, "You are about to take part in the biggest invasion in history. I know I can count on all of you to do your duty in what we believe to be a just cause."

Shortly after midnight on June 6, 1944, the ships started to move out. We didn't know how many ships there were until daylight, when we could see where we were going. We were headed straight for Normandy Beach in France. During the D-Day invasion, which was indeed the largest in history, there were thousands of ships and first-line airplanes, probably thousands more US and British paratroopers. Overall, there were hundreds of thousands of soldiers and troops of one sort or another headed for the beaches of France.

All the beaches were coded. The area of the beach that the *LST 408* was assigned was coded as Sword Beach, and that first morning we were going directly toward it. There was a lot going on that morning. Our crew had a hard time putting things together to be optimally effective. As we were going toward the beach, we passed a row of about twenty British and American battleships firing their two-ton shells at the beach.

The goal of the Allies was to knock out the German big guns that were trying to stop the troops and tanks from landing on the beach. I remember the noise was almost impossible to describe, only that it was "like a train going past your head." You could hardly hear anything being said, and you just had to concentrate on the job you were doing. Despite the German gunfire, all our ships kept going with determination to make it to their part of the beach.

Some of the ships got hit going into the beachhead, and some hit sea mines and sank. We were not allowed to stop under any circumstances. There were smaller boats arranged to be there for the purpose of rescuing survivors. To make matters worse, that day, June 6, 1944, was a stormy day. The wind was blowing on the shore, and as we got about two miles from the beach, we could see the sea rolling up on the beach about ten feet high as we were going toward it.

Our ship was rolling and leaping almost out of the water. A lot of the soldiers were seasick, and I knew they would like to be on land again. When we got about a half-mile from the shore, my friend and I had to go up forward on the bow of the ship. We were ready to open the bow doors. It was a dangerous place to be, because if there were any mines on the beach, that part of the ship would be the first place that would be hit. But everything worked out all right, and my friend and I were the first two from our ship to land on Sword Beach that day.

We unloaded our cargo of tanks, fuel, and food in an hour and a half, but because of the storm of wind that was blowing in on the beach, we were unable to leave until the next high tide. While we were waiting on the beach, we heard planes coming in over the convoy. Everybody nervously looked up toward the sky, and suddenly we saw the planes coming in over the ships. There was a big sigh of relief, since fortunately they were our planes, both British and American.

It was a hard-fought battle, but within three days the Allies knew they couldn't be pushed off the beach. They were there to stay!

As the days passed, Allied ships and LSTs were pouring on the shore with thousands of tanks, guns, and ammunition, plus food and fuel, with very little interference from the German ships or planes. Ours was one of the hundreds of LSTs that landed on Normandy Beach on June 6, 1944. We continued going back and forth from England to France, Belgium, and the Netherlands, carrying supplies and troops over to the war zone and carrying prisoners of war back to England.

All told, our ship brought back to England some 6,000 prisoners of war plus thousands of soldiers who were wounded. Part of our job was to look after all the wounded. This included both our own and the enemy soldiers. With the enemy soldiers who were wounded, there was medical staff to take care of them. On the other hand, the non-wounded prisoners were just given water, as it was only a couple of days and they would be back in England.

One morning as the *LST 408* was going back to England, my friend said, "I just saw a plane flying toward England, and there was smoke coming from it, so I reported it to the captain."

Then, sometime afterward, I saw one going toward England, and just like my friend had reported earlier, there was smoke coming from this one as well. Shortly after that, we heard an explosion and assumed that the plane we saw was one of our own planes and that it had been hit by anti-aircraft gunfire.

When we arrived at the London docks, however, we heard that the plane we saw earlier with the smoke trailing from it was in reality a new kind of German plane called a V1 or "doodlebug." It was an unmanned small plane that had been converted into a crude missile. I later read that these missiles came from over fifty catapult sites in France that launched thousands of missiles, with about maybe a quarter of them hitting London in the last year of the war.

After we arrived at the London docks, we were hoping to have a break for a couple of days. The first day we were there, my friend and I were standing on the afterdeck of our ship. We saw a V1 coming in toward us, but it passed us by about 200 yards. Then the V1 ran into a big high crane in the dark. I was standing opposite the ship's door, and there were double cover screens across the door as a blackout curtain at night. When the missile hit the crane, it immediately exploded, and I was blown into the canvas curtain and well into the inside of the ship.

I was shaken up for a few minutes, then I remembered my friend, who had been standing ten feet away from me. I ran out, and he was lying down on the deck. He wasn't as lucky as I was. I picked him up and carried him down to the first-aid quarters. We had three doctors on board because we were carrying a lot of wounded. When I reached the first-aid quarters, my friend was already dead. Of course, my hands and clothing were full of blood, which I thought was that of my friend. I didn't know it at the time, but I was also wounded in my shoulder, with an additional smaller wound to my head. These wounds were apparently caused by shrapnel, which might have hit me directly but more likely was a ricochet off the topsides of the ship. The wound in my shoulder was approximately two inches long, and the scar is still there. I guess I will carry the scar to my grave.

I was kept under observation for a few days, then I was checked over by a doctor who asked if I was feeling all right. I told him I was okay, and he then allowed me to go back to doing the work I had been doing for almost three years. Overall, and in this particular instance especially, I was fortunate that I wasn't badly hurt. Early the next morning, we left the London dock and proceeded to France again with another load of tanks for Sword Beach. The crew of the *LST 408* made so many trips that we pretty well knew where to go, since we had seen the place so often.

Of special note to me, on one of these trips back to England, the ship was boarded by King George VI. This was a big deal for the ship's crew, all of whom had worked so hard preparing and being an integral part of D-Day, landing on Sword Beach from just after daylight on D-Day. The King was inspecting the crew, and when he got to me, he recognized my "Newfoundland" shoulder lapel. He shook my hand and thanked me for my service, along with expressing his gratitude to all the Newfoundlanders who had served. I will always remember that event with fondness.

14 — Edie

TYING A KNOT IN HELL

November 1944 – June 1945

". . . but there was no need for her to worry. A couple of sailors were at the top watching, and when she got to the top of the ladder, they reached down and hauled her on board. I don't know if she has ever gotten over that."

— Willie "Bill" Lundrigan

As I remember events in late 1944, the relationship between Bill (Willie) and I unfolded very quickly. It was a romantic whirlwind that occurred more quickly than we ever thought. In those times, everything was influenced by the fact that we were still in the middle of a war.

One night in October, or possibly November in 1944, my friend Marge and I decided to go to a dance at one of the local hotels in Greys, Essex, called the Queens Hotel. There were lots of sailors and soldiers there from all the Allied forces. During the evening, we met two sailors of the British Royal Navy. One was named Jack Kerr from Wales, and the other one was named Willie Lundrigan from Newfoundland, a place we had never heard of before. We hadn't heard of anyone being called Willie, so Marge and I called him Bill, and he did not object. We danced with them and talked all evening. At the end of the night, we allowed them to walk us home. Actually, it was my friend Marge who walked with Bill that night, while I walked with Jack. We all agreed to meet again, but this time Bill and I danced and spent the entire evening together. There seemed to be a mutual attraction between the two of us, and that night we walked home together. That was the start of a friendship and later a romantic relationship between Bill and me.

It was wartime and we didn't have much time for dating, since every second week I was working until 10:00 p.m. each night, and sometimes later if there happened to be an air raid, which was, sadly, quite often.

From the time we met them that first night, every time their ship was docked and Jack and Bill had a chance to get off ship, they would come and meet Marge and me. At that time they were very busy going to France, trying to get as many tanks, fuel, and food across to France as they could before the rough weather started. They would be in France one night and back in England the next night. I was working at the margarine factory every day from 2:00 to 10:00 p.m., and of course Mum and Dad insisted that I should have to be indoors by 11:00 p.m.

I was quite struck by this quiet and handsome young sailor from some foreign place that we had never heard of, and from what I could see, he really liked me. On Christmas Day, 1944, Bill and his friend Jack, along with a number of other sailors from the *LST 408*, were invited to a Christmas party organized by Marge at her parents' house. We had a great time, with the party ending at 10:00 p.m., at which time we all went home and the sailors returned to the ship.

On one occasion, the captain of Bill's ship suggested that he and another sailor, Jan Wall, invite my friend Iris and me to have a tour of their ship and tea with the officers and captain. Iris and I were tickled to death, since we had never been on a warship before, so we got all dressed up. I put on my makeup, one of my favourite dresses, which was stylishly tight just below the knee, my best jewellery, and of course my high-heel shoes. I met Iris, and off we went to the Tilbury Docks, where many of the warships docked. Just before we got there, we met Bill and Jan and went to the ship. As we got closer to the ship, I was wondering and looking to see where the steps were to get onto the ship.

I turned to Bill and asked, "Bill, where do we get on the ship?"

Pointing to a long rope ladder, Bill replied, "Right over there."

Surprised and thinking this can't work, I looked to Iris and whispered, "That won't do!"

I looked down at my high heels and the lovely stylish dress that was tucked in tightly at the knees. "I can't possibly climb that," I said.

To which Bill replied, "That won't be a problem. I will help you get started, and the lads at the top will help you over the side."

I wasn't very impressed. I was nervous that I would fall, but it was also funny. Besides, Iris and I both had our hearts set on going aboard, so I thought I must at least try.

When we got by the ship, Bill said, "Okay, here we go."

As he passed me the end of the rope ladder, I was terrified to put my foot on the wooden rung—but embarrassed not to with so many sailors looking on. After passing my hat and purse to Bill, I moved gingerly over to the ladder. I put one foot on the rope and then took it back quickly when the rope started to move. Then I took a deep breath and started to climb.

The rope was wiggling, and it all felt so strange under my feet as the rope I was holding seemed to move uncontrollably in my hands. I climbed as best as I could, but my dress would not allow me to reach my leg from one rung to the next without sort of turning a bit to one side.

As I moved slowly up, I started to get a little used to it and seemed to be doing okay as I continued to climb with my eyes focused on the side of the ship and counting each rung as I moved farther up. Then, suddenly, when I was almost to the top, and as I made another reach up the rope, I could see that there was nothing in the space where the rung was supposed to be.

The missing rung gave me a fright, and I panicked and squealed for just a second. In the process, one of my shoes almost came off. After regaining my composure, I looked up, and there were several sailors laughing but also reaching out to me. I was close enough to reach up. One sailor grabbed one of my wrists and the second sailor the other wrist, and just like that I was pulled up and over the side of the ship.

A little embarrassed, I thanked the sailors and watched for Iris. While she didn't have the high heels or the dress to worry about, it was still fun watching her being airlifted over the side of the ship by the same sailors who had lifted me just minutes before.

After this, Bill and Jan both came aboard, and we had a lovely tour of the ship before going to the dining area to meet the captain and the ship's officers. We had a great meal, including a dessert of strawberries and cream. It really was a wonderful time.

But as I was eating proper dessert for the first time since the war began, I couldn't help think, *How the heck am I going to get back down that bloody ladder?*

In the end, it seems that my concern was justified, because getting off the ship did seem somewhat more perilous than getting on. But both Iris and I managed to get off without any injury or embarrassment.

In March of 1945, the war in Europe was almost over, and activity was beginning to ease off a bit. The air raids didn't happen as often, and there was a lighter, more optimistic air about. According to Bill, the official log of the *LST 408* indicated the ship and crew had made fifty-nine crossings from England to France, including several trips to Belgium and the Netherlands.

The *LST 408* was halfway across the English Channel on its way to Tilbury Docks, with a load of about 200 German prisoners of war on May 8, 1944, when the crew got the news that the war was over. As they arrived at Tilbury, there were five big army trucks and about fifty military police waiting to escort the German prisoners of war to a prison camp in England.

All the people, including the sailors and soldiers, were jubilant. When they arrived in England, there were great celebrations going on in the streets everywhere. Everyone was so excited that after almost six years this war was finally over. There were so many people that you could hardly get through the crowds. Bill told me that, several times, he was taken into a pub for a celebration drink. Eventually, he made his way to Charlton Street in West Thurrock, where my parents and I lived.

For my family, however, it was a day of incredibly mixed emotions. We were so very thankful and delighted that the war was over, and delighted that we were no longer worried about being bombed day and night. There was also enormous relief that my brothers Harry and Alf were no longer in harm's way. But then there was still absolute silence from the authorities on the whereabouts of my brother Sidney John Thomas.

It had been known now for almost two years that he was a prisoner of war held by the Japanese in Burma, but there had been no communication from or about him since sometime in late 1943. The news would come soon, but for now that dark cloud dampened everyone's spirits.

Now that the war in Europe had ended, Bill found out that his ship was going to the Far East war area to fight Japan. Of course, as far as we knew, he would be going, too, so we decided to get married before he left. My mother once again objected very strongly. It was hard for her to accept. She already had one son missing and possibly dead, with two more still in uniform, and now I was going to marry a complete stranger and possibly leave as well.

When Bill and I had decided to get married, my family did not know if my brother Sidney was alive or not. The stress for Mum, associated with his captivity, followed by complete silence from him, was incredibly difficult. It would not be hard to appreciate Mum's lack of enthusiasm or support for Bill and the whole marriage concept during the spring of 1945. Added to that, Bill's strong Newfoundland dialect made it difficult for Mum and Dad to understand what he was saying most of the time. Usually, they would both look at me to interpret for them. My father was easygoing and took it in stride, saying, "You must please yourself." But for Mum, it was just another reason why I shouldn't consider marrying him.

But by now the decision to get married had been made, and the process of getting permission to do so was under way. Apart from the intense worry of my brother Sid's well-being, the whole issue of making a wedding work during a World War was turning into quite an undertaking. Most everything around us was destroyed, and we were in the midst of a food and clothing rationing period. It was now the biggest and most immediate issue before us.

Even though the war in Europe was over, that didn't mean that, in the days and weeks after the declaration, supplies of food, clothing, and other materials would be widely available just yet. It would be hard to secure wedding supplies.

My sister Lil said, "Now, don't worry, I will take responsibility to collect ration coupons so you can get your wedding dress." Every man, woman, and child was given a ration book with an allowance of coupons. These were required before rationed goods, including basic foods such as sugar, meat, fats, bacon, and cheese, could be acquired. As far as Bill's clothing was concerned, he said, "There's no problem with my dress, because I will use my official Royal Navy uniform."

Fortunately, we did have an additional means to get some things, though, and that was from the ship that Bill served on, the *LST 408*. The captain, and particularly the crew of the galley, were very good to us, and so Bill was able to get most of the mixed fruit and other ingredients for our wedding cake. The cake itself was made by my

Auntie Lil. In addition to the cake ingredients, Bill was also able to get canned fruit and other food, including canned cream, to be used at the small wedding reception.

In the days after the war ended, Bill was able to get permission from the military for him to marry. After this permission was received, we met with the Church of England minister, who had some concerns about me marrying a military person. In particular, he was concerned that I was going to marry a service person who was not from England. Bill and I persuaded him that we knew what we were doing and assured the minister that we definitely wanted to spend our lives together. We convinced the minister that being able to marry now was in our best interests. After all of this was agreed upon, we came to the conclusion that the date would be June 2, 1945.

While wanting very much for us to get married, I think Bill understood all the resistance from both my mother as well as from the Church of England minister.

Willie (Bill) and Edie's wedding party. Picture taken outside Edie's parents' house in East Essex, June 2, 1945.

Bill always felt that my parents were not overly impressed that we were going to get married. And he could understand this. Also, there were many stories of sailors and other servicemen marrying English girls and never returning. Bill tried to assure both of my parents, especially Mum, that this would not be the case with him. He wasn't sure she believed him, but she still gave her blessing for the wedding.

After a lot of hurried arrangements, we eventually got married on the appointed date of June 2, 1945, in the small village church in North Stifford called St. Mary's Church. This was a very old church with a lot of tradition, and we really enjoyed being able to be married in such history, even during wartime. It was just a small wedding with a few family members and my closest friends. The ceremony was performed by Reverend Simmons with a special marriage licence. After the service, our wedding reception was only a very modest event at my parents' home, where we enjoyed a meal, including a wedding cake and dessert courtesy of the Royal Navy.

15 — Willie

NO LONGER NEEDED

January 19, 1946

"I couldn't understand how these people, who were just ordinary citizens who had been collected off the street and imprisoned only because of their race, could be released by Canada looking so badly."

— Willie Lundrigan

The celebration of the ending of the war in Europe erupted in May 1945 and dominated both the hearts and minds of the people and the media in Europe and North America. Hitler was dead and the Nazis were defeated. Freedom would prevail! It seemed that people were entirely consumed with this news, to the point that we didn't tune in to what was happening elsewhere. The war with Japan was still raging, and I was about to go there to serve.

Although the war with Germany and Italy had ended, Japan, which had been an ally to them, was not prepared to surrender. No one was surprised, since the culture of Japan was such that they did not really seem to recognize surrendering or giving up. As a consequence, the war, with its death and destruction, raged on there for several months.

Edie was thinking of her brother Sidney John Thomas and her family. She understood that the odds against him coming home were stacked pretty high. But they had not been told he wasn't coming back, so there was still hope.

The American power was vast and ever expanding with their production of military might, and now the rest of the Allied forces could focus their attention on the Pacific theatre of war. It was there, of course, that both Edie and I anticipated I would be going, now that the *LST 408* was stocking up on supplies to make that very trip. When I went back to my ship after we were married, the ship made several more trips back to France carrying supplies to the troops stationed there and brought back POW's, even though the war was officially over.

It would be hard for me to leave Edie after just being married, but my duty to the Royal Navy required me to go. We were so sure that I was going to Japan that I had the gold Afrika Korps ring, which I had been given by the German prisoner during the Italian invasions, cut in half. I gave one half to Edie, and one half I kept so that, when I returned to England, we would have the two half-rings reunited, as were we.

Then, ten days later, to the surprise of all of us, the ship's captain called me into his office and told me that I would not be going with the ship to Japan. The reason he gave me why I would not be going to the Pacific war theatre was my tour of duty ended on May 8, 1945. That was the date when the Germans surrendered, ending the war in Europe.

The captain explained to me that when I volunteered for the Royal Navy in 1939, I joined up for the duration of the war in Europe. Now that the war in Europe was finished, my time as a volunteer with the Royal Navy was finished. Although I pleaded with our captain to stay on the ship, this decision was beyond his control.

The sailor who was taking my place on the *LST 408* had been sent to relieve me. I met him when he came on board. I told him the situation, and he said, "I am sorry, mate."

As I was leaving the ship for the last time, I wished him and my entire former shipmates well. It would be several months before I was finished with the navy, but that was the last time I was on a naval vessel.

On June 23, 1945, I was then sent to a demobilization centre back in Devonport, where I spent some time just waiting to be officially released. During the period I spent there waiting, there were still German prisoners of war in the POW buildings at Devonport. These POWs were also waiting anxiously to return to their homeland. At this point, since hostilities were over, with the war declared officially ended, security measures for the prisoners were somewhat relaxed. Any prisoners considered trustworthy were allowed to choose to keep themselves busy within the POW camp as they chose.

I distinctly remember one young German soldier who had probably not even turned twenty years old. He was working in the carpentry shop and busied himself making all sorts of small objects with whatever scraps of wood and other material he could find. Increasingly, the beginnings of friendships emerged. I became personally comfortable, if not friendly, with this young man who had an eye for carpentry. I felt that maybe the friendship began because carpentry was a common interest that we shared.

Before I received word that I would be leaving the barracks, he pulled me aside one day and offered me a gift for what he called my willingness to help him. The item he gave me was a small wooden box. It was approximately 10" x 8" x 5", and considering the few tools available, it was neatly crafted from wood with a couple of modified metal hinges. I was surprised by the gesture and gladly accepted it. It became Edie's sewing box for the next fifty years and is still in the possession of our eldest granddaughter today.

While at the barracks, I also received a message from Edie saying that my elder brother Edward, whom I had looked for practically every day during the war, had arrived at her parents' home for a visit. I was granted a weekend pass to go and see him. We had a great weekend together, and I found it both funny and sad at the same time that Edie's mother seemed much more at ease around Edward than she did around me. Maybe she didn't have the same concern that Edward might take Edie away from them in the same sense as I might, now that we were married. More likely, though, it was Edward's warm and charming personality that captured her heart, as it did for most people he met. It was a gift I wished I could possess just a little of.

After a great weekend visit with him, I returned once again to the barracks in Devonport.

I would estimate that there were a couple of thousand sailors at the barracks waiting their turn to be released from the Royal Navy. From that number I could see it was going to be several months and a long wait before I was discharged. Then, surprisingly, in August 1945, I was told that I was allowed to go home to Newfoundland on leave for six weeks.

I took all of my belongings from the barracks and was sent to Liverpool by train. There I went aboard an ocean liner and travelled to Halifax. I then crossed the Cabot Strait to Port aux Basques by ferry, on to Whitbourne by train, and finally home to Upper Island Cove by taxi. I spent the next six weeks at home with my family. While I was there, I stood as godfather to Edwin Lundrigan, son of my first cousin Josiah and his wife, Cavell Lundrigan.

After my leave period was over, I went to St. John's by train, and then also by train to Port aux Basques. Once I crossed the Cabot Strait and on to Halifax, I boarded an ocean liner to Southampton, England. I was anxious to get back to Edie.

During our time waiting in Halifax for the ship to leave, I bought a few things to take back to England. I brought a whole box of Crispy Crunch bars. After all, there was still food rationing in Britain, and we wouldn't see sweets any time soon. Not surprisingly after that, Edie, a lover of chocolate, had a lifelong love affair with Crispy Crunch bars.

It was an interesting trip back across the Atlantic. While in Halifax, I met two friends who had just been discharged from the navy and who were not going back to England again. Both of them had a parcel to send back to their girlfriends there, and they wanted me to take the packages back for them.

I explained to both former members of the Royal Navy that the British customs officers at Southampton would be checking on my entire luggage, and I could not afford to pay the duty fees on their parcels. Unless they could provide me with the money for the duty fees, they would probably lose their parcels. Ultimately, though, I felt badly for these friends. Reluctantly, I agreed to take the parcels for them and take my chances with the duty fees.

A couple of days later, the ship left Halifax on its journey to England. On this trip, in addition to all the regular passengers, the ship was transporting back to England 150 Japanese internees. By now the war in the Pacific had ended with the nuclear bombings of Hiroshima on August 6, 1945, and Nagasaki August 9, 1945. As a result, these civilians were going back to England, and then likely to Japan.

These men and women were not military personnel but just regular citizens who, only because they were Japanese, had been held at internment camps in Canada for over four years. Generally speaking, they did not look like they were in great physical condition, which surprised me somewhat. During the war, even the prisoners on our ship were treated well, and I wondered about the treatment of these ordinary citizens who had been collected off the street and imprisoned in Canada.

One of the stewards on the ocean liner asked some sailors if we would help the ex-prisoners of war until we arrived in Southampton. Many of us, including me, said that we would be glad to do what we could for all of them.

While even then still under the watchful eye of the ship's crew, ex-prisoners were allowed to talk back and forth to explain anything that they bought in Halifax duty-free. I looked after three of the ex-prisoners all the way over during the six-day trip. Their entire luggage was in big canvas bags about six feet long, and all of them had bright yellow markings on the bags marked "EX P.O.W."

They were allowed to take back to England anything they wanted, and duty-free. The day before we arrived in England, the fellows who I was looking after thanked me for all that I had done for them. They offered me money for helping them. I told them that I could not accept their money and that it was a pleasure to have helped them.

But then, one fellow said he wished there was something he could do for me. That comment sparked a thought for me, and then I explained to the gentleman that I had been carrying some items for friends. I explained to him that I was concerned I might have to lose their parcels because I did not have enough money to pay the duty on them.

After this conversation, I left and went out on deck for a walk. When I came back after about an hour, my new Japanese acquaintances told me they could solve my problem as far as the customs office issue was concerned. They each had three bags with all their belongings. The three of them told me to open their bags and put the parcels of my friends in them. I placed the parcels of my friends in these bags and then marked them so that I would know them from the other bags.

When we arrived in Southampton, all three bags were taken ashore by the ex-POWs and put in a separate place. When I went through customs, I had nothing at all to declare except Edie's Crispy Crunch bars. When I went ashore, I got a taxi and took all my things plus the ex-POWs' bags to the train station. There, together with the Japanese passengers, we opened up the luggage, and I had to sort out the things that I had to somehow get to the girlfriends of my former navy friends.

I had the address of their friends, and when we met, I told them the story of how the Japanese internees helped me get their parcels through customs. I wished them well and then boarded the train to Greys, Essex, and then made the short trip home to West Thurrock.

My official service in the British Royal Navy came to an end on January 19, 1946.

During the next two months, Edie and I started to get to know each other as a married couple. This was complicated somewhat by having to make this matrimonial transition while living with her parents. This kind of live-in arrangement was standard in living accommodations in Britain at that time. There was a severe housing shortage because of the damage to so many residential buildings during the war.

Edie was still working at the margarine factory, and I was now looking for work and eventually found a job. In the meantime, Edie eventually gave up her wartime job, and we settled into married life. We continued to live with her parents in the small family home. Despite a coolness I initially felt from Edie's mum, things were starting to work out quite well. I still felt that Edie's mother didn't especially care for the foreigner in her midst, but I was determined to make the best of it.

Service record of William Lundrigan, DJX 181701, British Royal Navy WWII. Note: Russia Service Medal is missing, out of production.

16 — Edie

CAN I EVER FORGIVE?

September 1945

"When he came back inside the house, my father had changed forever."

— Edie Lundrigan

For many years, I did not tell my children the precise details of how we found out about my brother's death in 1945. I did tell them that we were officially informed of his death in a telegraph that was delivered to the house in September of that year.

Mum never really recovered from the tragic death of my brother Sidney John Thomas at the hands of the Japanese in Myanmar, October 1943. This news devastated all of us, including my two brothers, Harry and Alf, who had both served in the army and who had both returned home safely. This dreaded news was received just one month short of two years since the last communication with my brother. The official cause of death was never known, but my understanding was that he died as a result of "disease and starvation."

One day, sometime after that telegraph had already arrived, a visitor came to the house to meet with my father. While my father never said directly, it was my sense that Dad had asked to see this particular visitor. I found out later that the visitor was also a POW who worked on another section of the Death Railway and who survived the captivity.

I went to the door and opened it. Standing before me was a tall young man, who removed his hat and asked, "May I speak with Mr. Alfred England, please?"

I said, "Yes, of course. Let me get him for you."

The young man stood outside the door, and I immediately turned and found my father sitting in the front room, reading his newspaper. Before I had a chance to tell him what had happened, he was putting his paper aside while also laying his pipe in the ashtray sitting on the side table near him. He simply said, "It's okay, Edie, I'm on the way."

Dad went to the door, stepped outside, and closed the door behind him. They both walked away from the door. I did not recognize the young man, and since we didn't have many visitors, it was odd that Dad did not invite him in. While my father was outside, I found myself wondering if this man knew something about my brother's death. I just stood motionless for what seemed like a long time while they were both outside talking. After a while the door opened, and Dad stepped back inside.

The young man was gone, and so too was any colour in my father's face. I have never forgotten the look of such anguish he carried that day. To me, he seemed to have aged twenty years in the twenty minutes he had been outside. As he walked slowly toward me, he said in an almost trembling voice, "Go upstairs and tell your mother to come down, please."

I did as my father asked, and Mum, having heard the knock on the door, was already upset and bracing for the expected, but dreaded, news. My father shared with us that the man at the door also served in the Far East in Sid's army division. My father said that the young man told him he felt he "was fortunate to survive." He also told Dad, "It was a terrible place to be." Even though Mum and I probably thought the opposite, Dad said there was no other information.

Although Mum and I asked him more questions after that, he steadfastly refused to share any other details. He simply placed his hand on Mum's shoulder as she sat on the couch sobbing. Dad hugged me, then walked to the door, and reached for his hat on the coat hook. He walked out the front door and did not come back home until sometime later that evening.

That was really all my father ever said about it to Mum or anyone else, that I know of. Whatever else he was told about how my brother was treated, or how he died, Dad simply took to his grave when he passed away eleven years later.

But it was news that changed my parents forever. Mum was almost always sullen and stern, but now she carried a weight that drained life from her. My father, who didn't speak often, continued to live in that same reserved way, except that the tremendous sadness rarely lifted to allow a smile.

Life went on, however, and eventually their spirits were lifted somewhat. The first time I saw my father really smile was after our first-born, Jean, was born in December 1946, and more so when she started to crawl and ask for her "pop." Having a child in the house did not happen for over a year after that visitor came, but Jean also helped lift Mum's spirits somewhat. Both Mum and Dad doted on her, and she seemed to become the central figure now in both their lives.

Then, in July 1948, our eldest son was born. When I was asked why Bill and I named our first-born son Sidney John, my response was that Bill and I decided to name him Sidney John Lundrigan, after my brother Sid, who must have been strong to go through that terrible ordeal before his death. We felt that naming our son after my brother also brought a degree of peace to my mum and dad. It was our way to honour my brother while also giving our son a strong and fitting name.

Over the years, knowing that getting to see where my brother died or to see where he had been laid to rest was likely not possible, I read everything I could find on the subject. This included the well-documented cruelty employed by the Japanese at that time. The experience of knowing he was in captivity, the learning of his death and the horrors associated with how he and many others were deliberately mistreated, was at times just too much. My hurt turned to disgust, and my disgust became generalized as an intolerance of the Japanese people.

The horror of my brother Sid's treatment at the hands of his sadistic captors tore a piece out of my heart. I felt that such inhumane behaviour, endorsed by Japanese leaders, could never be justified or forgiven.

Never forgotten, the war was slowly being pushed behind me while we were busy living this new life.

17 — Willie

UPPER ISLAND COVE IS CALLING

April 1949

One thing I was sure of was my love for Edie.

Even the first night when Jock and I met Edie and Marge, I knew there was a connection between Edie and me. As it turned out that night, I walked home with Marge, but it should have been Edie. I know she felt a connection between us as well. The second night, just as Jack and I walked in the Queen's Hotel, Edie and I sat together and danced together the whole evening. By then I could tell this was going to be something special. There was no doubt who I would be walking home with from there.

If I hadn't truly loved her, I guess you could say, I had the perfect opportunity to leave Edie behind without a trace. I was told in June 1945 that my war service was coming to an end and that it would be official once the military could have my official release processed. In the interim, I was given leave to return to Newfoundland while this backlogged discharge system was able to process my official release documentation. In Upper Island Cove, some of my friends were now gainfully employed, with the influx of postwar (mostly American) money, for infrastructure projects in centres across the island in locations such as Gander, Stephenville, Pleasantville, Port aux Basques,

Argentia, and others, including Goose Bay in Labrador. I spent about six weeks in Upper Island Cove and enjoyed every minute of it. Some of my friends were enticing me to stay, but it couldn't happen, because I was also very anxious to return to England to be with Edie.

Willie and Edie, June 2, 1945

After that period of leave, I returned to Devonport and was informed my official re-entry into civilian life was set for January 19, 1946. With that, suddenly I transformed from a relatively carefree young fellow from outport Newfoundland, going off to war, to now being a married man and living in England as a civilian. There was a whole new world of possibilities, and challenges, that lay before me, but for some reason, this was something I could not seem to fully grasp.

My time in the navy was filled with tight schedules. Even at sea, everything, except for enemy engagement, happened in an organized, time-compliant, and sequential fashion. I just followed orders. Now I missed that neatly ordered life.

I missed the fact that I was part of something bigger. In that world, somehow my life had meaning and made sense. I took some comfort that someone else was always responsible for how my life unfolded. I was spared these adult decisions that I was forced into, but ill-prepared for, when I came back to England after my final period of leave. Now, suddenly, for the first time since the war started, I had to fit into a world where I ultimately had responsibility for how my life, as well as to a large extent the lives of others, unfolded. So, what was I to do now?

It was interesting to now become aware of how life after the war was not something that was ever talked about while we were engaged in war, either by my comrades or by the navy brass. And although it was not my intention to leave the navy, I was now out, whether I liked it or not.

Both the war effort and now the demobilization and rebuilding were so massive that providing any type of training for re-entry into the workforce was simply not logistically possible. In my specific case, I was provided with two amounts of cash called a War Gratuity and War Credit of Wages for a total of seventy-two English pounds. That wasn't going to last very long.

One night when her parents were out, I said to Edie, "Edie, I know that I have to find work somewhere, but I don't know where to start. Where do you think I should start? What kind of employer will want me? I don't have any work skills, and I don't know where to turn."

Edie's response was, "Oh, Bill, I'm sure you will be fine. A lot of the companies are crying for men to work in the limestone quarries and to help rebuild all that was bombed during the war. Maybe Lil's husband, Fred, would have a better idea. He works as a bricklayer."

I took Edie's advice and spoke to Fred about finding work, and he said, "Lucky you. I'm looking for a crew of men. I don't care if you have experience. I will teach you."

So off I went daily, on my bicycle, with my lunch tin in the parcel carrier to wherever Fred had a job to be done in the local area. Fred Bakewell was a great fellow. He taught me a lot about both living in England as well as about masonry work. But for some reason I couldn't seem to conquer the masonry skill and, after a short time, left that work. I don't know if my issue here was about adjusting to masonry work or about adjusting to post-navy life in general. I was also almost always fantasizing about living back in Upper Island Cove.

With Jean's birth in December 1946, Edie and I were ecstatic, and to my delight, so too were Edie's parents and the rest of her extended family. Life was good despite my tinge of homesickness, which I kept close to myself. Both Edie and I were beginning to find our way together in this new postwar England.

As far as work was concerned, next I found work with a cement company, but it didn't last long, either. I then moved on again and started work with a paper and box manufacturing company called the Thames Board Mills. I stayed working there with them until the winter of 1949.

During this same period, I had been experiencing bouts of colds, then pneumonia, and ultimately pleurisy. I spent a lot of time sick, including a couple of bouts in hospital.

A lot about life had changed for both Edie and me. I was gainfully employed, and even though I was still having adjustment issues, there were good times, too.

During the time Edie and I lived in England, I wanted to learn to read and write better than my very basic skills, most of which I had picked up after I left Newfoundland. I didn't know a lot about being literate, but I knew enough to realize I needed much more. Edie spent a lot of time helping me with these basic literacy skills of reading, writing, and arithmetic. I felt I made great progress, and by the time we left England, I could better communicate and understand the world around me through reading. Edie and I sat for many hours with pen and paper, along with quite a few of her old secondary school text and reference books. We also visited the local public library on a regular basis. Through all of this, it wasn't long before I was able to read and write at a much higher level.

By joining the Royal Navy in 1939, I leaped from a place of low expectations and little hope in Newfoundland into a world of immense danger. That world had, at its core, an incredible sense of structure and purpose and enormous opportunity.

In addition to this new world, where I had to find a way to retool both my brain and my hands to adapt, I was still caught up in thoughts of a war, the horror of which still caused strong emotional reactions at the least expected times. The sound of someone dropping a pot could send my heart racing. As the months passed, I felt myself thinking that even though I was no longer in Newfoundland, the growing sense of self-doubt in this new place reminded me of that pre-war time in my life. I kept thinking about down in the Meadow and how there was work in Newfoundland now. In my mind I kept seeing Edie being fascinated by this new place and the children being free and safe.

In the end, my physical illness postwar was such a concern that big decisions had to be made. I was arguably not in an emotional position to make them. In reference to the constant and worsening respiratory illnesses I was going through, my doctor told Edie, "If you love this man, you must take him away from here." This comment was apparently in reference to the especially damp climate, coupled with the heavy industrial pollution in England, which the doctor related to my impeded physical condition. After a lot of soul-searching, including some consideration of many options, one of which was moving to Australia, we eventually decided, in early 1949, that we would go to live as a family in Newfoundland. I felt a sense of joy with the prospect of moving back home, but I also felt a strong sense of guilt for this new upheaval in our lives due to my situation. Overwhelmingly, though, I was so thankful that I would again be able to live in the Meadow, feel well, and share this beautiful place with my family.

The decision to go to Newfoundland was not an easy one, since Edie would be leaving her home and family. This was a time when transatlantic travel was almost exclusively by boat, and we all knew that leaving England would mean Edie and the children might never see her parents again. It had to be an enormous blow to these two elderly people, who had already lost one son to the war. It was something, however, that I think Edie felt would probably help me with my health issues and help us as a family. I am sure she also hoped it would rekindle in me a sense of purpose that seemed to be missing. Now I was looking forward to returning to a world I knew and a community of people I loved and felt comforted by. It was a place where the economic challenges I had known were steadily slipping away and were being replaced by postwar economic development, which was happening as a result of the strategic location of Newfoundland to transatlantic travel.

Edie's parents had treated me well, even though I always felt Edie's mother was not very fond of me. On more than one occasion, I heard Edie and her mum talking about whether or not Edie and I should consider going to Newfoundland. On these occasions, Edie would get quite upset with her mum, telling her that any decision on going anywhere had to be made by her and me. Although she realized how difficult such a move would be on the lives of her parents, Edie would stress to her mum that this must be a decision made by us alone.

Edie later told me that she did a lot of thinking about what it would be like to leave her home and country and especially to take our children away from their grandparents. She also knew the medical advice was that I could get very ill or even die if we stayed, so she felt there was only one choice she could make. She said, "Once that choice was made, I made up my mind that everything would be fine."

And that was Edie's attitude in life. If it needed to be done, she would often say, "Now, get on with it."

I also knew it was hard for Edie to leave and likely never return to England. I always felt she probably believed that, irrespective of what the doctor said about leaving because of my poor health, I would never be content to spend the rest of my life in England.

18 — Edie

MY FIRST OCEAN VOYAGE

April 5-11, 1949

"One of the crew members of the ship asked me, 'Is this home for you?' I said, 'No, but it is going to be.' He replied, 'I feel sorry for you!'"

— Edie Lundrigan

Bill didn't speak much about what conditions were like in Newfoundland. I don't believe he was hiding anything from me, but it was just the way it was to him. Certainly he had said enough for me to understand that living there was so completely different to living where we had lived. In my mind, I felt that the way of life in Newfoundland might be similar to life in parts of rural Great Britain away from the cities.

Knowing what living conditions were like on the island of Newfoundland was not something you could really understand without ever living here. Poverty was systemic. And although there were deep pockets of poverty in many British cities, living conditions on this sparsely populated island were certainly quite unlike almost anything in Britain. The standard of living was even substantially lower than most everywhere else in Canada at the time. This is something that Bill's love for the place may have, in a way, blinded him from, or maybe he was afraid to go too deeply into it with me before we arrived. I think he made himself believe I would understand it much better when I got there.

It is true that the realization, by the United States and Britain, of Newfoundland's strategic location during World War II had begun a level of development in various Newfoundland communities that was quite unprecedented. Even that, however, was just enough to make a start on providing people with hope for the future. Some change comes with the money, but real change in a society happens more gradually. It takes time for people to accept and embrace new ways. It seemed to me that such was likely the case for post-confederation Newfoundland. The way of life, borne out through decades of a history of sporadic and isolated fishing establishments, would not change substantially outside some centres of development in the province for many years after we came to Newfoundland.

My thinking at the time was, even if Bill was still physically weak, his spirits had been raised by the prospect of going home, and more still by bringing his wife and children home to be part of his family down in the Meadow. That meant an awful lot to me. I so dearly loved England, but I loved Bill and my children so much more.

I knew there would be an adjustment. I just couldn't fathom how much and how long it would take for conditions in this new Canadian province, and in particular in our lives, to return to a level that I had just stepped away from. Then again, the war had wreaked such havoc and created so much dysfunction in Britain that even staying there was never going to be like it was in my childhood.

The world had changed everywhere, I reasoned. My family needed me, and I was ready for the adventure. Despite any lingering doubts about making this plunge into a land of ice and snow, I was entirely committed to making this new life, in this new land, work for my family.

LOVE AND WAR

While the rest of the world seemed to have been changed remarkably by the industrial revolution, Newfoundland's almost singular dependence on the fishery as an economic driver had not seen nearly such change.

The talk was that living conditions would improve with confederation. When Bill and I arrived here in April 1949, just days after Newfoundland became a province of Canada, I was about to find out that any change was not highly visible, at least not yet. The living conditions and the way of life seemed to be decades behind a place like England was before the war, not that England was the royal standard for living conditions.

I was about to find out what living in the early days of Newfoundland's confederation with Canada really meant.

Mum was very opposed to my decision to uproot the children and go with Bill to his home. That was very understandable, really, but of course it was not her decision to make. These kinds of things didn't cause me to stop loving my mother, but it did make it hard for me to live my life as she felt I needed to. I sometimes felt that Mum, with all the best of intentions, sometimes tried to exert her influence in our marriage, and I swore to myself that if one of my children was ever to get married, I would never want to be an "interfering mother-in-law."

On April 5, 1949, after a very emotional goodbye to my parents, Bill, two-year-old Jean, nine-month-old Sid, and I, along with a few bags containing our meagre possessions, boarded a train and travelled from Mum and Dad's to London. There we boarded an express train to Liverpool. After some delay there, we were passed through customs and embarked on the Royal Mail Ship (RMS) *Newfoundland*.

I had never travelled outside of England and certainly had never been on a large oceangoing ship. In many ways I felt that the trip to Newfoundland was going to be an adventure, even though Bill had told me about the likelihood of bad weather and seasickness along the way.

119

That wasn't quite the way it worked out, and adventurous might not be the way I would describe it once we finally got to dock in the harbour at St. John's. Leaving was a combination of sadness and nervous anticipation for me, and I really felt terrible as I waved goodbye to my mother and father, who were standing so alone, outside the only home that I had ever known. But in the only way I could deal with such emotion, I simply pushed the emotion deep inside to be processed at another time.

Once on board the ship, the RMS *Newfoundland*, we found our cabin and were ready to sail from the present into the past. We huddled together on the deck in the light rain as the ship steamed slowly out the harbour and away from English soil. Within a very short time, any sign of land, and my previous life, disappeared, and only ocean surrounded us. Bill was fine, but this was unsettling for me.

The first day of the boat ride was a real novelty. Even with two small children, the sense of adventure was able to keep any sense of trepidation or regret suppressed. But then the fog and rain and rough seas gradually turned our adventure into discomfort. My preoccupation was to keep the children from getting seasick. I lost that battle, but after a few more days, there was the sight of land to the west.

After a very stormy trip, we arrived in St. John's on April 11, 1949. It was very early in the morning, around breakfast.

I remember Bill saying, "Edie, you should go up on deck to see the ship go through the Narrows."

It was a cold, wet, dreary morning, and as I stood on the deck and looked at this bleak island of rock, my first thought was, *Oh my God, where have I come to?*

All I could see were tall cliffs with little wooden houses clinging to the rocks. I must say that I was not impressed at all.

One of the crew members of the ship asked, "Is this home for you?"

I said, "No, but it is going to be."

He replied, "I feel sorry for you!"

It certainly wasn't much of a welcome, but I was glad we had finally arrived. I was looking forward to getting off the ship and getting on solid ground again.

But it was not to be, at least not yet. As we docked, Bill went on deck to see what the procedure for going through customs and disembarking entailed. I was busy getting the children ready and picking up our luggage to go through customs.

I heard Bill open the door, saying, "Damn the like of that!"

I said, "Goodness, Bill, what's the matter?"

Bill, obviously angry and flustered, replied., "The bloody Canadian immigration officials won't let us leave the ship. Or, should I say, he won't let you leave the ship."

"What do you mean?" I asked. "Why?"

"Because you are a British citizen, and we don't have the correct papers for you to enter Canada. Why in the heck did Newfoundland join confederation, anyway?" he sputtered.

"But we have all the paperwork. Mr. Davis, the trade commissioner for Newfoundland in England, had it all arranged for us," I said, now worried about what would happen next.

"What about the children? Do they qualify to enter Canada?" I asked, concerned now that someone might suggest that Bill and the children leave the ship without me.

"Yes, apparently the children are fine to get off the ship, since as their father I am returning home. But don't worry about that, we are not going anywhere without you," Bill said, trying to reassure me.

I had so many questions Bill was unable to answer fast enough. In answer to the previous question of why I wasn't allowed in, Bill said, "Yes, that's correct, Edie. The paperwork in England was all good. The problem is that the paperwork was done for us to hand over to the Newfoundland authorities—when Newfoundland was on its own and not a part of Canada. Unfortunately for us, as of March 31 past, we are now a province of Canada. The people at the Canadian customs here are insisting we need the correct paperwork for Canada. Their main concern is that you don't have the correct medical clearance."

While still taking care of Jean and Sid, Bill and I were in the middle of this discussion when there was a loud knock on our cabin door.

Bill opened it, and a man introduced himself as a doctor with the customs office. He was a man of few words but basically said, "Ma'am, you will need to go directly to St. Clare's Hospital and have a chest X-ray completed. If that comes back negative, you will be free to go."

We had to arrange to have Bill and the children wait on the boat while I was gone. I was taken to St. Clare's Mercy Hospital on Lemarchant Road for the X-ray. As expected, it turned out just fine, and back at the ship, my passport was stamped, and all four of us finally got to officially disembark.

Bill did not have a strong appreciation of French-speaking people.

This feeling had been developed during World War II, where there was an overall sense among sailors in the Royal Navy, and maybe even with the British people, that France didn't do as much as they might have to resist the German advance. As a result, it was felt by many that England, in addition to its own war-related responsibilities, was forced to do much of the heavy lifting that it had expected France to do. Many believed that a quick surrender by France gave Germany a significant and early advantage in the war. The chatter among sailors was that many British lives had been lost in trying to re-establish democracy there.

This feeling of resentment or annoyance against the French was really ramped up for Bill after, and because of, my being prevented from entering Newfoundland when we arrived on the RMS *Newfoundland*. Bill always felt, in this circumstance involving our entry into Canada, that the French-speaking Canadian representative was not only hard to understand but that his response to this situation was not fair, compassionate, or necessary.

Both Bill and I thought that, in consideration of his service to Britain during the war, it should have been a much more welcoming experience when he returned home with his wife and children to make a life with us here. We already had permission to enter Newfoundland, and even though Newfoundland had joined Canada, our experience with the Canadian authorities was anything but a welcoming one.

As a result of this experience, Bill was forever wary of the Canadian government and always saw himself as a Newfoundlander, not a Canadian.

19 — Edie

MEETING AUNT SIS

April 1949

"On a closer look, I saw that in this bench there were two round holes about a foot in diameter. I got closer, and when I stepped inside the door, I was mortified by the absolutely putrid stench. Well, I thought, that won't do!"

— Edie Lundrigan

When we did finally leave the RMS *Newfoundland*, we piled in one of the two taxis waiting on the pier and went to visit Bill's uncle and aunt, Mr. and Mrs. Walter and Rosanah Baggs, who lived in the Battery area of St. John's. We were hugged and kissed when they found out who we were. They also made a big fuss of Jean and Sid.

Suddenly, I realized that I was now standing in one of the small houses clinging to the cliffs that I had seen as the ship entered St. John's harbour. I wondered why anyone would wish to live here on the edge of the earth. Deep inside, I knew that generally people would likely have good reasons for this, but I didn't ask for fear of exposing my ignorance.

We had a lunch and a rest there, then with the help of Mr. Baggs, we made our way to the bus station, where we could catch a bus to Upper Island Cove. That's what I thought, but there wasn't any bus station, just an old bus parked on the side of the road on George Street.

While waiting for the bus to leave, Bill saw his brother-in-law Arch Drover and his cousin Josiah Lundrigan loading freight onto their truck to bring around the bay. They both came over to see us, and Arch came on board the bus and gave me a hug and a welcome to Newfoundland. He also hugged the children and gave them each a twenty-five-cent piece. Despite the seasickness and the trouble with the Canadian authorities, it gave me a good feeling. It was an encouraging start to this new life. Now we were off to meet the rest of the family—in goodness knows where.

During my life, I had regularly used public transit from my home to London to go to picture shows, to go shopping, and for other reasons and occasions. I was used to taking a bus or a train from just at the end of Charlton Street, off London Road, to exactly where I intended, and arriving at that location at a time that had been scheduled.

I was soon to discover not only that there was really little in the way of public transit in Newfoundland, but more importantly, that somewhere while out on the Atlantic Ocean, the ship must surely have gone through a time warp, taking us back in time so many years.

At the risk of sounding dramatic, which is certainly not the way people would generally characterize me, I was not aware of just how much difference there was between what life was like in Newfoundland compared to life in England before I came here. I was now realizing that I was in for a rude awakening, but over the years I came to understand much more about why it was so different.

When we started off on the yellow school bus, I thought we would only be travelling a short while, but we seemed to be going for hours on a dirt road with only miles and miles of fir trees (Christmas trees to me then). There were some houses to be seen, but as it was near dark at this time, they didn't seem to be very plentiful.

We arrived at a place called Spaniard's Bay, and the bus driver said, "This is as far as I go."

I couldn't believe it! We were going to be put off the bus with two children and luggage on the side of the road!

Someone on the bus suggested that we get Ray Murrin to carry us to Upper Island Cove.

I thought, *Okay, we have to change buses. That's fine.*

But even that was not what I expected.

When Mr. Murrin arrived, he was not in a bus but rather in a small pickup truck. We put our luggage in the back and jammed four of us, along with Mr. Murrin, in the single-seat cab of this pickup truck. Once he found room to manoeuvre the gear shifter, which was mounted in the middle of the truck floor, off we went.

By this time I was beginning to wonder where this place of Upper Island Cove was. The children were tired and hungry, and I was losing my enthusiasm for this journey. But then I thought this must be the last leg of the travelling. We were still on the dirt road, and it would be many years before we travelled on pavement.

I couldn't see much of this place. By the time we arrived, it was practically dark. I didn't care, really. All I wanted was to be inside the house, where it was warm when we arrived in the Meadow at the bottom of Lundrigan's Lane.

Bill said, "Come on, Edie, we have to walk the rest of the way."

"How far now?" I wondered out loud, questioning if this was ever going to end.

The luggage was left for someone else to handle, and off we went. I followed Bill and, with Sid in my arms, hopped in over the wooden stiles.

"That's the brook there," Bill said. I looked but could only see a hole in the ground.

He said, "That's the store." All I saw was a shed.

There was a small, two-storey, unpainted wooden house at last, with a faint glow shining from the window.

Thank God, I thought, *at last we are here!*

I wondered briefly what kind of reception we were going to receive, or at least what I was going to receive. The words my father privately said to me the day we left England now rang out in my mind. Unlike Mum, my father never opposed my decision to go but simply said I must please myself.

What he did say as we were preparing to take the train to Liverpool was, "Don't let anyone make a fool of you." I would never forget those words.

The moment was at hand. Bill knocked on the door, and a tall, grey-haired, stately looking lady came out, and he said, "Hello, Mother, may we come in?"

She was so overjoyed, she couldn't speak. She put her arm first around Bill and then me before turning to the children. Before I realized it, she was holding Jean's hand and leading her into the house. Once inside, we met Bill's two younger brothers, Ray and Ian, the youngest of nine children.

I often wondered what Bill would have done if she had refused us, as some of the parents did to daughters-in-law who came to Newfoundland.

I was very fortunate to have such a caring mother-in-law. She made us all very welcome, especially the children. All the family were very kind and helped, with everyone doing their best to make us feel at home.

But life was full of surprises

Elizabeth (Smith) Lundrigan, Willie's mother, commonly known as Aunt Sis

for me in this new world. The whole immigration issue as well as the erratic journey to Upper Island Cove were unwelcome surprises, but the next surprise . . . well, let's just say it was gut-wrenching!

After meeting everyone and getting the luggage into the house, I realized that I hadn't had a chance yet to go to the toilet. I looked around and didn't see one on the main floor. To my dreadful surprise, I found out that there weren't any toilet facilities in the house.

I pulled Bill aside and said, "Bill, what about the toilet?"

"Oh, there's no toilet in here!" Bill said.

I'm sure my jaw just dropped as I stood there staring at him in utter disbelief!

"Don't worry, the toilet is outside. Come on, I'll show you," he said so calmly and in such a matter-of-fact manner.

Bill took a kerosene lantern and walked toward the door. I, still trying to process what he was saying, followed him. *Did he say outside?* I questioned whether I was hearing correctly as we stepped outside. As I followed him out in the front garden, I wondered how that could work. There wasn't any running water in the house, and they had a toilet outside?

Bill stopped at a tiny shed. As he held the light from a distance, I could see inside the open door. There was a single window high up in the door of this decrepit-looking shed, and I could see a wooden bench along the back wall. I took the lantern, and on a closer look, I saw that in this bench there were two round holes about a foot in diameter.

I got closer, and when I stepped inside the door, I was mortified by the absolutely putrid stench. My stomach rolled over, and I urged but managed to avoid throwing up.

"Well," I said, "that won't do!"

After an animated discussion where Bill saw humour that completely escaped me, let's just say a solution was found, at least for now! This was only the beginning of a seventeen-year battle with toileting issues.

Back inside the house, Bill helped me find water. It was not coming from a tap but rather was sitting in galvanized buckets out in the porch. It came from that small hole down at the middle of the lane that Bill had pointed out earlier. The buckets of water had to be carried up to the house several times a day.

I think that all of these changes from what I was used to made me realize what a difference there was in my way of life and the way Bill had grown up. It truly explained a lot about Bill that I could never have understood without being in Newfoundland.

20 — Edie

GOING BACK IN TIME

1949–1960

After World War II, war veterans who returned to Canada were provided with a re-establishment credit (monetary grant) by the federal Department of Veterans Affairs. In Bill's case, the total qualifying service credit was $547.50. Additionally, he had a qualifying overseas service credit of another $535.50, based on $0.25 per day served in active service in Europe. This provided for a total amount of $1,083. It was this amount that Bill and I used to start building our home down in the Meadow at Upper Island Cove.

Bill was able to work in 1949 in Upper Island Cove and was placed in charge of a local "make-work" project, part of which was record keeping. Then in April 1950, he was employed for a short time on a reforestation project. Young people might be surprised to know it was largely World War II veterans who planted the tiny pine trees throughout the area between Upper Island Cove, the Thicket, and Spaniard's Bay Barrens area. After the pine tree setting, he acquired a job on a whaling vessel for the Polar Whaling Company, which operated out of Harbour Grace. He was fortunate to have worked right through the summer that year.

The thing is, though, that despite the difficult circumstances of his childhood in Newfoundland, Bill never stopped loving Upper Island Cove. The Meadow was very much his home. So, while coming back to live here was not an easy decision, over time I began to understand that it was likely the only place in the world that could provide solace for him. For sure it was difficult for me to give up my life of comfort to allow him to do this. Bill always saw me as strong, but that was not always true. I do believe he tried to see things from my point of view. But during his own struggles, I'm afraid he was not able to fully understand how coming to Newfoundland truly impacted the rest of my life.

The reality of life in Newfoundland when we returned from England with our family was that it was a difficult, if not still a pioneering, way of life. Conditions for disease and illness were ripe here compared to England. In 1951, our eldest child, Jean, became quite ill and remained unwell for a long time. It turned out that she had contracted a strep throat and scarlet fever, which ultimately resulted in a diagnosis of the autoimmune disease of rheumatic fever. Jean was what I often called a sickly child after that, but in time she seemed to improve. While her symptoms abated, though, this disease was not about to let go of Jean any time yet.

Many times during those early years, Bill had to go away to different places such as Goose Bay, St. Anthony, St. John's, Port aux Basques, or wherever work was available. He also found work, for a while, at the mines on Bell Island, where he worked as a carpenter. In the meantime, his health was already in serious decline. He had previously suffered from pneumonia and pleurisy. Before long, medical evidence showed there was a problem with his spine that was deteriorating.

There was sporadic work in areas such as Argentia, Pleasantville, Gander, and Stephenville that had just really gotten under way after the war. While better living and economic conditions were beginning to evolve, much of the province was likely economically similar in mid-1949, when Bill and I came here from England, to what it had been for the previous decade or more. As a result, there were quite a few things I had to learn and adjust to that most of England and other developed societies had long since left in the past.

One very visible difference was that the residential areas in England, for instance, were laid out in an organized fashion and often joined together into duplex or row housing. Additionally, the building material for the exterior was primarily bricks and mortar. Some of the houses were owned by the occupants, but many were rented or leased.

Here in Newfoundland, the houses were all single-family detached homes (at least in the rural areas) and haphazardly scattered here, there, and everywhere, but always as close as possible to the ocean. Almost all of the dwellings were constructed of rugged wooden exteriors, often left for years without any paint on them to protect them from this harsh climate.

The Lundrigan house where Bill and I and the children were going to live was itself wooden. It was a very old wooden structure and had never seen a lick of paint on the outside. It was a small, two-storey house built by Bill's grandfather and had three small bedrooms and a kitchen with just one wood-burning stove.

I was fascinated with the way the people chose to arrange the inside of their homes. I was surprised to know that the house Bill grew up in was substantially bigger than the house that I grew up in back in England. Putting aside the issue of indoor plumbing, the biggest surprise for me was that the kitchens in these houses were huge.

In England, a kitchen was a very small area where food was prepared. It was laid out efficiently but compactly, allowing for additional room for moderate-sized bedrooms and a bathroom. In Upper Island Cove, on the other hand, the kitchen was a large room where people gathered. The main floor of the house consisted of a kitchen on the west side, stretching from front to back, in which all the family gathered. In the kitchen there was the wood-burning stove, which was used both for all cooking and baking services as well as serving as the only source of heat for the house.

When I first arrived there, I was alarmed by a distinct smell in the kitchen.

"Bill," I asked, "what's that awful smell?"

Bill first said, "I don't know. What does it smell like?"

"I don't know, but it smells like something rotten," I replied.

Bill laughed and said, "Oh, you will have to get used to that, Edie. That's the smell of the socks and boots drying there by the stove."

The aroma of both the burning wood and the socks and boots drying near the stove was one of those things that grew on me. Something that I first found revolting eventually became so comforting on the many cold and snowy days I spent alone in our house with Jean and Sid while Bill was away working.

Everything about the kitchen had a very specific and useful purpose. Two windows gave lots of natural light as well as a great breeze through the kitchen in the summer, when the wood stove was in use baking the almost daily batch of bread. Another window was located on the front or south-facing wall, and there Bill used to place a pair of binoculars that were used regularly by him and others to look out over the bay.

The kitchen also had a "daybed," which was really a sort of couch, allowing the possibility of a nap by the stove or just extra space for visitors to sit. There was a large kitchen table, which was used for everything from meal preparation and eating area, making bread, and baking. When not otherwise in use, it was a place for Bill's mother to do her sewing work. I would soon learn how much sewing she did and how much it was needed and valued by the community.

Bill showed me the rarely used room he called the "parlour" next to the kitchen. It had a painted floor and minimal furniture. Bill said, "That's where they laid out Father and Mabel."

I asked, "What do you mean? Is that a place where they used to lie down?" (Thinking to myself that it must have been awful cold in here without a stove!)

Bill laughed and said, "No, no, Edie, I meant that's where they laid them out . . . you know, when each of them died."

I forced a grin at his dark sense of humour and said, "Next room, please!"

Despite the well-worn floors and faded wallpaper, the house was very clean. This cleanliness was such a reflection of Bill's mother's work ethic. Since the house didn't have any electricity, just our kerosene lamps for light, nor running water, this made the spotless condition all that much more impressive. It was very strange to me to see these conditions, since electricity, central gas heating, and hot and cold running water with flush toilets and a bathtub were all that I knew of growing up in England.

From the time we met, even though that night I walked home with Jock, I was in love with Bill. In our own right, Bill and I were the children of two very different cultures and worlds. It seemed to me that I had stepped back in time. And as I often said, this was now my new home, and I was determined to get used to this new place and the new lifestyle.

But how was I going to get used to this snow and the cold? I simply found it hard to understand how people here managed to get through the long winters when they had so very little. In England, an inch of snow once or twice a winter was a big deal.

The first winter I spent here, 1949–1950, was a culture shock and a learning experience for me, for sure. Jean and Sid settled into this way of life very well. I don't think they knew there was any difference in their lives. Of course, they were too young to realize this. Jean was two years and four months, and Sid was nine months old, just babies, really. It was cold, intensely cold and snowy, and so much of it. I had never seen snow like it. I wondered how people could survive in this sort of weather with only one stove in the house.

The four of us slept in one bed, mostly to keep warm. I remember waking one morning and feeling the cold on my face and seeing my breath rise in the cold air. Just lying back there in the early morning light, I noticed that the ceiling had a rather unique sparkly look to it.

"Bill, did your mother apply some kind of texture to the ceiling paint?" I asked.

Bill looked at me in some bewilderment until it occurred to him what I was seeing.

"Not at all, Edie. What you are seeing is the effect of the heavy frost on the ceiling paint. This causes the whole ceiling to glisten."

One Monday morning (it was always Monday), I was determined to wash the clothes for us. I had watched Bill's mother and thought, *Okay, that seems easy enough*. So, I grabbed the water buckets from the old porch with the intention of going down the lane to what Bill had loosely referred to as "the well." I put my hand on the door latch leading from the porch to the outside, but it was stuck.

Bill wasn't home, so I said, "Mrs. Lundrigan, the latch is stuck and I can't get the door opened. Is there something I'm doing wrong?"

"Edie," she replied softly, not wanting to embarrass me, "I don't think the latch is broken. We had a lot of snow last night, and the door has about three feet of snow blocking it from opening."

"Bloody snow," I said under my breath.

Fortunately, Bill wasn't far. He was just outside shovelling the front door and was on his way to the porch door to do the same. We got through that year, and things seemed better after that. There were many more cold winters, but that one always stayed in my mind.

In 1950, we decided to start building a house. Bill's health improved quite a lot, and he was looking forward to going to work and getting a home ready for us. In May 1950, Bill left the Meadow for the first time in a while and went to work on a whaling ship in Labrador and was away till November. In the meantime, his brothers Ray and Ian, along with George "Deaney" Lynch, started building the house. They started with Ray and Ian digging a ditch with a pick and shovel in order to pour a concrete foundation.

Once that was done and the forms for the cement were in place, they had to go to the small neighbouring community of Bryant's Cove in someone's truck and get the sand from the beach. Again using only shovels and a wheelbarrow, they mixed the sand and cement and poured the mixture into the wooden cement forms. It may not have been sand that would be of an approved building standard today, but some seventy-two years later, the house foundation appears to be as strong as ever. By August 1950, there was enough done with the little 22' by 24' house that the children and I were able to move in. This was a good day for me. I was on my own, at last!

I had settled into this new way of life and had made some friends. The children were healthy and growing. Life was peaceful. I still missed my family and that way of life, but I couldn't dwell on that. I was really looking forward to Bill coming home from Hawke's Bay.

Willie and Edie's house being built, summer 1950

I have often thought about those early years. I would look around at this place, so rugged and harsh-looking with so much rock and stone, houses everywhere as if they had grown out of the hillsides. Oh, how I missed England's soft green meadows and hills. What was I doing in this place? Getting used to the ways of the people was challenging.

One day in the early 1950s, Bill and I spent a Saturday afternoon with Arch and Myra and their children. Arch took us in his truck to Glover Road, where the children played in a small field area while we boiled the kettle and had a lunch. It was all very lovely. When we came back to Bill's mother's, I could smell something quite strong as soon as we opened the door. Bill's mother was cooking something on the stove.

I said, "Mrs. Lundrigan, what's that strong smell?"

She said, innocently enough, "Come over and have a look."

I went over, and as she lifted the cover, I could for just an instant see what looked like feet in the boiler. The smell was so strong that I ran immediately to the back door and became stomach sick. Bill chased me outside to see if I was okay.

"My God, Bill, what is that in the pot?" I asked.

Bill said, "That's seal flippers."

I became sick again. I'm sure Bill was grinning, but I was both stomach sick and a bit upset.

"What's wrong?" Bill asked.

"I'll be fine, but I will not be having supper today. The last time I saw a seal flipper was on a seal at the zoo in London!"

Later that evening, still trying to process the smell and the sight of cooking seal feet, I remembered before I left England speaking with a relative who had lived in Norway during the war years. She said, "Don't leave your country. You'll be sorry."

I was beginning to think she might have been right. And maybe that's the way Bill felt when we were in England.

There were many times in these early years that I was hopelessly homesick and there were tears shed in the privacy of a small bedroom. I don't think anyone realized what an upheaval this was for me, especially Bill. He was happy to be home, although he was still sick and continued to be for most of that first summer. As his body adjusted to the climate again, his health improved. It was clear to see his adoration for this place, and in particular of the people of Upper Island Cove.

What really stood out was the kindness of Bill's mother. This relationship was always important to me and continued to grow over time. I had become aware over the years of how some war brides were not treated very well by their husbands' family, and in some cases a large portion of the small community in which they had settled. In Upper Island Cove, I was accepted very well. Given my status of an outsider, I knew I could never truly be accepted as "one of them," but I was respected and accepted as someone who married into the community.

Aunt Sis, as Bill's mother was affectionately known throughout the communities of Upper Island Cove and Bishop's Cove, was a woman of great strength and character who did much over the years to allow me to cope and adapt to this new life. She had such a warm and comforting demeanour, and yet with a rather subdued personality, who had a lot of sorrows in her own life. She was also a strong woman who had raised her family without the help of her husband, who had died many years ago. She had fully supported me in this new life, taught me many skills, traditions, and local customs, and I will always be grateful to her for her concern and care for us.

Bill's family, neighbours, and friends were all kind and helpful to me over the years as well. The only person I felt any disrespect from in the community was an older man who Bill simply called Crooked Jim. He always spoke gruffly to me when I went to Les and Lydia's grocery store up on the Back Road. He cursed a lot and grumbled something at me, which I could never understand, but he always finished with the words "bloody limey."

There were two other war brides in Upper Island Cove—Nellie Crane and Kay Parsons, who had arrived from England shortly after the end of the war. At least having three of us provided some comfort that we were not completely alone. Kay eventually moved with her family to Toronto. In the early years, we spent some good time together. Bill and I spent a lot of time, when the children were younger, with Nellie and Nath Crane, as well as Harold and Phoebe Coombs. We would often go to their place or they would come to ours for a game of cards and an evening of fun, remembering good and difficult times, and often just enjoying a lovely friendship. Life was often challenging, but there were these gems that produced such good memories.

One night in particular, we went to Harold and Phoebe's and decided to play cards, a game of "forty-fives," to be exact. In those days Bill and Harold used to like to play for some kind of prize. I can't say exactly how it came about, but that evening, Bill won what he rather redundantly referred to as a "laying hen." Of course, we didn't have a barn or henhouse as the Coombs family did, so the deal was that Phoebe would keep the hen, and every second day, Bill would take the eggs. It was a comical arrangement, with Bill coming home with eggs in the pocket of his jacket that winter. On the bright side, the children had eggs more often than they ever had them before. We also had milk from time to time. I would send Bill or one of the older children, empty bottle in hand, down to Uncle Dick Mercer's, who had a cow. To be clear, many families had canned Carnation Milk in their homes during the 1950s, but few had fresh milk. The older people used to call it "cows' milk," not to distinguish it from the milk of another animal, but to distinguish it from the Carnation canned milk.

Besides the crude physical facilities and the harsh and rugged environment, there were so many other aspects of life in the Meadow for me to get used to or become acquainted with. It was not unusual for a group of women to have to take care of the home and care for the children by themselves for much of a typical year. Work was scarce, and other than the short summer fishery, most men followed the work around the province. For me and the other women, this led to strong bonds of friendship during difficult times. In addition to Bill's family, two such friends of Bill and me were Rudolph and Agnes Mercer, who lived next door.

When Bill was away working, there was still a need to keep the fire in the stove. There was no one available to either cut wood or to go to the Avalon Coal shed in Bay Roberts or to the Munn's Coal Shed in Harbour Grace. In the absence of Bill and Rudolph, Agnes and I would get together. The two of us would have someone deliver two huge truckloads of coal and dump it in the small garden between the two houses.

We would then literally "dig in," shovel the coal into wheelbarrows or coal buckets, and alternate in carrying the coal into the basement of each of the two houses. This was hard work that simply had to be done, and we would continue this until we were exhausted or were needed for other family responsibilities. Next day we would start again and continue until every piece was all put in the coal pound for the winter. It usually took a lot of time and physical effort, since each home would need, and often purchase, as much as three tons of soft (regular) coal along with a ton of hard coal. I distinctly remember the year I was pregnant with Robert. Bill didn't have much work, but the very time he was away was when the coal was delivered. Agnes wanted me to look after her children and mine so that she would do all the coal, but that could not be. So, just like when she was pregnant with their son David, we did it together.

I was never that much interested in politics, but Bill was. I think his interest was more about who he wouldn't support as opposed to who he felt he should support. This may have had something to do with us, me in particular, being prevented by the government of the day from entering the country a year or so previously.

One night in November 1951, he came home laughing about

something that had occurred, but I knew from his actions that he had not really found it to be funny. I asked him what happened.

"Well Edie," he said, as he picked at the supper of meat and potatoes, "a couple of friends and I were standing toward the back at an outdoor Liberal political rally this evening near the Hearse House. The premier, Mr. Joey Smallwood, was speaking, and the crowd was cheering and clapping, except for my friends and me. Instead, we chose to contribute a few courses of jeers and boos.

"Joey (as he was commonly known and referred to) was aware of us disrupting his event, and when he next spoke, it was with hard-hitting and insulting comments, the gist of which was, 'Well, I hope the people of Upper Island Cove ignore these hooligans out there and that they do vote for Jim Chalker on November 26, because if not, Upper Island Cove will be like the label on the bottle. You will always be on the outside looking in.'"

Bill always swore that he never forgot that episode and never, ever voted for a Liberal candidate.

My concern, really, wasn't politics but rather adjusting to life in our new house. I discovered one of my biggest issues was that of "the pail."

When I left England, I was used to going to the toilet, being able to get a bath, and brush my teeth at a sink in the bathroom. I was mortified when I realized there was no indoor plumbing in the old house. Instead, people used a chamber pot in the bedrooms, and either a pail or the old outhouse for other toileting needs.

In our new house, we were without either a toilet or an outhouse for the next sixteen years. As a result, a pail was placed in the basement of the house that had been dug out enough to get inside. The contents of this white enamel pail had to be emptied somewhere.

There really wasn't enough room on our property to place an outhouse, and when I asked Bill what we were going to do now, he simply replied, "Throw it over the Kettle Gulch, I suppose." Like how I felt about the outdoor toilet on my first day here, I was speechless!

I knew that the men would be away to work, and I knew how steep the path was to the Kettle Gulch. I also knew that I would have no choice but to go there to dump the pail, at least when Bill was away working.

The only place to do this was down the steep garden below our house, about 200 feet to the cliff area overlooking the ocean. Bertha, Cavell, and I would meet and walk down the garden, pail in hand. When we reached the wooden railing at the edge of the cliff, we would dump the contents of the pail into the waters of Conception Bay. Then, together we would walk back up until the next agreed time.

Although I didn't say much about it, I remember being discouraged that Bill hadn't told me about these issues when we were still in England. Maybe he was afraid that if I knew about the outdoor toilet and the pail, I might feel differently about coming to Newfoundland.

If that's what he was thinking, he might have been right!

But if I thought that coming to a small community on the Avalon Peninsula, located two to three hours by train or bus from St. John's, was like stepping back in time, I had another consideration yet to process . . .

Bill and I had to continue the struggle to provide the necessities of life for our family. Every effort was made by Bill to find work, and he had some success during the period of 1950 to early 1953. For some reason then, the opportunities seemed to dry up. So began a new adventure for Bill and me, in company with Jean and Sid.

In the spring of 1953, having no work in sight, Bill found out that his Uncle Will Duncan Smith from Bishop's Cove, who ordinarily took a crew of fishermen to a fishing village called Dark Tickle, on the Labrador coast, would not be doing so that season. His uncle told Bill that he was welcome to use both his boat and his fishing gear as well as his fishing residence, which were all located on the mid-coast of Labrador at the mouth of Groswater Bay.

Bill and I discussed the possibility of going in Uncle Will Duncan's place and decided to take up the offer. This was a routine thing for lots of families in the summer, although none of them seemed to get very rich through this process. It was a daunting endeavour for us, though. One thing was certain—even though Bill had lost the opportunity to develop carpentry skills as advanced as many from the area, he was not afraid of work and not afraid to take on a challenge that most people would never do. So, off we went, children in tow.

Many people from Upper Island Cove often talked fondly about the trip down and back from the Labrador on the SS *Kyle*. I found the boat trip quite different than my impressions from those romantic, if not misguided, stories.

We went on the *Kyle*, not knowing where we were going, guided again by blind faith. Oh boy, was I in for a rude awakening! I honestly believe that the *Kyle* was a ship meant, and certainly more suitable, for transporting supplies and equipment than people. Women and children were in one part of the ship that was called the "steerage travel." The men were living and sleeping in the hold of the ship, a place normally reserved for cargo material only. For the most part, there were just some crude bunks in the place for women and children, but no provision of chairs or tables. During the part of the trip along the Northeast Coast, as far as I could see there were many people who succumbed to motion sickness. I did not but, on one occasion, came very close. A friend of Bill saw that Sid and Jean had been sick, and obviously I didn't look too well.

He approached me with a bowl of soup, saying, "Here, Mrs. Lundrigan, maybe this will help you. It is really good soup."

I took the soup from him, saying, "Thank you very much. That's very kind of you."

As I accepted the soup from him, I could see that both his thumbs were sitting on the inside of the bowl, being washed by the soup. As he handed the bowl off to me, he simply nodded and licked his thumbs before wiping them in his shirt. We didn't have soup that day!

We arrived in Dark Tickle, Labrador, after five or six long and stormy days. Considering the poor condition of the ship and the rough seas pounding all the way, especially in the open area of the Northeast Coast, the boat trip to Labrador felt much worse than the trip we had taken four years earlier from Liverpool, England, to St. John's.

Here we were on the isolated coast of Labrador, where the way of life in Upper Island Cove felt privileged compared with life in a tiny seasonal fishing shack in a place that was cold, entirely rugged, isolated, and literally in the middle of nowhere. Additionally, it was unquestionably the permanent home of a host of furry, four-legged creatures who didn't take kindly to our intrusion and had no intention of vacating their home just because we arrived in June that year.

Cooking for a hungry crew of men, along with Bill, Sid, Jean, and me, was difficult with the crude and rusty stove and the few banged-up pots and pans. This was even more difficult to accomplish with few supplies and a leaky roof. The ultimate insult was having to chase the odd rodent from the small kitchen area. The nearest supply store was in an area known as Smokey. With the need to be fishing or salting the catch every day, there was little time to make that journey, except on Sunday, if the weather was suitable for the trip in Uncle Will Duncan's small motorboat.

The whole trip to the Labrador coast was really of little financial value to us. Bill didn't know anything about fishing, especially using cod traps the way they did at that time. Only for the hard work and guidance of our Meadow neighbour turned crew member, Harris Mercer, the trip would have been a complete disaster. The other crew members were Theodore Smith from Bishop's Cove and a young man named Johnathan from a neighbouring community.

Really, the idea of taking on such a trip came about out of desperation because of the lack of other gainful employment. When we began to prepare, it was already too late, in the spring of 1953. Bill had been told by fishermen who had spent a lifetime fishing on the Labrador that, in addition to the fish, berries were plentiful, as was the presence of small game and the occasional seal. We were also warned that, although rare, there was the occasional sighting of a polar bear. As a result, just before we went to the Labrador, Bill purchased a twelve-gauge shotgun from Harold Gosse in Spaniard's Bay for $20. The shotgun didn't have a fore stock, so he fashioned one out of a piece of birch, and it worked out just fine. He always tried to be very careful with how, where, and when he used it.

By the time we got everything together and arrived there toward the latter part of June, it was considerably later than crews who had arrived and started fishing weeks before. In addition to transforming the small living quarters into a livable condition, the men prepared the sole cod trap, anchors, and other fishing gear. We realized that some of it was showing signs of age and disrepair, especially the rotten twine in the cod trap, but there was no turning back now.

On one occasion, the other fishing crews in the harbour helped sew a new bottom in the trap. Our crew used the trap for a short while and, seeing more damage, pulled it back out of the water. All of this was preventing them from catching and curing (by salting) the codfish we came for. Finally, we realized that the trap was beyond repair, and handlining would never get us the quantity of fish we needed to even pay for our trip.

Only through the wonderful generosity and kindness of Mr. Lewis Sheppard of Spaniard's Bay were we able to borrow and use a spare trap that he had. This kind act ensured that, while well behind in the catch as the summer was slipping away, the season would now not be a complete loss. It was heartwarming to see some of the other crews offer at least a little support. It was Mr. Sheppard, before now a stranger to us, who came to us, provided us with expensive fishing gear that saved our summer, and would accept only a "thank you" in return.

Even when it came time to put out this new trap, it was our friend and neighbour, Harris, with the help of Mr. Sheppard's crew, who had the knowledge and experience to do it properly. When we came home in September, we "broke even," as I often said. Probably because of the poor experience of that summer, we didn't bother to take on that responsibility again.

Looking back on it, I often wondered what I was doing in that barren land. Being pregnant with our third child also contributed to this being a punishing experience for me, and one I did not wish to repeat. We arrived back in Upper Island Cove in September 1953, and I was so glad to see our little house in the Meadow again. I said then that I would not travel anywhere else by boat. I had had enough of both stormy seas and boats in general.

The summer on the Labrador provided a wonderful experience for Bill, but that's not what I would call it. I was thirty years old, pregnant, and could not have offered the word "wonderful" to describe the place or the experience.

21 — Willie

'TIS ALL RIGHT ... BUT 'TIS NO GOOD

1949–1961

"Willie, this new boat you have is all right ... but it's no good, really."

— "Little" Joe Crane, Upper Island Cove

Once we returned to Upper Island Cove, I was on the search for work, and luckily I was able to secure the occasional short-term job, but nothing of any duration. I continued to hunt regularly while we needed food that I was able to bring home. Just after Christmas in 1954, our third child, Robert, was born. Indeed, he came into the world on Old Christmas Day, January 6. He was a small child and did not seem very strong. Mother always used to say, "Don't make too much fuss over that child. I have poor thoughts of him." Edie didn't approve of such talk, which I generally ignored, as just the sayings of older people, which were not founded in anything factual. Robert did struggle, though, and it took a long time before he really began to thrive.

If I wasn't working somewhere, I was hunting, except in the summers, of course. There were many occasions when Little Joe, John Billy, and I went out together in a small boat and hunted anywhere from Ben's Head to down the bay as far as Harbour Grace Island. I remember that on March 11, 1955, it was a decent morning on the water, so Joe, John Billy, and I left Upper Island Cove in a small boat owned by John Billy. We didn't see many birds down along the shore as far as Bryant's Cove, so we decided to go down around Harbour Grace Island. As we approached Souther Rock, we saw a lot of ducks and drakes flying around the island, so we decided to go and investigate. We also noticed that the wind had increased fairly strongly from the south-southwest, but we kept on going, as we were more interested in the ducks at that point.

We shot a few birds, but quite suddenly we realized that the wind was a lot stronger than we thought. We picked up the couple of ducks we shot and then decided we'd better try and get back to Bryant's Cove Point. We used the oars on board. I sculled while Joe rowed the boat. We got just part of the way to Bryant's Cove when we took on a nice drop of water over the bow. When I looked up, I could see an even bigger wave about to hit us. I thought, *This is bad. We already have more than a barrel of water on board from the last wave, and now this . . .* The wave hit and we took on more water, but not as much as I feared.

As I bailed the boat with the bailing can, I said, "Joe, turn around. Fast, now, before another wave hits us."

John Billy was scared and the wettest of the three of us, since he was sitting in the bow when the waves hit.

"John, come down here and sit on the middle thwart. That way we won't take on water over the bow when the wave hits us from behind and pushes us forward," I said.

John Billy did as I asked and stayed there, dripping wet. By now it was clear that the wind was too strong for our little boat. We were forced to go back to Harbor Grace Island.

John Billy was a very worried man and said, "This is not good, Joe. I'm a bit worried. Are you?"

Joe, who knew what we had to do and was confident we would be okay, told him, "No, this will be fine. The wind will drop out later this evening. Just listen to what Willie tells you."

Joe knew that John Billy had confidence in me because I had spent a number of years in the navy. I wasn't as confident, though, as John Billy was in me. But after Joe spoke to him, he seemed to be fine.

The wind wasn't dying out, so we decided we should wait out the storm there since we were reasonably safe at the moment. We needed some sort of shelter, so we hauled our boat up on the beach and turned it bottom up. We could crawl underneath if it rained during the night. Sometime later, all three of us went on top of the island and got some blackberry bushes that we used to start a fire. Joe cleaned a couple of the ducks that we had shot earlier. We had some molasses bread plus a roasted duck to make a fine lunch. We lit a fire and shoved a stick through the ducks in order to roast them. We had a feed of duck, molasses bread, and boiled tea.

We crawled under the boat for a while, but the temperature had dropped below freezing.

Joe said, "Willie, turning over the boat is all right . . . but 'tis really no good."

He was right. Turning over the boat would keep us from getting wet, but it was so terribly cold we were unable to stay there. We walked around the beach most of the night, trying to keep warm. It wasn't the last time Joe used that expression, and I may have used it myself over the years.

When daylight finally broke in the eastern sky, through a combination of walking and climbing, we went up on top of the island. I looked all around with my binoculars, and in the distance I saw what I thought was a schooner. Before long, I was able to see more clearly and confirmed to Joe and John Billy that a schooner was coming toward us. John Billy, who had a bit of a speech stoppage, was so excited he couldn't get a word out. We climbed back down to the beach and turned our boat back on her keel. Joe got in first, since he was the lightest of the three of us. John Billy and I pushed the boat the short distance to the water. Joe and I then navigated out the narrow gulch, which was barely wide enough to get our boat through, since the tide was low.

Within fifteen minutes, we had sculled our punt out to the schooner. In no time, we were on board the schooner, with the punt in tow. The vessel then headed for Carbonear. When we got on board, we were all given a large drink of rum and a good breakfast. By then we were in Carbonear. We thanked the captain and crew of our rescue boat and tied up our punt to the wharf. With that, three of us got a ride home to Upper Island Cove in a police car. The name of the rescue schooner was the MV *Philip*. It was sixty tons. The captain was William Jones, and the crew members were Max Rogers and William Sheppard. The vessel was owned by Ralph Mercer, whose father, known locally by his nickname, Jimmy Dood, was originally from Upper Island Cove. This was the same Jimmy Dood on whose radio I had heard the speech of King George VI back on September 3, 1939.

Even though things went differently than we had planned, we agreed that we wouldn't have missed the trip out on the water that day for anything.

Something funny about that night was that, even though we had a fine lunch eating roast duck and molasses bread, when daylight came and we were able to see each other better, the combination of blood from the partially cooked duck and molasses from the bread painted quite a picture on each of our faces. When they first saw us, the ship's crew had quite a laugh.

Sometime in the next few years, John Billy purchased a small outboard motor, which was marvellous for the three of us. We were able to get out more, not work so hard, sometimes sculling and often rowing the boat, and not worry about the wind quite the same. John Billy's boat was getting old and untrustworthy, so I purchased a punt from our neighbour, Rudolph Mercer. Joe, John Billy, and I used it a lot during the winter. We had great success, although there were a few times we got stranded when the ice blocked us from getting back in the cove. On more than one occasion we had to pull up the boat in Bryant's Cove and walk home. I also remember one evening we got as close to the wharf as around the Dog Gulch but no farther, so we pulled up the small boat on a skittery rock down behind where Warren "Deaney" Lynch has his house now.

We also got good use of it in the summers. Sid and Robert loved to go down alongshore with me on a calm day to try for a lobster. If it rained we would get wet, but in summer we didn't mind. Robert, who was only six or seven years old, wouldn't get wet because he could fit in the small cuddy in the bow of the boat. Unfortunately, the boat was near the end of its life, and one day in July 1961, with the help of seven-year-old Robert, I started to take it apart. Coincidentally, we didn't get a lot done that day, since it was the day my brother Edward, who after the war married and lived in Scotland, was returning home after a visit to see us, especially Mother, who by then was seventy-one years old.

22 — Willie

COMRADES

1957–1963

"When I signed up with the British Royal Navy, in my mind it was for the purpose of helping win a war and continue to be a member of the navy. And for me, this whole new way of life in the navy actually became the only real life that I knew. I had no interest in leaving."
— Willie Lundrigan

While the family grew, I continued to work, when and where I could. As time passed, I was becoming less able to do the heavy work of a labourer or carpenter's helper than I had been able to do in the earlier years. During the time that my health and employment challenges were ongoing, I got involved in something that helped keep me in a positive place.

Upper Island Cove had over forty men living in the community who had served in World War II, most of whom were still alive during the 1950s. Additionally, there were approximately thirty survivors of World War I who called Upper Island Cove home. Many of these older war veterans were members of the World War I organization known as the Great War Veterans Association (GWVA). They sometimes held meetings in St. Peter's School, and many people saw this organization as the natural forerunner of the Royal Canadian Legion as we know it.

During the 1950s, to provide support to these members who had served their country in war, some veterans in a variety of other towns in the province had established, or were in the process of establishing, branches of the then Canadian Legion. The GWVA, in July 1960, through a special Act of Parliament, became known as the Royal Canadian Legion, or locally as the Legion.[7] This movement was of keen interest to some war veterans in Upper Island Cove, who, while never expressing their true feelings about how war had changed them, nonetheless felt that an organization of this sort would provide a venue in which they could have a place and a forum to support each other and the community generally.

Sometime around 1956 or 1957, a number of local veterans, including me, started to consider the benefit of having such an organization with its own building in Upper Island Cove. I felt that in consideration of the fact that the past was being relived continuously by many veterans, this could be a good thing. I never shared my most inner and tumultuous feelings with anyone. Unfortunately, I could not hide from Edie my body's response to the night disturbances. She was also often awakened by me talking or yelling in my sleep. She was often the one who woke me and handed me pyjamas to replace the ones that were now drenched in perspiration. I knew others had to be similar, but there wasn't much opportunity to share and possibly lighten the burden with my fellow veterans.

For many of us, the motivation to become part of such an organization was very much tied to the concept of being able to come together as a group of people who had experienced many difficult, but shared, experiences. A Legion would hopefully be a place to share a story and laugh about some of the comical encounters, but ultimately

---

7   Legion website, Our History

an organization and a place in which to feel supported. I could truly call these people my comrades—our service to our country and King created a bond that had always been very strong.

Finally, after a considerable amount of discussion, we began the process of forming a branch of the Legion. After working with the Provincial Command in St. John's, Branch 22 of the Royal Canadian Legion, Newfoundland Command, was formed in Upper Island Cove. Forming a branch was just the beginning, and once we started, it seemed that there was no turning back. An executive board was elected, and one of the first orders of business was to find a place in the community where we might acquire a parcel of land on which to build our own Legion building.

There were lots of organizational meetings, some held at St. Peter's School, but many held in the private homes of members such as Nath Jones, Les Reid, Nath Crane, Harold Coombs, and others. During these meetings, there was a great deal of collaboration but also heated discussion about how to proceed to acquire a Legion building. Many of the new members agreed to begin by cutting logs, which could then be sawed into framing for the structure. One of the new Legion members, Hayward Mercer, acquired a permit from the Department of Forestry to cut the logs. Over that winter of 1957–1958, there were many truckloads of logs cut on the Salmonier Line, near Father Duffy's Well. They were transported to Josiah Lundrigan's sawmill. Not being a veteran himself, but as a way to support us veterans, Josiah sawed the logs free of charge for the newly minted Legion branch. In many ways this passion of ours became a community endeavour, with people in Upper Island Cove and area. Many friends and relatives of veterans jumped in to cut logs and eventually helped with the building construction.

The Legion building was constructed down in the Cove area, fittingly overlooking the fishing boats moored in the Cove. It became a location for veterans to meet and plan events. More importantly, however, it became a positive addition and a sense of pride to the community. It was appreciated by both veterans and non-veterans alike. Practically, for veterans, it was a place exclusively created for their benefit and a place where, it was hoped, the camaraderie of the group could help individual members in coping with the past.

Throughout the province, the sanctuary of the Legion has helped many on their postwar journey. Some veterans enjoyed the camaraderie of others and the opportunity to talk about or talk through any issues they were experiencing. Not everyone could benefit as much from that kind of social engagement, and so not every veteran was active in the Legion.

It seemed to me that, during the last half of the 1960s and through the 1970s, right across the province, fewer people appeared to value the real purpose of the Legion. During those years, I also felt that fewer people came out to Remembrance Day ceremonies. With all that I had going on personally, I also lost a lot of interest.

Eventually feeling a significant amount of personal duress related to my health and inability to earn, I decided I needed to step back from the Legion. I continued to pay my annual membership for a number of years after that, but eventually I just stopped my involvement altogether. I look back on it with some regret, but it was the right decision for me at the time.

23 — Willie

FIVE-POINT APPLES

1963–1972

"I didn't leave my family and come all the way from England to this little community in Newfoundland to have my family fall apart. My mother always accused me of being strong-willed, and I used that quality to pick us up when we were down and to help move us forward when I could."

— Edie Lundrigan

Edie was not from here but was very much welcomed into the community. From what she could see, life was not easy for anyone living in Upper Island Cove or other similar small towns during the decades of the 1950s and 1960s. I used to tell her that the economy was improving, but it was hard for her to see. Personal financial challenges were very prevalent. Town infrastructure, up to now almost non-existent throughout rural Newfoundland, was just being recognized as a need.

But there were two especially bright lights for Edie and me. Our son Philip was born in May 1960, and it would be fair to say that Edie and I, the proud parents of new-born Philip, were surprised when several months later we realized that Edie was pregnant again. Then in September 1961, our second daughter, Mavis, was born at home. Mavis was the third of four children born in Newfoundland after we brought Jean and Sid across the Atlantic. Although there was one more child to come, Mavis would be the last child to be born in our little house at Upper Island Cove. Having already supported Edie in the birth of Robert and Phil, this would also mark the end of Aunt Maggie (Coaker) Lundrigan's midwifery skills for our family. This incredible lady, who had supported so many women before, during, and after childbirth, was so appreciated by the community. She, along with others, such as Aunt Sus Sharpe and Aunt Mary Margaret Drover, were true unsung heroes of the community.

A growing family, late 1961. Standing: Sid and Jean. Sitting from left to right: Phil, Willie, Robert, Edie, Mavis. Not yet born: Boyd.

Challenging times were even more challenging with two small children, who before long would require extra resources from the income we were getting from my sporadic employment. Like many families in the community, we did not have running water or indoor toilet facilities. We had to use the bit of money we had put aside for a furnace to pay for coal for the kitchen stove, which was essential for both cooking and heating at least a portion of our small house. As far as indoor plumbing was concerned, it would take a long time before carrying the pail under the bank would be a thing of the past.

One of the people who I felt really understood me was my younger brother Ray.

Ray was about four years younger than me and had become recognized as a good carpenter and a well-respected worker. He also had developed a good understanding of some of the many struggles we were having, including my difficulty finding work. As was his character, Ray did everything he could to help his elder brother get work. If Ray went to Port aux Basques for work, or if he went to Goose Bay or Holyrood or elsewhere, he usually came down to see me to say, "Willie, I got word that there is a job for us in Port aux Basques, if you are interested."

Invariably I would say, "Well, Ray, that's wonderful news. Did you hear that, Edie? When do we start, Ray?"

When we made eye contact, Ray would just smile. A knowing nod of acknowledgement from me as he was going out the door was more than enough to satisfy him.

But by 1963, Ray couldn't help us anymore. I had had a long history of health issues, beginning with pneumonia twice in 1940, pleurisy, pneumonia in the period of 1946 to 1949, and a deteriorating spinal condition throughout these years. Objective medical evidence (X-rays) now confirmed I was unable to continue with the only work I knew. At that point my doctor turned me down from working. I was just forty-two years old.

Thankfully, and to Ray's credit, the relationship between him and me never changed or faltered, and Ray's loyalty never failed to lift us up over the years. We might see Ray any time during the week, but regardless of that, almost every Sunday for decades, Ray would come down the lane to our house for a visit. There was always something to say—a story from the past or some local news that Ray would put a funny twist to. It was always a very pleasant way to spend a Sunday morning for Edie and me. It was also a way for Ray and me to remain close as brothers and best friends through to the end.

I was never a person to get caught up in what other people thought. That included what they might have thought abut me during this time of great financial strain. It did matter a lot what Edie thought. I know she understood that the doctor determined I could not do heavy work, but I guess I wondered from time to time if Edie thought I might try another type of work. I never again returned to gainful employment. Although it didn't diminish our relationship, my absence as a breadwinner during that period, I believe, made her very sad. It was something I think she struggled with for many years. Very late in her life, I think she may have understood the impact of years of intense war service on me.

During this time, and although she would never speak of anything, I was also aware that, from time to time, Edie was having her own challenges. While she was emotionally strong, having left her family in England over a decade ago, this permanent separation had to be difficult, especially knowing that the separation would likely be for a lifetime.

Edie had always supported me as I struggled physically and in my attempts, previously, finding work. She must have been frustrated with our financial condition or, even worse, disappointed in me. I wondered from time to time if I saw the edges of that frustration, but she never once verbalized it to me. I don't think she would admit that she was disappointed, because doing so would largely confirm her mother's view that she should never have left England in the first place. Nevertheless, she must have seen me as facing life's challenges rather poorly compared to how she was doing. She was not born into the same culture as I was. Either genetically or because of her upbringing, Edie seemed to have a tenacity and a resilience that few people possessed. While the struggle for each of us was different, we would continue to try to make life better for our children.

In 1963, Sid and Jean were both in their final years of school. Phil and Mavis had not yet started school, and Boyd had not yet entered this world. Robert was in grade four and at an especially vulnerable age. That year, as usual, the students always had a Halloween Party in school. During the party, they had the standard treats such as a portion of an apple, Purity Hot Knobs, and a few assorted unwrapped candies. The children did have a few simple decorations and usually a small paper mask of some design. The year before, in grade three, I believe Robert had the Lone Ranger mask.

"Mom, you know it will soon be time for us to have a Halloween party in school again. Can you buy me a mask, please?" Robert asked one day in early October.

"We shall see. Halloween is still a way off, yet," said Edie.

We knew having the mask was important, and it wasn't a lot of money. But when you have none, even a little is a lot. Now, toward the end of October, Robert came back and asked again, "Mom, can I have that mask now?"

"I don't think we will be able to get you a mask this year like we did last year. But you can still have lots of fun, and I'm sure we can come up with some way to get a mask for you," replied Edie.

With this disappointing news, nine-year-old Robert went to his room and slammed the door. He wouldn't come out for a bedtime snack and didn't say good night to either of us, as he always did faithfully. Next morning, he didn't say much and didn't eat much breakfast. We also noticed that he went off to school by himself rather than wait for Roslyn Mercer and Dorothy Coombs, as he regularly did.

We tried desperately to make him feel better about not having a mask, but it didn't do much good.

"Willie, you stay with the children. I have to run down to Mary

Emma's for a few minutes." Edie needed a few groceries, and Aunt Mary Emma Crane had the closest local general store. There she purchased some needed groceries, which were placed in a medium-sized brown paper bag. This was good, because she could now help with Robert's mask situation.

After she returned home, she took the groceries out of the bag.

"Come over to the table with me, Robert, and help me with this mask," she encouraged.

As Robert watched, she carefully cut out holes for the eyes, nose, and mouth in the empty bag. With some encouragement, she persuaded Robert to help her colour the bag in a fancy orange design. I looked on, and when they finished the design, Edie told Robert he could use this tomorrow for his Halloween mask.

Robert said, "That's okay, Mom. I am in grade four. Some of us aren't wearing masks this year." Edie knew this was not accurate. The next morning, she made sure he had the paper-bag mask in his school bag. Off to school he went. No one took out any masks or treats that early for fear that the teacher would not allow them to have a party in the afternoon.

After lunch, everyone excitedly put on their masks and, as was the custom, waited for parents to drop by with a few treats. From what Edie could see, peeking in from the corridor, everyone had a mask except for Robert. Thankfully, not all parents attended these Halloween parties. Robert didn't know that Edie saw him without the mask, and we never spoke of it again.

We found out later that Robert told his friends he had lost his mask in the drain, which ran along the side of the road all the way from the school to the Cove. After he went to bed that night, Edie opened his bookbag, and there as we thought, was the paper-bag mask.

Next morning, she asked, "Why didn't you wear your mask?"

After a minute of silently hanging his head, Robert said, "I'm sorry, Mom, I know we can't afford it, and I know you really wanted me to wear it, but I would have been made fun of, and people would know we are poor."

Of all the struggles we had, I think this hurt Edie as much as anything. She would sacrifice anything to see the children happy. It upset me, but I didn't say much about it. Instead, I went for a walk down alongshore. Edie must have wondered if I even noticed. But I did notice and felt a great deal of responsibility for the fact that we couldn't afford much, let alone a mask.

I'm sure Edie sometimes wondered what she had signed on for when she agreed to come across the Atlantic. I felt deeply hurt for Robert and for Edie but also awful mad about the place that all of us were in. Even though I loved my family, avoiding or tuning out these situations became a coping mechanism that followed me throughout my life. To Edie it must have seemed that I didn't care, but that was not at all the case.

In 1963, Edie had helped me make an application to the federal Department of Veterans Affairs (DVA) for a financial benefit for veterans known as a War Veterans Allowance.

"Now, Bill, I have that DVA form filled out, and I want you to sign it. If this War Veterans Allowance gets approved, at least we'll have a little bit of money coming in, especially now with Christmas approaching," said Edie.

I signed the form and went over across the back to Mrs. Foley's, the lady who looked after the local postal service, and mailed it. After about a week, we started to wonder if we would get a reply. In the letter, Edie reasoned that there was a clear link between the now severe condition of my lower spine and the amount of time I spent in the water because of the torpedo, or incidents while I was on the *Laurentic* in November 1940. It seemed to take such a long time. Just before Christmas in 1963, I went to the mail and received a letter, the return address of which was the Department of Veterans Affairs. I took it directly home and gave it to Edie. We looked at one another, anxious now to get a positive response after so many times having an application for benefits rejected.

Edie opened the letter with a kitchen knife, unfolded the paper, and began to read. It only took a few seconds observing her facial features to realize the news was not what we had hoped for.

"What is it, Edie? What does it say?" I asked.

Edie read one line from the letter. "I am sorry to inform you that we are unable to approve your application for benefits at this time."

For me it was quite upsetting, as I'm sure it must have been for Edie. Giving no indication how she felt about it, Edie simply said, "Well that's that."

"We will continue as we were. I'm sure they must have made a mistake, and somewhere, someone must realize that you qualify for some benefits because of your war service. But for now we must just get on with it and give the children the best Christmas we can."

With no money coming in and the application turned down, Christmas was about to become a challenging time.

But none of this deterred Edie. She once told me, "I didn't leave my family and come all the way from England to this little community in Newfoundland to have my family fall apart."

She used to say her mother always accused her of being strong-willed. She certainly used that quality to pick us up when we were down and to help move us forward when she could.

But while I was not well, I would never give up trying to make life easier and better for our family, sometimes in ways that, as a person from England, Edie could never have imagined.

For instance, I had great success in acquiring food through an ability to hunt. I knew and loved every nook and cranny of this unique community of Upper Island Cove, and in particular the area known locally as "down alongshore." There were always seals and a host of migratory birds around in the waters of Conception Bay in the fall, winter, and spring, and I always successfully acquired a fair share. It was a regular occurrence during the 1960s for us to have wild game as part of our meal.

Edie worried that I would get hurt while hunting by myself on the steep cliffs and slippery rocks. But I knew these rocks and cliffs so well that I think I was able to give her a bit of comfort that I'd be okay. I had my shotgun, but buying ammunition was expensive. We had little money, so, ever conscious of our financial plight, I always picked up the spent cardboard cartridges when I fired my twelve-gauge shotgun. Later in the evening, after the children were in bed, I would take them and carefully repack them with a firing cap, gunpowder, and #12 shot.

For years that shotgun was hung in the kitchen over the door going to the porch. It was never loaded, and the ammunition was kept close by but far out of reach of any child.

The location was no accident, since seeing wildlife such as a seal, a Baccalieu bird (murre), or a loon required me to move quickly, because whatever I saw with the binoculars was not going to stick around forever. But the gun was also hung close by because others in the community, such as the Cranes (nicknamed Pops) over in the Cove and the Coombses (nicknamed Cockys) down in the Meadow, were no slouches when it came to being the first to get that shot and have the prize in the pot in short order.

Early in the morning and before the sun came up, no matter how cold and wet, I would often go down alongshore, between Upper Island Cove and Bryant's Cove, any time from October until well into the spring of the year to hunt for seals and whatever migratory game bird I could find.

Fortunately for us, Jean had finished grade eleven in June 1963 and immediately went to summer school for basic teacher training in St. John's. The school course she enrolled in was designed for preparing new teachers who had recently graduated from high school.

Through that summer school, Jean acquired what was known as

a "D" licence, which enabled her to teach in the public school system that September. She had a few offers of a teaching position, but the one she chose was in Gander Bay North. The school itself was located in the tiny village of Davidsville. As a result of being employed as a teacher, Jean was able to help us a little by purchasing a few children's Christmas presents.

In addition to the support of Jean, the Christmas of 1963 also saw an outpouring of support from some of my other family members as well as some of our friends. Our children always looked forward to the regular Christmas parcels from Edie's mother, as well as her elder sister, Lil, in England. They always sent nice packages with special "English" candies, but this year the parcels seemed to be that much bigger. The gifts from England were all bundled up and stored in our bedroom, however the cupboards were bare.

Late one afternoon during the week before Christmas, Edie and I were alone, since the children were up in Ray and Bertha's garden playing in the snow. I thought I heard a vehicle door open and close. Edie looked out the front window. There were no street lights, so she could not see who it was. She decided to go and have a look, but before she got to the door, someone opened it from the outside. This wasn't unusual, since people coming to your house didn't usually knock. When the door opened, Edie could see someone behind a large cardboard box.

"Hello," called the voice. "Anyone home?"

Edie recognized the voice as that of her brother-in-law Les Reid.

"Oh yes, Willie and I are here," she replied.

"Lydia is coming behind me," Les said. "May we come in?"

"My goodness, yes," Edie replied, and at the same time she shouted out to me, "Bill, Les and Lydia are here!"

I came out from the front room, saying, "On the way."

Les and Lydia both walked into the kitchen and laid two boxes on the table and left to go back to the car.

"Lydia, what's this you have here?" Edie asked as Lydia was going back out through the porch.

"Wait now," Lydia said. "I'll be right back."

We peeked into one of the boxes and saw oranges, red grapes, cornflakes, and Purity Fancy Biscuits. I looked at Edie, and uncharacteristically, I could see such strong emotion show on her face. She started to cry and turned to me. I held her and could feel her tears on my cheek. Both Les and Lydia came back inside with two more boxes.

Edie and I could not speak.

Lydia hugged us both while saying, "Merry Christmas to the both of you."

Edie hugged them both back, and Les and I shook hands as he patted my shoulder. Edie and I thanked them sincerely. Lydia, too, was emotional and said something about Santa Claus coming, just to change the subject.

The reality was that we lived in a small and caring town. Lydia and her husband, Les, had a small supermarket that supplied most families in the Meadow, across the Back and the Rocky Hill area, including us. They were not wealthy people, yet they took groceries from the shelves and gave them to us so that we would be able to have a Christmas with our children.

And they were not the only ones. We soon realized there must have been a plan.

Within a few minutes, we saw our sister-in-law Bertha, along with Ray, coming to the door. Bertha made some great raisin bread as well as a very tasty dark Christmas cake. Ray, sporting his infectious smile, came in the porch carrying a sack of potatoes on his strong back. Later that evening, we also had visits from Rudolph and Agnes as well as my sister Myra and her husband, Arch, who also helped out. There was a regret, and for me a lingering sense of guilt, that we were in a very poor situation, but I can say with certainty that our family and friends so readily helped Santa Claus do what was otherwise likely impossible that Christmas.

Willie and siblings. Left to right: Willie, Myra, Lydia, Ian, Ray. Missing from the photo are John, Edward, and Mabel.

Having a turkey cooked for Christmas dinner was already a tradition for many people in this part of Newfoundland. One of the children asked if we were going to have turkey for Christmas dinner. We were so appreciative of all that we had. As I looked through everything, I realized the only thing we didn't have for Christmas dinner was a turkey. The children were hoping for one, and we weren't done yet.

I was always an early riser, and on Christmas Eve I left the house early and didn't come back until around lunchtime. When I walked out the door dressed in my warm old sheepskin pants, made years ago by my mother, I was determined to find a way to save our Christmas dinner. I went down to an area called Grandma Young's Path, just below Freshwater Beach, about halfway between the Meadow and Bryant's Cove Point. As I looked out over the cliff, I could see two loons diving for food in the shallow water. I went back farther from the edge and climbed slowly down nearer the water without being seen or sensed by the birds. The trouble was that the loons seemed to take turns diving, and they usually only dived for a short period of time. Unless both dived together, I couldn't afford to move.

Eventually, both dived at the same time and I moved to within a gunshot, but when they came up again, they were too far away. I had to wait patiently and hope they would eventually move closer instead of leaving. Finally, that happened, and when they dived again, I cocked the shotgun and placed it to my shoulder, waiting anxiously. The loons came up, and to my delight, they were not only in range but positioned so that, if I was fortunate, I could possibly get two of them in the single shot. I knew one shot would be all I could get.

Bang!

I watched as both birds slumped, motionless, on the calm water. I was delighted, but now to get them in to me. I took my floating jigger, made of a piece of wood about a foot long, which was full of small fish hooks embedded all around it and fastened to a long rope. After a number of attempts, I had the birds at my feet.

Later on, when I walked in the house, I brought with me two large loons. Edie, not one to usually like wild meat, was delighted, especially for the children. I cleaned the birds, and since we didn't have a refrigerator, I placed them in the cool basement until next morning.

Then everyone prepared for Christmas Eve. The routine was to have the children leave a bit of molasses bread, maybe a cookie, and some Purity Syrup for Santa, place their stockings by the foot of the bed, and off they went. Later in the night, Edie or I would take Robert and usually Jean and Sid to the Christmas Eve church service at St. Peter's Church for 11:30 p.m. There was always a big crowd, so we didn't stay for the whole service. But even then it was after 1:30 a.m. before we got back home.

The next morning was an early rise as usual. Under the tree, the big hits were the tricycles that Phil and Mavis had, thanks to Jean. The children also made a big fuss of the other gifts from England, along with a small item from Edie and me. We both felt more emotional that Christmas than I remember any Christmas since we came back from England. We had fewer presents for the children, but they didn't notice. There were oranges and red grapes and chocolate in all stockings hung neatly under the tree. We had apple juice for breakfast along with the luxury of bacon and eggs.

For Edie and for me, the warmth of the fire was that much more comforting that Christmas of 1963 because of what all our family and friends had done to make it special for the children. I couldn't help but feel a bit guilty, which Edie hushed away quickly, and said I should get out and light the fire and "get on with it." I knew she was happy, too.

After the children got up with their gifts, Edie and I started preparing food. The birds, along with the food from the Reids, Uncle Ray's potatoes, and baked goods from the others, were huge hits for all of us. They were served up as a big part of our Christmas dinner. The loons didn't quite taste the same as turkey, but everyone seemed quite happy that we had at least some sort of a bird that we could have for Christmas dinner.

An appeal of that DVA decision was made on my behalf by Branch 22 of the Royal Canadian Legion in January 1964, and in March of 1964, the War Veterans Allowance was approved. The War Veterans Allowance of $112 per month wasn't very much, but it was coming in every month, so we had some security.

24 — Willie

A LIGHTER LOAD

1964–1972

Unfortunately, but predictably, the difficult financial times didn't just end after the Christmas of 1963. This was but the beginning of a period of time when, after putting the basic food on the table, heating the house, and clothing our children, there was pitifully little left for anything else. This wasn't as much a complaint as it was an observation of how we were challenged to make things work over the next decade. And we did.

The last place I worked before having to stop was at the United States Naval Base in Argentia with Ray. There were a lot of people from Upper Island Cove and area working there, some longer-term and some, like me, usually for only a few months at a time. One of the kind gestures of the working dads, on their Saturday night trip home for an abbreviated weekend break, was to stop somewhere on the base and purchase some treats. These were then given to the children when they reached home. Favourite treats included items such as Turkish Delight bars and five-point apples. When I stopped working, of course that, too, stopped for our children. Occasionally, one of the other dads would buy extra and drop it off to our house. This practice dwindled away over time, and I know it bothered our children that these treats were no longer a regular part of their lives. But changes were occurring at our house as well.

At just sixteen months younger than Jean, our son Sid was going to turn sixteen in July of 1964.

"Mother, I'm not going back to school. Myself and Gordon Mercer got a job on the Labrador," said Sid out of the blue one day in the spring of 1964.

"My goodness, you must go to school, my son. You're only fifteen," replied Edie.

"Yes, I know, Mother. But I'm not interested in school, and Gordon is not, either. We want to get out and earn some money. I don't want to be in school," said Sid.

"But Sid, you will be sorry for leaving school. You need to stay in school to get a good education, my son," said Edie.

"Mother, I just don't want to be in school. There's nothing there for me. I want to go out and earn money, and you mark my words, I'll be just fine without any more education," said a determined Sid.

When I got home, Edie and I discussed it. We both came to the conclusion that we could not really force him to go to school if he didn't want to. After all, he would be sixteen in July, and many of his friends had already left school.

But even before that, he left school in the spring and went fishing on the Labrador coast with Robert John Clarke. At that point, Edie and I could only support his decision and wish him well. With both Jean and Sid now somewhat independent, over time things were getting a little easier for us.

Sid didn't earn a massive amount of money that year, but he did bring home a couple of barrels of Labrador salted codfish, cod's heads, Arctic char, salmon, and of course Labrador bakeapples. He described the summer as a learning experience, and it made him feel a little independent.

During the next three years fishing on the coast with Fred Mercer, he earned a bit more money. He also made several trips to Toronto for work during the fall and winter.

Parenting correctly is an issue for all of us. In my case, I just didn't seem to be equipped with the skill to be an effective parent. I found knowing what to do as a parent was daunting. I had never experienced a warm, nurturing childhood. As a family, we seemed to be always in survival mode. As it was in my childhood, so too was it also common in the 1960s for children to be punished for wrongdoing, using physical force such as with a strap.

It was, after all, the era of "spare the rod, spoil the child." There was a close call in that regard for Robert in the winter of 1965.

One day, a young fellow from down in the Meadow knocked at the door, and when I opened it, he said, "Willie, Robert was down by the wharf jumping between pans of ice and went down between two pans."

"Where is he now?" I asked.

"I dunno. We didn't see him after that."

Edie was pregnant and about to give birth within days. She overheard this conversation, and I could see her reaction when she held on to her stomach with one hand and gasped while holding on to a chair with the other.

With my help she sat down and calmly said, "Bill, please go and bring that child home."

I probably needed that direction, since I always depended on Edie to be the voice of reason. I grabbed my coat and shoved my bare feet into my tattered winter boots and bolted through the door. I don't know what I was thinking, or where exactly I would look for Robert, but I was headed as fast as I could right for the Cove. It was slippery, and I had to be careful in order to stay on my feet. As I approached the top of Mercer's Hill, there was nothing but a glare of ice, and with caution to the wind, I let myself slide on both feet, accelerating as I went. Other than a strange look from a few people out shovelling snow from the door, I made it down the hill okay.

I started to sprint past Willie Hussey's when, suddenly, I saw the form of a boy trudging slowly toward me. His hood was up, and his head was bent down. I immediately recognized his walk and his clothing. My racing heart began to slow a little, and as we came closer together, any sense of anxiety quickly turned to relief, and then to anger. It was Robert, alive and well and soaking wet.

I don't remember the exact sequence of events after that, but I was equally glad and mad. I would deal with the reckless behaviour later. I must admit, the fact he was cold and wet was a low priority for me at that point. I still had to get him to the house as quickly as possible to provide proof to his heavily pregnant and distraught mother, that while he was wet and maybe even injured, he was alive and well. Within minutes we were back at the house, and Edie had her arms around Robert, yelling at him as she hugged him. It was after the hugging Robert and I retired to his bedroom for a lesson in not going on the harbour ice again. And while I had a good leather belt with me, Robert's remorse was more than sufficient punishment.

Despite all the fuss involving Robert and an ice pan earlier in the winter, our youngest child, Boyd, took his own time and arrived right when he was expected. A year and a half after his eldest sister and sibling, Jean, left for her teaching position in Gander Bay, Boyd, our youngest child, was born at Carbonear Hospital in mid-March 1965. All was well.

By 1965, Jean had been teaching in Gander Bay for two years. She came home for a visit on Good Friday, April 16, 1965, to see Boyd, who had been born less than a month earlier. It was during that visit that Jean announced she was getting married. Only then did she ask what we thought about it. This was quite a surprise for Edie and me.

While I did not really like it, Edie quickly reminded me that, at eighteen years old, Jean was an adult and a very responsible one. I'm sure Edie was also concerned because she was so young, but Edie put the answer in the same manner to Jean as her father did to her when she told him about taking her family to live in Newfoundland. "You must please yourself." Jean's fiancé, Lloyd Eveleigh, accompanied her on that trip, and he seemed like a nice man. Before they left to go back to Gander Bay, they told us that the wedding was planned for June 25, just two months away. They wanted both of us to be there for the wedding. On their last day of that Easter visit, Edie pulled Lloyd aside and said to him, very directly, "As long as you look after our daughter and treat her with respect, you will always be welcome here."

Even though Boyd was just three months old, on June 23, 1965, we farmed out the children to Bertha and Agnes (Rudolph was fishing and Ray was away working) and took a taxi to the train station in Whitbourne. There we boarded the Newfie Bullet, travelling from Whitbourne to Gander, where Lloyd picked us up and took us to Gander Bay. It was all very emotional, but we had a wonderful time at the small wedding celebration and returned as we arrived on the following Monday.

Travelling to Gander Bay would have been so much easier if I'd had a car. Indeed, in the mid-1960s, Sid offered me his car. I was too afraid of hitting and injuring or killing someone, especially a child, to even consider applying for a driver's licence. I don't know why, but I just couldn't do it.

With a new baby, having to do without water and sewer was taxing, to put it mildly. But a quiet woman with a strong will was about to have an impact on that issue, which would also change our lives. At one point after years of this regular routine of dumping the pail in the Kettle Gulch, Edie and Bertha were joined by Jessie, who had recently married my youngest brother, Ian.

One day after a period of snow, Jessie asked, "I wonder, is it slippery going down there?" Followed with, "I'm half afraid to go down there, buddy. Ian said don't forget to hold on to the rail."

She had not made this dangerous trek often before and had been following the lead of the more experienced ladies. But Jessie was becoming more frustrated with this archaic activity every trip she made. Now at the end of her rope, and standing three feet from the edge of the cliff with the sea boiling seventy feet beneath her, with her fingerprints now firmly embedded in the wooden railing, Jessie said, "My God, buddy, this is an awful way to dump the pail."

Edie and Bertha agreed but deposited what they came to deposit. When it came to Jessie, she said, "Well, I didn't like this from the first day I came down here, and this is my last day doing this!"

Now it was Jessie's turn. She left the cover on the pail, held the railing even tighter, and with as much might as she dared to give without stumbling, she fired everything in her hand, including the pail and its contents, over the Kettle Gulch, saying, "They are going to have to come up with something better than this, buddy!"

Edie said she and Bertha looked at Jessie in amazement and burst into a fit of laughing.

It wasn't long after that we had indoor plumbing.

We had just come through a very cold winter with only the stove in the kitchen to warm the house. Edie and I had hoped to have the water and sewer installed soon. We also realized that having a small baby in the house with very little heat anywhere, except in the kitchen, was a big concern. While having only a small amount of money coming in, we had to make difficult choices. Maybe we could get running water, but a bathtub was a luxury that would have to wait. We did have a small space allocated in our little house for a bathroom, but up to now it had been an area that we generally stored off-season items, such as my big and cumbersome hunting clothing, winter coats, boots, and so on. At least that was the adult view. The children saw it as a great secret hiding place, which meant any and all stored items in there were never very organized.

The summer of 1965 was also the year we said goodbye to Mother, everyone's seamstress and a very kind mother and mother-in-law, Elizabeth "Aunt Sis" Lundrigan. Her health had been gradually deteriorating, and by June she was using a cane to walk, when she could walk at all. On July 6 she became immobile and lost consciousness. In the early hours of July 7, 1965, she slipped away, with most of her children around her.

As a family, we continued on our journey. Even though we didn't have a lot, it was only less by a degree than most people around us. It wasn't as though we were destitute in a land of plenty. Most everyone did their best to make ends meet, while wages and the still relative scarcity of work provided favour to no one. Our children had a pretty bland diet, largely of potatoes and fish, or maybe fish and potatoes, but I don't think they went hungry. I also believe that, for the most part, the children had fun, were happy, and were well-adjusted overall.

For instance, each morning I got up early and lit the fire in the kitchen stove. It was cold, since the fire, stoked before going to bed, had usually burnt out by four or five o'clock. I also put three shovels of soft coal and one shovel of hard coal in the Warm Morning stove situated in the front room, but it also went out by about 3:00 a.m. After I lit the fire, I cut up a loaf of Edie's homemade bread, placed a cushion in the oven for the older ones, and then went in and called them to come out for breakfast. When they came out, I removed the cushions from the oven and placed them on the cold wooden chairs. The children then sat on the warmth of the cushion while I got to the issue of breakfast.

We had an old grate for use when making toast, but I preferred to place the bread directly on the stove. It was so hot that the toast immediately sizzled and I turned it over. After about five seconds, I grabbed it, buttered it, and gave it to one of the children with a cup of hot tea. I then did the same for the younger ones, beginning with Phil and Mavis. When Phil, Mavis, and Boyd were each tiny and still using a crib at night, I would wheel the crib out to the kitchen. There wasn't much room, but at least this way the child was warm, and I didn't have to worry about him or her going too close to the scalding hot stove until Edie came out to the kitchen. By the time she came out, I had the window open to dissipate the smoke created by burnt toast, although I'm sure I never fooled her, since the smell stayed in the air for some time.

Edie was not a person fond of the early mornings, so usually when she came out to the kitchen, we had the same conversation. She would say with frustration in her voice, "Bill, why do you have that stove so hot? For God's sake, we can't breathe here. And why don't you use the grate for the toast? Those stains will be so hard to come off." These comments were accompanied by a "tut, tut, tut" from her.

My response, which wasn't always useful, was often something like, "Well, Edie, we don't want the children cold, and when they finish breakfast, we can open the door to the hall and warm up the bedroom area. And as far as the toast is concerned, the children love it that way, and I will clean the stove later on."

Of course, I usually did clean the stove and clean up from breakfast. Edie never mentioned the stove until we had the same conversation the next day.

25 — Willie

LIFE IS A ROLLER COASTER

1964–1972

Over several years, even though I chose not to be an active member in the Legion, Edie, to her credit, stayed with and supported the Royal Canadian Legion Ladies' Auxiliary. One of her most called-upon tasks for the Auxiliary was, together with Nellie Crane, to call bingo at the Legion, usually a couple of times a week. Many times I heard people who had been there say how captivating it was to hear these two British war brides calling bingo. I believe Edie and Nellie attracted many more patrons, just so people could hear their accents, especially when they were talking to one another in front of the microphone. Calling bingo was something they both enjoyed and continued to do for the benefit of the Legion for many years.

Just seven years after we left England, Edie's dad, Alfred England, died. It was 1956, and there was no money to allow Edie to return for the funeral. Mostly because of the challenging financial times, by 1966, Edie had still not been able to go back to see her family in England. That year was "Come Home Year" in Newfoundland. Ironically, it was Edie who went home to England that summer, for the first time since leaving there in April 1949. This could never have happened without the help of our daughter Jean as well as Edie's sister, Lil, and her mum.

It was very therapeutic for her, and she had a great visit with her mum, her sister, as well as her brothers, Alf and Harry. It was the last time she would ever see her mum or her brother Alf.

It was good that she had a chance to see her family. It was only by going back to England that Edie realized that the England she left was no more. After, and as a result of the war, so much had been rebuilt and so much had changed that it did not feel like her home. After that visit, she still spoke often and had fond memories of England, but it was really about the England she left in 1949, not the England that she saw on her return visit.

Edie returns to England for a visit, July 1996.

She returned home to the Meadow after her first visit to England, to continue what was probably the most challenging decade of our lives together, but she felt different now. Now she felt Upper Island Cove was home. She still fondly referred to England as home, but I believe in her heart she knew that was mostly to keep it close to her. The question now was how to raise a young family of four children (Sid and Jean were now independent to a large extent), ranging in age from just over one year old to twelve years old, with the most minimal of resources.

By now Sid was pretty much finished fishing on the Labrador and instead, was spending most of his time working in Toronto. He would return home for what seemed like shorter and shorter periods of time until eventually he stayed there most of the year.

Although it was something I would not have admitted, I did not feel very comfortable when it came to travelling by airplane. The reality was that this uncomfortable feeling also manifested itself in any number of ways, especially when it came to the children.

One day, Phil, who was a young boy with a mouth full of questions all the time, asked, "Father, can I have your axe? I want to chop some wood."

I quickly replied, "No, my son, you can't have the axe. That's very sharp."

"But Father," he said, "all my friends chop wood for their fathers. Why can't I?"

"Because I'm afraid you will cut yourself."

"But Father . . ."

I stopped him before he could press the issue further. I was so mortally afraid of him being cut that it was much better for me to do these tasks myself. I didn't allow Robert to do it, and I wasn't going to allow Boyd or Phil to possibly be seriously injured. Sid had already mastered these tasks while fishing down on the Labrador coast. Even though he was experienced, whenever he was with me, I preferred to do any tasks where I was afraid he would be injured.

I also recall the day Boyd was sliding down through Ray and Bertha's yard into the front area of Ian and Jessie's yard. He had been lying on his sled headfirst and was travelling downhill fast behind his friend Hubert. Hubert stopped suddenly, and one of the slide runners tipped up just as Boyd came up behind him. Boyd couldn't stop, and the sharp metal runner tips hit him directly in his left eye. As soon as someone alerted us to this incident, I immediately found Edie to make sure she could attend to Boyd's needs. Then I disappeared down the Meadow and continued for a walk down alongshore. Robert and Bernice were visiting that day, so Edie and Robert took Boyd first to the doctor in Harbour Grace, and then on to the Carbonear Hospital. Fortunately, he was not seriously harmed and recovered in about a month. I'm glad Edie was there to take over.

There were also times when our children just wanted to do what their friends were doing. I was often unsure if allowing them to do these things was okay or not, so I usually said no.

I remember one day when Phil wanted to do something or another, and as soon as he asked, I said no in a very abrupt manner, apparently.

Phil's response was, "Just listen to Father. Father, this isn't the navy. Can we just talk about it?"

My response the second time was "No," and with that I left the house and went for a walk down the Meadow. I felt the need to remove myself from the situation, or alternatively to be strict and uncompromising. That way it was done with and over.

I also remember when our youngest daughter, Mavis, was in high school, and the popular show for many young people was *Jesus Christ Superstar*, and it was playing at the Arts and Culture Centre in St. John's. There was a bus going to St. John's from her school, and many of her friends were going to see it. Mavis asked Edie and me for permission, and Edie decided she should speak to me.

"Dad, there's a show playing in St. John's I would like to see. The school is putting on a bus, and a lot of my friends are going. I have some money saved, so I wouldn't need a lot. Can I go?"

"What's the show about?" I asked.

"*Jesus Christ Superstar*, and Dad, they say it's really good. The teachers are encouraging us to go," she said.

"No, Mavis," I responded quickly.

"But Dad, why not? It's a good show."

"No, Mavis, if you want to know about Jesus, then go to church. Now that's all."

Phil asked the same, only with his usual greater insistence, but the answer was still no.

Sometimes Edie would ask, "Bill, why did you say no? What harm is there to it?"

"I can't say why, Edie. I just feel it's not a good thing, not a good idea for them to see, and that was that."

"Bill, you must realize that when you say no all the time, the children get very frustrated," said Edie.

"But Edie, this kind of show seemed to question everything about respect for the church. I'm not a regular churchgoer, but this sort of show can't be good," I responded.

I have often reflected that when the children were young, I probably could have spent more time with them, but that wasn't the norm in the 1960s and 1970s. In the later years, I did spend more time with them, but really more so with the grandchildren when they would come to visit. I sometimes took our own children on short excursions such as fishing, berry picking, and on other adventures and tried my best to be a good father. I truly loved each of our children dearly. As they got older and began to be curious and question everything, I found it more difficult to know how to respond, and I suppose that's why I shied away somewhat.

I am pretty confident that, other than Jean, Sid, and Robert, the other three children were so young, they didn't realize how difficult times were for us. This circumstance of their childhood of course became clearer to them as they became older, but the fewer children home, the more Edie and I were able to provide. Each of them has various memories at Christmastime of Edie or me coming from the post office with these two huge parcels from England. Like every year, we would put these in our bedroom at the foot of the bed, and none of the children would touch them. Once they arrived, they knew Santa would come!

Our daughter Mavis and I were chatting one day, and Mavis said that she never realized until later in life that, for quite a few Christmases, we couldn't provide much in the way of presents. Despite that reality, she never felt deprived. In fact, she told me she felt privileged because we always received such different gifts from England that none of her friends had. She relayed a memory of one Christmas in particular when I had made her a wooden sewing box with her name on the cover. She told me that she was so surprised and happy with this gift and thought it was so very touching.

Mavis also noted that, as she got older, she started to realize we didn't have as much compared to her friends, whose parents were generally younger and working and seemed to have everything that she did not. Mavis told me, "We always knew we were loved and that Mom and Dad would do whatever they could to provide for us."

She relayed a particular instance when she was in elementary school and was on the volleyball team. At the end of the year, there was a banquet, and all team members were offered the opportunity to purchase a coat with the school logo and volleyball team crest on it. Mavis said she knew we couldn't afford to purchase the coat, so she didn't even ask for one and told her physical education teacher that she didn't want one.

Her teacher and volleyball coach, Mr. Tony Bowring, had called us to say that she was the only one who was not purchasing a team coat. He was very kind and offered for us to purchase the coat and pay for it in installments. When it came time for the sports banquet, Mavis and Edie attended together, and this was when the coats were being distributed. Mavis was very surprised when her name was called to come forward to receive her coat. She looked at her mother and said, "Mom, I didn't order a coat!" Edie just smiled, pushed her forward, and said, "Go on up and get it."

Mavis said, "I walked up to the stage but with much confusion. How did this happen? I wondered. Was this all a mistake? I had previously decided I would not order the coat because I didn't want to burden my parents with paying for it."

When she got back to her seat, Edie told her the story of her teacher having called to say she was the only one who didn't order a coat. Mavis said she treasured that coat like it was made of gold. The reality was that Edie and I were humbled with the opportunity to do this for her.

At the house, there was always lots of homemade bread and custard and jelly on Sunday. If you were really lucky, you might even get a glass of juice on Sunday morning as well. We didn't have a refrigerator, so Edie or I would put the jelly and custard in a secure container and place it in the basement or in the attic to set up before Sunday supper.

The winter nights were cold, with frost having painted pictures on the windows. The frost also sparkled on the bedroom ceilings. It was relatively warm first when the children went to bed, but it got cold quickly, since we no longer had the Warm Morning stove in the front room. We had to sell it because we couldn't afford the coal to go in it. The children joked that they often woke up finding it difficult to move under all the winter coats that Edie and I threw over the blankets before we went to bed.

One morning, Phil said, "Mom, why do you keep putting all the coats over us? I can't move my legs."

"That's all right, Phil, your legs will be fine and warm under those coats," she replied.

We felt putting the coats over them was necessary, since there weren't enough blankets to go around. The summer, however, created almost too much heat in the bedrooms, especially the one facing the ocean, even with the blinds closed. Unfortunately, there wasn't much we could do about that except open the window, which offered a whole different issue.

In the summer, the sun burst in through the southeast-facing bedroom window as well as the kitchen window. With the windows open, even a crack, you could hear all the boats returning to the wharf after the crews had hauled the cod traps. Edie didn't notice them much, but this sight never got old to me. I often watched them with my binoculars as they came in, but I didn't need to see them. I could tell the difference between most boats just by listening. I knew the way Uncle Ernest Bishop steamed in fast, and then the "make and break" engine stopped suddenly. Then there was the way young Ernest Bishop slowed his engine speed far out from the Bishop's Rocks to avoid a direct hit to the big rock they sometimes tied up to. I often wished I had a boat and could go on the water.

Edie had a little strawberry garden behind the house, and I remember her being proud of the plants and flowers, since she often said, "This reminds me so much of England."

She tended to the plants and weeded and thinned them each summer. She used to show the children, especially Mavis, how to do the planting and how to care for them. When she brought in a bowl of freshly picked strawberries, you could see that it was a rewarding experience for her. Looking back now, I suppose it was something she treasured because it was her little garden and something that represented a bit of tranquility in a hectic and sometimes difficult life.

26 — Willie

OCEAN THERAPY

1972-1992

By the 1970s, I was feeling increasingly better and stronger, physically. There is no doubt that, over time, something happened to my back medically that caused me to be able to do more than I had been previously able to do. Certainly, from about that time until I was no longer able to walk on a regular basis, people in Upper Island Cove often told me that they knew me from a distance long before they could recognize my face. One morning as I walked in the Mash around Aunt Theresa Drover's, I could see Little Bert leaning over the fence in front of his house.

As I continued to walk and approached, he said, "Willie, is that you? My son, I could tell it was you when I saw this fellow walking in the Mash as straight as a gun rod." He followed that with, "Why, Willie, you walks some straight. I suppose that were you was in the navy."

That might have been partially true, but I felt it likely had a lot more to do with structural changes because of my severe spinal arthritis that had been diagnosed many years earlier. I felt more inclined to get back into a more active community life, similar to my involvement a decade or so earlier with the Legion.

Politics was always a lively topic in Upper Island Cove. We were all glued to the TV to see the results of the historic October 1971 provincial election when, even though defeated, the governing Liberals tried everything to cling to power. In March 1972, I formally joined the Haig Young PC team and helped at the Upper Island Cove campaign office, which was in the former snack bar owned by Leander and Irene Greeley up in the Back Road. Ed Neil was the campaign manager.

This was, I suppose, another historic general election when the PC Party, led by Frank Moores, finally defeated Joey Smallwood's Liberal government after twenty-three years in office. I was involved again in the 1975 provincial general election.

While I did not become a political organizer until 1972, my decision of which party to *not* support had been made clear on numerous occasions in my life.

In the years prior to that, my favourite local politicians included people such as Hank Murphy, Gerry Ottenheimer, Frank Moores, Haig Young, and of course Uncle Joe and Aunt Cavell's eldest son, John Howard Lundrigan, who I always felt was the best premier Newfoundland never had.

I was also elected to the Upper Island Cove town council in 1972. My municipal career, however, was short-lived. The town council had locked horns with the then Progressive Conservative provincial government's Department of Municipal Affairs on a funding issue for the community. We could not make any progress. Frustrated by having been denied action by government on a previously committed solution, the whole council, including me, resigned.

One morning about that time, Edie received a letter from one of her relatives in England.

"Bill, I just received this letter from a lawyer who was looking after Mum's estate. It says that there's a small amount of money that I'm going to get soon.

"Bill, there are lots of things we can use this for, but I think we should buy a bathtub and upgrade the bathroom. If we have any money left over, maybe we can get the phone company to install a phone for us."

When the money came, we purchased the tub and plumbing supplies, and I installed it. The phone also got installed. For a short while it was just a party line, which meant that you shared the line with someone else. Not long after, the telephone company revised the system so that we all had "private" lines.

I still very much preferred to spend a considerable amount of time on my own, often going for a long walk. Being alone was good for me. My long walks were rejuvenating and even instructive for me, in that they taught me one of the most incredible life lessons, which was to understand the critical importance of solitude.

I can truly say that I never felt lonely when I was alone. Quite the contrary, these were the times when I was most at peace with the world and with myself. I never measured lonely by how few people were around me. Rather, if such a measurement existed, it could be measured by how I tended to be better connected to myself outside of the noise and static of the crowd. That crowd could sometimes be just one other person. The mental energy I gathered by going for long walks alone was as close as I ever came to any kind of formalized therapy activity. I understand that Edie may not have had a great appreciation for why I left her alone at our house so frequently, and sometimes for hours, but for me, these times were essential components of my life. How could I tell her I needed to be alone without her feeling I didn't want to be with her?

Although a step up from the last decade, our family continued to struggle financially. By 1972, however, as our third-eldest child, Robert, turned eighteen, he left home to attend school in St. John's. This allowed a little more flexibility with the family income, to the benefit, in particular, of the three younger children, Phil, Mavis, and Boyd, who were, at that time, twelve, eleven, and seven years old.

Our eldest son, Sid, had worked many hours with Clifford Lundrigan at a variety of jobs associated with Uncle Josiah's very successful sawmill and hardware store business. Sid and Clifford had become great buddies, and at some point around 1971 or thereabouts, likely in exchange for some work he had done, Clifford gave Sid what was known then as a "speedboat," or one designed to be used with an outboard motor. Of course, Sid didn't have an outboard motor, and he was by now spending a lot of time working at construction sites in Toronto.

One day I asked, "Sid what are you going to do with that boat, my son? You just can't leave it outside. It will crack to pieces in the hot sun."

He didn't have a place to put the boat, so we stored it in our basement. Sid insisted, "Now, Father, you take it and use it."

"Yes, my son, but without a motor, it's too big to get around. I'll never be able to scull that size of a boat," I told him.

In the spring and summer of 1973, Robert worked at construction work in St. John's as a student, trying to put aside some money to help pay for his room and board for school in St. John's. Then one day when I came from a walk down the Meadow, there was an outboard motor lying outside the back door of the house.

I went inside and said, "Edie, who owns that motor out there by the door?"

"I don't know," she said. "You'd better ask Robert."

Robert came out of the bathroom and said, "That's yours, Dad. Put that on Sid's boat, now, and you'll be all set."

I was speechless and had to insist I didn't want the motor. But Robert knew I did and that the boat was useless without a motor. It was small, but then, the boat was only about sixteen feet.

I didn't know it at the time, but his goal was to give this motor to me in order that I could use it together with Sid's boat. This would allow me to get out on the water for the first time, really, since the summer of 1961. My family all knew I dearly loved to be on the water, but they also knew I had no means to get there. After the motor was purchased, I took Sid's boat out of the basement and, with the motor on it, moored it out on the collar in the Cove.

My world changed.

It is hard to overstate the positive impact this boat and motor helped create for me. During the previous two decades, I found it hard to develop interest in anything. Now I was feeling like a person who didn't have enough time in the day to do the things I wanted to do. For the next two decades, I was never without a boat and motor, never without time on the water, and always enjoyed the peace, tranquility, and solitude associated with this passion. The ocean also served as my sanctuary, and the fishing grounds of Crab Ledge my personal favourite place to be. For sure, I enjoyed taking people out fishing, but I was entirely at peace when I was out there alone.

I also came to find this was a way for us to supplement our income. During that period, beginning in 1972, I sometimes caught and sold between twenty and thirty quintals (a quintal is 112 pounds) of dried salt fish.

In the spring of 1972, Sid, still living and working in Toronto, married Ivy Porter from Port de Grave, who was also living in Toronto at that time. Both Sid and Ivy wanted Edie and me to attend their wedding, but given our limited finances, coupled with my aversion to flying, we decided that Edie would go alone. Then, just over a year later, in 1973, our first grandchild, Craig, was born. Sid and Ivy returned to Newfoundland that fall and came to live with us.

This became a wonderful time in our lives. Besides having our own three younger children at home, we now had a four-month-old grandchild with us as well. We have dearly loved all our grandchildren, but having Craig live with us created a very special bond. Not long after Sid and Ivy arrived home, Sid and I began to go, almost daily, to the area of Fox Marsh Resource Road to cut logs in preparation for a house they hoped to start in 1974. Throughout the course of the winter, we cut and brought home over 1,000 logs. This was hard but wonderful work. We would wake early, dress warmly, and pack a good lunch, including lots of molasses bread and tea. We would then go into the woods to spend many days cutting. Sid was young and much stronger than me, but I did my best to help him. I wouldn't dare see him go into the woods to do this dangerous work alone. Robert, still attending post-secondary school in St. John's, often accompanied us, especially during term breaks and between school semesters.

Additionally, in the years after we finished cutting logs, I began the process of almost annually building a boat. I built nine wooden speedboats, eighteen feet in length, in the small basement in our home. Three of these boats I used myself, two I built for family members, and four I sold to people who asked me to build one for them.

One of Willie's speedboats taking shape in the backyard

The process of building a boat required quite a bit of work, which involved lifting, bending, and reaching. While it was sometimes difficult,

I could manage. This generally took all winter and well into the spring to complete. I loved to take my time and work alone. It certainly was a labour of love for me and obviously something that I was able to do. I was quite pleased with the level of skill I had acquired over the years. In the 1950s, when I needed work, I often dreaded the responsibility I felt to complete work to a skill level that I had not yet acquired. Doing this work gave me a great sense of purpose, and it helped me find a way to occupy myself. It was another place of solitude, but the freedom of being alone in my boat, on the bay, was by far the most spiritual place for me.

Starting in 1973, and for the next two decades, you could find me any day, between May and December, alone and content on the fishing grounds. I guess that was my safe place. Though unspoken, I felt that my children were becoming increasingly aware that my contribution to the war effort was taking its toll and that time spent like this was a big part of my health journey.

One day many years after the war, Edie and I were sitting in the kitchen looking out the window over the bay. Edie must have seen the sense of peace I had looking at the fishing boats bobbing gently in the Cove and said, "Bill, you have lived the life you always wanted to live."

That statement didn't surprise me, but deep down I wished it were as simple as that.

What Edie could sense, throughout all these years, was that I loved Newfoundland and longed dearly to live in Upper Island Cove. The reality for me, however, was not that I lived the life I wanted to live as much as I lived my life the only way I knew how. It is true that I loved Upper Island Cove, but living here was much more about finding sanctuary, a feeling I had but for years found hard to explain to others. It wasn't just Edie whom I felt couldn't understand. I don't think any of our children really understood that living in Upper Island Cove, for me, was more about the only place I could live rather than the place I just wanted to live. The kindness and support I felt from the people of Upper Island Cove, and the peacefulness of the land and the ocean, were incredible and what, to a large extent, sustained me even when I didn't realize it.

Yes, I was born here, I was from here, and I felt like I belonged here.

Our eldest daughter, Jean, was still living in Gander Bay but was having a lot of health issues. It was during these health issues that she became pregnant. Through all these various health concerns, their only child, Trevor, was born in April 1974. Edie went to Gander Bay to help support Jean, while I stayed and kept a schedule for the three younger children.

1974 was also the year my eldest brother, John, died. John was the business person of the family, having a small takeout food service up in the back road next to where he had built his house. During the 1960s, his place and his food were quite popular, especially with the young people who gathered there in the evenings. His death, as a relatively young man of sixty years, was quite sudden and a big shock to his wife, Mary, and two daughters, Mabel and Mary. John's loss was a big blow to the whole extended family. As a young man, his efforts to provide for us after Father died can never be overstated. Fortunately, it would be about two decades before we lost another sibling.

In the summer of 1975, Robert married Bernice Roberts from Spaniard's Bay. They had both just finished post-secondary school and were about to start their first permanent jobs. The night they held their wedding, all the family and all the Mercer family were included as guests. Sadly, late that afternoon, one of my war veteran comrades and a close neighbour, Hayward Mercer, died. The wedding went ahead, but the Mercer family felt it inappropriate to attend.

In the next while, Edie began to talk of us returning to England for a trip. I had an aversion to airplanes, but in 1977, with considerable reservation, I did fly with Edie back to England. It was my first and her second trip back since 1949, and by all accounts and from what I can recall, we had a fine visit. We spent lots of time with family and friends, and we did a lot of exploring old stomping grounds where we met as well as where we both worked. We also had the chance to visit with many ex-military and civilian friends. The trip was great, but I had no plans to get on a plane again any time soon.

I had a great love for all life, of all creatures great and small. Of all the hunting I did during the 1950s and 1960s, one of my biggest regrets was going moose hunting. I appreciate that many people thoroughly enjoy this sport, but it was not for me. I could see absolutely no pleasure in killing one of these majestic animals. During the late 1970s, when we did this, I felt we no longer needed to hunt for food. My elder sons, Sid and Robert, wanted to go moose hunting, so I went along with them—but not often, and I never did shoot a moose. I began to realize that I had changed from a hunter to someone who did not wish to see any creature harmed. We would all venture outside our personal comfort zone to see our families prosper.

Some people may have viewed the change in me from hunting to someone who appreciated all living creatures as being a bit odd. It didn't matter to me. I distinctly remember one day, on one of my early morning walks through the community, I saw some snails that had taken advantage of the early morning dew to ease their trip across the pavement. By the time I saw them, the pavement was dry and the snails had stopped in the middle of the road. I thought about walking by but knew that, possibly within minutes, these creatures would be flattened by a passing car. I chose to pick them all up and placed them off to the side in the grass to help, at least temporarily, preserve their lives.

Sometime during the mid-1980s, one morning while out fishing, we saw a basking shark just lying on the water. It was right out in front of our house, about a hundred yards from the shoreline. We got ready and went down alongshore. There was no sign of any shark. We caught our fish and were returning home.

It was a flat-calm day. Our youngest son, Boyd, was at the motor, while I was standing forward between the second and third thwart holding the painter for balance and all the while scanning the water. I was looking for anything that we could possibly run over and damage the boat or motor, such as a piece of an old wharf or stage. We neared the Head, and something caught my eye. I motioned with one hand, without turning around, for Boyd to slow the motor. He reduced to about half-speed, and I pointed toward something on the water. We approached it slowly, and I saw that it was a fin. As we got even closer to it, we could see that it was a basking shark. I touched it gently with the sculling oar, and it gave a flick and dived but within seconds resurfaced about a hundred feet away from us.

Later that afternoon, I went over to the wharf, where I met Robert to go out on the water to go cod fishing When we were about to leave the wharf, I saw that another fisherman was standing on the wharf and placing a twelve-gauge shotgun in his boat. Someone asked him what he was doing with the gun, to which he replied, "I'm going to shoot that shark down off the Head."

I was not impressed, but I said nothing. I started the engine and turned to Robert and said, "You take over the motor and go down to where the basking shark is." Robert did so, and as we looked at the shark, we could see another boat leave the wharf with that fisherman we saw earlier standing in the bow, brandishing a shotgun. I told Robert to position our boat between the oncoming boat and the shark, thereby preventing the person with the gun from being able to shoot. I then took the sculling oar and gently prodded the shark until it decided to dive and leave the area. I know the person with the gun was annoyed, but it was a good day for the shark and a good day for me.

Our own family was constantly growing now. We already had our three eldest married, and we had been blessed with four grandchildren. In May 1981, our younger daughter, Mavis, married Kevin Squires from Gander Bay.

And then the talk of getting on that damned plane started again! One day in 1982, Edie said, "Bill, we should go back to England for another visit." The trip was being planned, including me flying with Edie. Even though I was not at all fond of airplanes, I really wanted to go back to England with Edie, since we had had such a great time just five years earlier. In the months leading up to the trip, however, I had a bad stomach and started to verbalize my concern about flying.

Finally, Edie said, "Bill, maybe you shouldn't go to England."

I must admit I didn't put up a lot of resistance, and after the ticket cancellation, my stomach issues resolved and I was feeling fine again. I was relieved that I did not have to get aboard the plane.

The following year, our fifth grandchild, and first granddaughter, was born. Jennifer was born to Bernice and Robert. She already had cousins—Craig, Collin, and Keith of Ivy and Sid, along with Trevor of Jean and Lloyd.

"Life is what happens when you are busy making plans" is an expression often used to describe how, no matter what or how carefully you plan, the unexpected is always possible. In our lives there were yet to be unexpected events, presenting even greater challenges.

One such event occurred while we were on vacation in the summer of 1988. Other than going back to England together in 1977, there were no vacations. This event with Robert, Bernice, and their young daughter, Jennifer, was the first time going on vacation outside the province together for Edie and me. It was also our only time travelling in a motorhome. We had stopped the first night in Gander Bay to visit with our daughter Jean, her husband, Lloyd, and their teenaged son, Trevor. Next morning, we were off again, crossed the gulf to Nova Scotia, and then on to Prince Edward Island. We were having a wonderful time visiting various tourist attractions. Even though it was still early in August, one of the places we visited was Santa's Woods. It was a magical place, with Santa Claus being a captivating old gentleman who was so kind and gentle with our young granddaughter. After that visit, all of us were feeling wonderful but tired, so we returned to the campground to prepare some supper. It was about five o'clock on what I recall was the fourth day, and as we were relaxing at the National Park in Cavendish, we received news to call home. Robert did so and was told our son-in-law, Lloyd, whom we had spent the night with just four days before, had died suddenly. It was a devastating blow.

Bernice simply looked at Robert and said, "Robert, we have to go to Gander Bay."

It was a very stressful time, but Robert and Bernice were logically focused on a plan to return there with the rest of the family to support our daughter Jean and grandson Trevor. We were in a rush to get home, but I was very aware that they had a young child with them and Bernice was pregnant. I could see that Robert didn't want the stress of this circumstance to have any negative impact on her.

"Okay, let's pick up everything and head for the ferry to Nova Scotia. We can get food along the way, and of course there's lots of food in the vehicle," said Robert.

When we got there, and after a short conversation with the staff at the boat terminal, our vehicle was placed right at the front of the line.

When we got to Nova Scotia, I said, "Edie, I think we should stop for some supper."

"Bill, maybe we should just get something to eat in the vehicle so Robert can continue driving," Replied Edie.

"No, I need to stop, Edie. Can you stop at a restaurant to have supper, Robert, please?" I asked with a sense of near-panic.

As Robert had pointed out, we had food in the motorhome, and we had to catch a ferry back to Newfoundland. My actions were not meant to impede our progress of getting back to support Jean.

We stopped at the nearest highway stop at the Canso Causeway, and as I left the vehicle to go in, I heard Robert say, "Mom, tell Dad we can't stay long. We must get to North Sydney before the ferry leaves at midnight."

"Yes," said Edie, "he just needs to have time to absorb everything that's happening, I think," she replied.

I think stopping to have a meal was my attempt to bring a sense of order, a sense of calmness and control to a situation that was very much outside the control of all of us. The sudden death of our son-in-law triggered something to rise inside of me that I felt powerless to control and equally powerless to explain to anyone else.

Once we got back to Newfoundland, Robert dropped Bernice and Jennifer off at a friend's house in Stephenville Crossing, and we proceeded to Gander Bay to support Jean and Trevor.

We were all concerned that the trauma of this event might have caused issues with Bernice's pregnancy. It didn't appear so. However, Stephanie was born to Bernice and Robert the following March, and only eleven days after her birth, she was diagnosed with a serious health issue that required surgery a few years later.

Overall, I tried to live a good life, but my feelings about going to church were mixed. As a child, and then as an adolescent, I found myself in a small community where there was not a lot of interaction with the outside world. I didn't pay too much attention to church when I was growing up, but it is fair to say that few people in a community were more persuasive than the local priest or minister. Of course, my parents wanted me to attend church on a regular basis, and very likely as most children in rural Newfoundland did, I did as well.

How much of my moral compass, good or bad, I learned from my churchgoing versus from my parents, my friends, or my general environment will forever remain a question. I'm confident, if you looked closely, you would find the initials WL carved in the back of the second-last pew on the south side of the church. Many of us as young boys attended, but few of us were really tuned in to what the minister was saying most of the time.

I believe I always had a strong sense of obligation to my family and to society generally. If this were not true, my feelings of guilt about not being able to help my family in my youth would not have been so strong. It is also unlikely I would have gone off to war, even if I wanted adventure, if I did not feel the need to do right by society.

No doubt there was a lot about me that reflected the Christian tradition in which I grew up. For instance, I always made a valiant attempt to not swear and never used profanity. For me, an expression of frustration would sometimes erupt into the phrase "My goodie gracious," and when I had a really high level of frustration, I sometimes used the phrase "Damn the like of that!" And no matter where I was, either alone or with others, people could hear me singing, whistling, or humming, "How Great Thou Art," or "Nearer My God to Thee," or "Amazing Grace," among others.

When we returned from England, my churchgoing habits were rather varied. There were long periods of time, often spanning several years, when I attended church regularly. At other times, I must admit, likely far too often, I just sent the children instead of going with them. I never really figured out if I did it because it was the right thing to do, or whether it was what was expected of parents, by the church and the community generally. I didn't feel like talking much about religion or what I believed. One thing I did feel strongly about, and which I found especially bothersome, was the held-over remnants of sectarian thinking or actions. In my opinion, this sort of thinking often represented the opposite of what organized religion or religious-based thinking should stand for.

During my years in the navy, it didn't matter the colour of your skin, your religious beliefs, or any such artificial categorization of people. When it came to facing some sort of danger, such as an enemy attack, everyone worked together as one unit. That was what was important in that circumstance and what should have been the golden rule in life. Taking that idea to its natural conclusion would mean war should never exist.

As I became more literate, I read a lot about religion, various deities, and topics related to spirituality. As a churchgoer, I probably fell short as a good Anglican, but I did feel a strong spiritual connection with my fellow human beings. Yet I was also trapped between that broader spirituality and the more traditional view of the church of my youth.

Edie seemed to feel far less of an obligation to attend church or have the children attend church than I did. She used to say that, when she grew up in England, church was not something she felt pressure to attend. She certainly did believe in God, although I know her faith has been tested, and maybe temporarily weakened, on occasion.

But as Rev. Greg Mercer, who was also her godchild, said to one of our children, "Your mom had great faith."

He probably saw and felt something that I didn't see, but that is what faith is, isn't it?

Edie didn't talk much of religion, either. I certainly sensed that she seemed to find a level of comfort through the church rituals she participated in throughout her time here in Upper Island Cove, and especially so during the burial service of our daughter Jean. I remember Mavis asking her to go to church on more than one occasion, but she had no inclination to do so. It would therefore be hard for me to draw real conclusions about the level of her faith or sense of spirituality, but there is no question that the Christian traditions did provide her with a lot of comfort.

One of the biggest gifts that I felt Edie and I shared was that of our love of reading and literacy.

Books, books, and more books!

Edie and I gathered many books, rarely by purchase in the early years, sometimes borrowing from a friend, sometimes from Edie's mum or her sister, Lil, in England. Sometimes we got them from the local school library, and even sometimes from the small collection in the Anglican church rectory. In the long summer evenings, I would often walk the short walk farther down the Meadow to the home of Master Coombs, a former schoolteacher in the Roman Catholic school system. He was an avid reader himself and, as a teacher, was also eager to lend us a book. His only policy was that we read and return one book, in good order, before he would loan another. A little later, we also received books as gifts from the elder children and their spouses.

Edie and I did not usually read the same kind or genre of books, although Edie was sometimes inclined to read a book I had finished. For the most part, though, she read fiction, probably as an escape from her daily challenges and her ever-present loss of a life left behind.

I didn't see the purpose of reading fiction. Unless I was going to learn something new, I thought it was a waste of time. I grew up knowing very little about the world. I felt that reading books of fiction gave me little or none of the knowledge that I yearned for and was so desperate to absorb. For me there was an urgency in reading. Sometimes I read almost all day long. I loved to read about the strategies of the Allies as well as the Axis powers during the war. I think it helped me make more sense of my almost six years of military service.

Sometime in the 1970s, Reverend Fred Rowsell asked to see both Edie and me. We went to the rectory one evening, and he said, "Willie and Mrs. Lundrigan, the church would like to support the idea of having a public library in the community. We will need a volunteer board to help organize and run it. Would both of you agree to be members of the board?"

Without really knowing what we were agreeing to do, Edie and I both said, "Yes, Reverend, that sounds like a wonderful idea. We would certainly like to help."

So, along with several others, including my sister Myra and her husband, Arch, we became founding members of the town's newly minted library board, a branch of the province's public library system. There is little doubt that the good reverend's knowledge, that both Edie and I were such eager readers, led to this invitation.

The importance of literacy, to both of us, propelled an active membership in the library board for approximately twenty-six years. Reverend Rowsell became chairperson, and I immediately became the vice-chairperson. Reverend Rowsell eventually left Upper Island Cove for a new parish assignment, and for the last six years of our tenure, I was elected as the chairperson of the board. During that time, I vigorously advocated for and represented the local library. As a result, I was mixing socially with chairpersons of library boards in other communities. Most of the people I interacted with were teachers, school principals, or business people. All of them had significantly more formal education than I did. It was all a bit intimidating, but I did my best not to make my lack of formal education too obvious. For the most part, I think it worked out okay.

The Anglican church parish owned the former "schoolmaster's" residence, just a stone's throw from St. Peter's K to grade nine school. After it was no longer used for that purpose, it was converted into a space for the library. Rev. Greg Mercer grew up as a next-door neighbour, a son of our great friends Agnes and Rudolph. I remembered at one point the church wanted the library board to pay rent for its use of the building.

The church had initially decided not to charge rent on the church-owned library building but for some reason changed their position. There was a meeting attended by the regular church minister, accompanied by Rev. Greg, who was helping the parish as a visiting clergy, and me. The regular minister and church representatives on the library board suggested strongly that the church was in a position where it was necessary to charge a rental fee to the library board.

I disagreed with the proposed fee and did so rather vigorously, noting that it would impede the library from its intended purpose. My feeling was so strong about this issue that my final position to the attending clergyman was, "If you charge rent for the use of this building, the church will never see a cent from me ever again."

I believe the church very well understood my point as well as my passion for the library.

I continued to serve as the chairperson for the library board until the Upper Island Cove Public Library was shut down in favour of one larger library in a more centralized location.

Before the decision to close was made, I had a conversation with our MHA, John Efford. I told him, "Mr. Efford, your government is doing the wrong thing here by closing this library. As a province, we have the lowest level of literacy in the country. I have always believed this policy of closing local libraries was a mistake. Government might save a few dollars in the short term, but limiting instead of promoting reading is not the way to improve our province."

Mr. Efford said, "Thank you, Mr. Lundrigan. I understand where you are coming from, and I will bring your concerns back to cabinet."

Even though the library closed, I have no doubt that John Efford did as he told me he would.

It often seemed that, although the six years in the British Royal Navy had been incredibly tough, for much of the rest of my life I spent large chunks of time reflecting on, and some would say reliving, those years. I was now more than ever fascinated and enthralled with world events during that period.

Neither Edie nor I ever saw a day when we would have any desire to stop reading—and we didn't. After all the children were raised and we were alone, it was always such a pleasure to be able to read, the only interruptions being the routines of our quiet lives. We became creatures of habit. I always sat, with my favourite book, on the sofa, feet up and with a pole lamp behind me. Edie always sat in the wingback chair, conveniently located by the front window for a view of not only her best book but also any passing activity on the Meadow Road. This location also gave her a heads-up on any incoming guest traffic.

Unlike reading, dealing with our family finances was not for me. I didn't trust my arithmetic skills that much. This was something that Edie did, and did exceedingly well, considering how she made everything work with so little money to work with.

"Edie, I would like to buy some salt to cure my fish. Can I have some money, please?"

"Yes, hold on, I will get you some. How much do you need?" she asked.

"I have no idea," I replied.

"What do you mean you have no idea? Do you need $10 or $100?" she asked in an incredulous tone.

"Edie, I have no idea of what salt costs, and honestly I don't care. If you tell me we can afford it, then give me some money and I will buy as much as I need, or else they will give me as much as the value of the money I give them," I replied, a little impatiently.

"In the name of God, wait a minute and I will get it for you."

As much as I read, and eventually wrote, from the time we came across the Atlantic, I had no interest in our financial affairs. As long as we were able to pay our bills, I was fine. Plastic cards had no place in my life. Edie looked after any money that came in or was paid out on our behalf. This included any money I earned or pension money I received. She paid all the bills, purchased all the groceries and clothing for everyone. She made sure we had enough bedding, kitchen supplies, and the like. Besides the regular writing she did to her mum, Lil, and some of her friends back in England, she did all the writing associated with applications for benefits for me to various agencies.

Throughout these years, our family was continuing to grow, and in December 1989, our youngest son, Boyd, married Nancy Jones from Upper Island Cove. There are two things I distinctly remember about the event. First, I remember our daughter Mavis spending most of her time in church trying to keep her young son, Christopher Squires, from cutting a bigger shine than the bride and groom. He was very active, and what was the fun celebrating a marriage if you couldn't run laps around the church during the ceremony? The other memory was that of the famous "cold plate."

This was a Christmas wedding, and as might be expected for an event that everyone looked forward to attending, the night was a blustery and cold one. At the Legion, where the event was being held, the morning and early afternoon were filled with preparations of the tables and, finally, the placing of food on the plates. Our daughter Jean was, unofficially, the senior organizer. All was going well until a discussion occurred about, of all things, the proper way to present a cold plate. Jean had her idea how to do this, and so too did this lady from the Legion Auxiliary. I don't recall the precise conversation, but it went something like this.

Jean: "Now, ladies when we place the food on the plates, the coleslaw goes on this side of the potato salad."

Legion Lady: "No, Jean buddy, that's not right. The coleslaw goes over here, and that's where the turkey goes."

Jean: "No, if you put the coleslaw there, it will be too close to the beet salad and won't look good."

Legion Lady: "Well, buddy, I've been doing cold plates here for about thirty years, and that's where we always put the coleslaw."

Exasperated by now, Jean's final response, as she turned red as a beet herself, was, "Well, I don't know what you always do, but today the coleslaw will be right here, and that's the end of that."

Both women smiled politely. All of us turned away, some trying to hide the grin from witnessing this absurd conversation. I didn't know what to do, so I went to the bathroom out of the way.

Regardless of the location of the coleslaw, the wedding cold plate tasted lovely.

27 — Willie

TRIALS AND TRIBULATIONS

1994–2004

"My doctor told me that I had two to five years to live ... five if I was lucky. I told Mother and Father the doctor informed me that I should stop paying into any pension fund, quit my job, and go home to spend the rest of my time with my family."
— Philip Lundrigan, April 1994

If there is any truth to the expression that the time when we get older could be classified as "the Golden Years," the period from about the early 1970s to the early 1990s was that period for Edie and me. The next fifteen years for us were among some very unpleasant.

In 1992, when the cod moratorium came into effect, it marked the end of my fishing endeavours. From 1973 until that time, I'd felt that I had a real purpose in life again. Now, at the age of seventy-one, my whole life was again lacking an essential piece. Some would say that fishing, for me at my advanced age, was unnecessary, and after all, it was just a couple of months in the summer. That's not the way it felt for me, though. I generally had my boat in the water from mid-May, but often earlier, until just before Christmas, except of course for the few years when I also used it in early January. But it was more than that for me—it was about having the slice of my life ripped away by a faraway government that had already failed my family once.

I felt upset with Canada in 1992 when the federal government introduced the codfish moratorium to all of Newfoundland and Labrador. Some people saw the cod moratorium as necessary in order to save the diminishing fish stock. But I, and most Newfoundlanders, saw it as the result of the federal government exploiting our resource for the good of central Canada.

"Edie, do you see what's happening again? Someone from up there in Ottawa is always taking from us. The fishery would still be strong if the bloody government didn't give a lot of it away to European countries." I was exasperated, and I wished I was at that protest with Crosbie.

John Crosbie, then federal Fisheries Minister, on behalf of government was right there on the TV saying, "I didn't take the fish from the goddamn water."

"Well, goodie gracious. This might not be your fault directly, John, but it is the fault of the Canadian government, and you know it," I said as I caught myself yelling at the TV.

Edie too was mad. She was mad for a different reason. She had become a Canadian citizen back in 1981 and, ever since, had resented giving up her British citizenship. She wasn't fond of Canada, and here was another injustice to confirm her opinion.

What was done with the fishery was done, and now I was done, too.

I kept my boat for a few years but eventually sold it to someone in the community. I never bothered to go on the water again. It was probably not long after that I started to wonder if my memory was beginning to fade, although it did not become acute for about eight to ten years.

Especially in the absence of my real love of being on the water, I turned to my other passion. One of the things that I continued to do was to read and read and read. And that, too, was with much thanks to Edie. She had spent a lot of time, effort, and energy, to take me from, pretty much, functional illiteracy to someone who could read and comprehend the written text at a reasonably high level.

During my life, but especially from the time of the cod moratorium, when I gave up on my boat and fishing, I tried my best to help people in the community, and I felt a sense of pride in doing so. This included the years I had spent volunteering with the Royal Canadian Legion, the Anglican Church Assistance Association (ACAA), the Upper Island Cove public library board, the Harbour Grace PC Association, and as a member of the Upper Island Cove town council. I also spent time just trying to be kind to individuals, especially shut-ins.

I always enjoyed trying to be a good friend and neighbour. It seemed to give me a lot of personal satisfaction to help others in the community I so dearly loved, and which, frankly, daily helped breathe life into me. For instance, over the years I established a good relationship with a gentleman named George Mercer as well as his wife, Betty.

George was a quiet man who was quite a bit older than me. He too was a war veteran, having served in the Royal Navy for Britain in the First World War. Like almost all of us, when we get older, both George and Betty weren't as able to get around as they once did, so I often walked to the drugstore to pick up their medications. I also went to the post office regularly to pick up their mail, and as best as I could, I always shovelled them out in the winter. In addition to that, I spent a lot of time visiting and chatting with them, just to keep them company.

I did much the same in the later years for Josiah and Cavell, who lived across the road, as far as picking up their mail for them was concerned. I also found it important to visit people in the community whom I knew were sick and shut in. It didn't matter who it was—I felt that having someone visit might help them get through another day.

While I had left the Royal Canadian Legion, I was very much carrying on the outreach work I felt was appropriate, visiting and helping all, both veterans and non-veterans. Now, after many years away from the Legion, I joined again in 1993. This time I joined the Corporal Matthew Brazil Branch (Branch 9) in Spaniard's Bay. My reasoning for doing that was because that was where five of our six children and their families all lived at that time. Phil was working in Toronto. Our eldest daughter, Jean, who lived in Tilton, also joined Branch 9 as well. Through the children and grandchildren, both Edie and I had seen such good community outreach work being done through the Legion. Just the involvement of the Legion branches in both Upper Island Cove and Spaniard's Bay, with the local school's Remembrance programs, was encouraging and inspiring to us.

Additionally, of course, there were now quite a few new war veterans who had come home from peacekeeping and recent conflicts such as in Afghanistan. They could benefit from a supportive Legion branch. Knowing that the Legion was largely focused on the young people, Edie and I were both persuaded that there was a renewed purpose for the organization. The Royal Canadian Legion continued to stay in touch with both of us well into our senior years.

During our lives, Edie and I had faced lots of challenges since we met near the end of World War II, and we were about to face another one.

In early March 1994, our son Philip made a surprise visit home from Toronto. Edie and I were delighted that he was home but had no idea why. The reality was that Philip wasn't doing well. He called Robert and Bernice to discuss his situation, and he continued to confide in them for the next few weeks until he was able to get to a place where he could better cope with some life-altering news. Shortly after arriving from the mainland, both he and Robert dropped by for a visit.

Edie was sitting in her usual spot in the wingback chair by the living room window. It was in the middle of the afternoon when we heard the car door close outside. As she was keen to do, Edie peeked outside by pulling back the curtain. She saw Phil, followed by Robert, coming in toward the back door. Edie said, "Bill, that's Phil with Robert coming. I didn't know he was coming home."

I nodded, and in anticipation that one of them might need to sit on the other end of the couch, I closed my book and swivelled on the couch, bringing my feet down to the floor. I then pulled on my slippers and reached back to turn off the reading lamp behind me. Before they reached the living room, I had gotten up, turned the furnace up a few degrees, and was sitting back down again.

I wondered why Robert and Phil were coming in together. It was lovely to see them together, since there was no hint that Phil was coming home at this time. Robert sat on the end of the couch, where I had moved my legs minutes ago, and Phil sat in the rocking chair. We chatted about the weather and some other ordinary things. Then Philip said he had something to tell us.

Phil simply said, "Well, Mother and Father, I have some not-so-good news. I saw my doctor recently in Toronto, and he told me that I have been diagnosed with HIV."

Edie and I both sat there in silence. Even though we had a good idea what this meant, Phil explained what exactly that meant for him.

Phil went on to say, "My doctor in Ontario told me that I should get my affairs in order and spend as much time as I could with my family. He also told me that I likely had from two to five years to live. He advised me not to take out any mortgage or long-term investments. When I told the doctor this was hard to absorb, because I don't feel ill, he told me I will know it when it happens."

Edie and I sat listening intently to what Phil was saying. At that point I felt as though I was looking in on someone else's life—like watching a TV show about another family. As I watched this scene unfold before me, I saw Edie respond to Phil and this difficult news in the same manner as she had handled almost everything in her life— with a calmness and reassurance that helped me, let alone Phil.

When Phil finished speaking, Edie paused for just a few seconds and simply said, "What do you need from us, my son?"

At that point, I watched as she moved the small footstool in front of her chair to one side, stood, and gave Philip a big hug. She gently rubbed his back with her right hand while saying, "Phil, you are my child! You will always be my child, and I will always love you."

Philip cried, and I could see Edie struggle, but she managed to hold back her own emotions. He would have expected that of his mother.

That was the point where I felt I had to escape. I felt as though I couldn't breathe. I went in the hall and down the stairs into the basement. I had to get space, had to be alone, to figure out what had just happened. Within a few minutes, Robert came downstairs to check on me.

He said, "Are you okay, Dad?"

"Yes, I'm all right, my son."

"Dad, I know this is hard for you, but Phil needs you now. Are you able to go back up and speak to him?" Robert asked.

"Yes... yes, I can do that. But I just had to get away. It felt so overwhelming," I told him.

Robert went back upstairs, and within ten minutes, I returned to the living room. I went directly to Phil and gave him a big hug, which was as touching for Phil, as it was unusual for me. No words passed between us. I wish I could have been more supportive, but that was the only way I knew how to handle such a situation. Coming upstairs and hugging Phil was a big thing for me to be able to do.

Handling strong emotions was a difficulty that I struggled with all my life. I remember dreading the two days in the year when the Legion held Remembrance ceremonies, July 1 and November 11. Earlier in my life, I found the strength to attend, but as the years passed, I found myself being unable to cope with the reminders of war and the carnage that it had created. I often found myself sitting on top of the mountain in Upper Island Cove, looking on as members of the Legion and my family, including Edie, attended the war memorial services in the town.

One year in the mid-1990s, I had decided that going to Remembrance Day school assemblies and war memorial services was taking the good out of me. They were important, and I was glad they were being held and well-attended, but I could not stand the strong emotional response that seemed to grow stronger within me as the years passed. On this day, just before Edie went to be with the other members of the Royal Canadian Legion Ladies' Auxiliary at the parade and service, I slipped out the door so as not to be there when she left. I gradually made my way, walking down the Meadow and up Mercer's Lane, to Rocky Hill, then in by our Dribbling Brook Garden, where I followed the sparsely used footpath to the back of the mountain.

I had walked this walk in over the mountain many times. Once you reached the precipice, the view of the community and of the surrounding area was breathtaking. How could you not be at peace in this place? The mountain usually protects Upper Island Cove from the strong and cold northerly winds. Today I hoped it would do the same for me.

I could hear the lone army cadet member, who was playing the kettle drum, beating out the standard marching rhythm as I moved to the west side of the peak. There, with my binoculars, on this cool but especially calm morning, I sat on a rock and could see the parade form up near the Anglican church, with my Legion comrades slowly making their way to chairs placed for them near the war memorial. This was a safe place for me today. I would be able to keep my emotions in check.

As always, the service began with a hymn and opening prayers, and soon I heard the cadet bugler play the Last Post. I told myself that this was the best place for me, until I could no longer focus. As I took my binoculars down, I noticed how much my hands were trembling. Why did I have to be like this? It would be nice to be able to go to the parade and show respect to my fallen comrades. I realized now, though, that my ability to do that, if it ever existed to any great extent, had faded with the passing years, and not much was likely to change.

In fairness to them, it would be difficult for our children to ever understand the real impact of war on veterans like us. And how could they? We grew up and went to war in a completely different era. My hope was that our contributions, among millions of others who contributed, had helped create a world safe enough today that the atrocities of that time really couldn't be imagined—and certainly never repeated. Many of us older veterans found it difficult to understand our own feelings about the past. It was obvious that feelings of strong emotions were now more easily triggered and increasingly present, generally, but especially around the times of war remembrance.

On Christmas Day, 2000, all the family were at Robert and Bernice's for our traditional family get-together. We were sitting around chatting, and Robert said, "Dad, the boys want to hear the new speaker system, so I am going to put on a movie, and it might be a bit loud."

I said, "That's okay, my son."

Robert followed up by saying, "It is a war movie I am putting on, so you will hear some sounds like explosions."

I was talking to someone else and acknowledged what he said by again responding, "Yes, that's okay."

I was involved in a conversation with one of the grandchildren when, suddenly, I heard the distinct and horrifying sound of a depth charge. I immediately lost touch with where I was. When I heard the sound, I froze.

Robert saw me and immediately turned off the sound. "Are you okay, Dad?"

I couldn't answer. I couldn't speak. All hands were looking at me.

Once I could move, I went immediately for the patio door. I felt I couldn't breathe. I was both overcome with images and sounds of the past and embarrassed that I had reacted so strongly. Edie and Robert both followed me outside as I walked around in the backyard.

Edie knew exactly what had happened and, in a firm but compassionate way, said, "Robert, that's okay. I will see to him. He will be all right. You go back inside with the others."

Robert backed away, and as she approached me, I remember saying, "Edie, we should go home now."

We got one of the children to drive us home. No one, including me, ever spoke of the incident again.

28 — Edie

DIGGING DEEPER

1994–2004

Today is June 6, 1994, the fiftieth anniversary of D-Day. My mind goes back to past challenges. Being here in Upper Island Cove has been wonderful, but I have missed so much back in England. There are so many memories, and at times like this I think about all my family members and friends who have died and whom I could not say goodbye to. Sometimes I feel pain of a lifelong separation, especially on days like today. This is my home now, but England is where I am from. From time to time, I have to shake myself because memories like this are best kept where they belong, deep in my heart where they can rest.

Some people have referred to me as a very strong-willed person. It is certainly true that, once I make up my mind, little if anything has been able to alter that path.

I find it is a matter of being practical. One of the most distressing things in life is the state of indecision. It creates the environment for a perfect storm of competing emotions. Therefore, my strong preference is to avoid that state of mind, if at all possible. When I can see or feel something that is happening or about to happen in my life, I prefer to take control rather than simply waiting for it to control me.

Being decisive worked well for me in 2004.

I had been feeling a good bit of pain and limited in my mobility because of a diagnosed spinal condition. My doctor told me the only real likelihood of having relief and staving off confinement to a wheelchair, eventually, was to have an operation he referred to as a spinal fusion. Given my age and medical circumstance, though, he was reluctant to recommend the surgery for me without further medical consultation.

When Bill asked me what I was going to do, I remember saying, "I didn't come all this way around the world to let life effectively stop now. The likelihood of no longer being able to get shopping, among other things that I still want to do, has played a big role in influencing my decision. Bill, I feel I must go ahead and have the surgery. I realize you and the children are quite concerned, but this is what I feel is needed for me right now."

Our son Robert was working in Spaniard's Bay then. When he heard this news, he called me and told me he would be down tomorrow (a weekday) to have lunch with his dad and me. I realized his motive in coming for lunch, but that was fine. It would be lovely for him to come for lunch no matter the motive. He came down the next day, and I had prepared a lunch of sandwiches and some cookies, with a cup of tea, of course.

Once he had started his lunch, he said, "Mom, I know you have decided to have the spinal surgery, but we are all concerned that it might be too much for you at this age. You are getting up in years, and the body probably wouldn't heal like a younger person would."

I smiled, looked at Bill, and then responded calmly, "I knew when you said you were coming for lunch that the surgery is what was on your mind. I realize I am eighty years old, but I still have a lot of go left in me yet. As you know, I have had two heart attacks and several stents placed in my arteries. But I've spoken to the cardiologist, and he says my heart is still strong, and there is no medical reason why I should not proceed. So, I have made up my mind that this is the right thing to do. Now, carry on and eat the rest of your lunch!"

After I finished, Robert chuckled. He said he wanted to have the conversation before I actually went in to hospital, but he was not surprised with my decision.

A couple of weeks after that lunch, I did have the surgery and was beginning to recover very well, although with quite a bit of pain. Even though I was fully prepared for the associated pain and discomfort, what I was feeling was more than I had expected. I began to think that I wasn't as prepared for this as I thought I was. My doctor realized that something seemed wrong. After further tests and a consultation with other doctors, he decided that further corrective surgery was necessary. It turned out that one of the screws inserted in my back was pinching a nerve. After the second surgery, I felt much better and progressed quite well. I was at the shopping mall with Jean in no time.

I guess, like everything, in later years that brave face and strong heart eventually gave way to a more emotional response to life events. This was especially true when it came to my recollection of the war years. Sometimes I had a hard time when I finally allowed myself to realize what we had all gone through. I often preferred to sit alone, watching the memorial services on TV, and could feel the raw emotion well up inside me. In years gone by, I was almost too busy with the children to take the time to sit and watch. But now, by contrast, I spent countless hours alone every July 1, and especially November 11, watching the war memorial services.

July 1 was important to the people of Newfoundland because of the sacrifice of Newfoundland soldiers in World War I, especially the Battle of Beaumont-Hamel. I greatly respected that. But November 11 meant a lot to me personally. It was then I thought of Bill, his brother Edward, as well as my brothers Harry and Alf. I remembered all those who had served for freedom. But most of all, this was when I felt closest to my brother Sidney John Thomas, who did not make it home from war.

Each year I seemed to remember even more clearly the whole ordeal of his captivity, finding out he was dead, and seeing the intense pain on the faces of my parents. As I sat there watching the TV but seeing little, all my own experiences also flooded back to me.

It seemed that, no matter how hard I tried to be strong and stop these memories and thoughts, the heartbreak and the tears came freely now. They could not be stopped.

The strength that people in the family and the neighbourhood saw in me, if that ever really existed, was a part of me that had changed. And I know Bill, too, found it difficult. Just as the experiences had haunted him, I realized I was not immune to the aftermath of what I experienced.

The years had passed by quickly, and Newfoundland was my home. I could never have left here and returned to England. The England I knew no longer existed. This was my home, but more importantly, it was the home of our children, grandchildren, and great-grandchildren. But none of this could ever take away the inexplicable recurring sense of homesickness and the need to sometimes be with my English family.

Right after Phil moved home from Toronto in 1994, he started a long and dedicated period of advocacy for people living with AIDS and HIV. This work helped many people and took Phil to several cities around the world, attending and speaking at conferences and the like. In the summer of 2000, he attended an international HIV/AIDS conference in Durban, South Africa.

Phil organized his travel so that he could stop in England for a few days prior to the conference. He had not been to England previously, and this would allow him to connect with my family there. He arrived in England on a Thursday morning and by early afternoon met my only surviving sibling, Lil. When they met, Phil was immediately struck by the resemblance between his Aunt Lil and me. They spoke for about a half-hour, after which Lil went back to her own house.

Very early the next morning, my cousin Jack Cox drove Phil to Portsmouth so that he could catch the ferry to France. Phil later told me he wanted to try to imagine what it might have been like when his father's ship was part of the D-Day invasion. The ferry landed near Sword Beach, which is where Bill's ship landed. He spent some time on the beach, where he picked up some sand and other miscellaneous items.

While he was waiting for the return ferry, he called home, at which point I told him that Lil had passed away the previous night. Having just met her the same afternoon, Phil was quite shocked.

After returning to England from France, he went on to the conference in South Africa. The day after he returned to England from South Africa, the funeral for Lil took place.

A few days later, he returned home to Newfoundland, and the next day he came down to our house to see Bill and me. It was an emotional reunion, and we both hugged, as did Phil and Bill. It was as though our relationship had changed. Phil could now share the privilege with me of having met and talked with Lil, something, as adults, none of the other five children had been able to do. We talked about the events of the past two weeks, and I was happy he got to meet my sister. It seemed like Lil was waiting for someone from my family to visit.

Phil looked at Bill and said, "Father, I have a bag of sand and some cockle shells, along with a piece of brick that I picked up on Sword Beach."

Bill opened the small plastic bag and gently ran his fingers through the sand. He stared intently at the bag for a minute and then, thoughtfully and in the sincerest way, looked up at Phil and commented, "Yes, my son, I didn't have time to get any when I was there."

29 — Edie

ALL ROADS LEAD HOME

2005

"I have noticed that time does not really exist for mothers with regard to their children. It does not matter greatly how old the child is—in the blink of an eye, the mother can see the child again as the child was when he or she was born, learned to walk, or as the child was at any age, at any time, even when the child is fully grown and a parent him or herself."
— Edie Lundrigan

I had enjoyed the quiet life with Bill as we continued to live together down in the Meadow. It was now the early years in the new millennium, and the children came regularly to visit so that we could share in their lives as well as in the lives of the grandchildren. They brought so much joy to our lives. Bill had long since retired his once incredible desire for fishing or hunting for birds and seals.

The decade certainly started on a really good note. Our granddaughter Angela (Boyd and Nancy) was born in 1991, as was Adrienne (Mavis and Kevin). Our youngest grandchild, Andrew (Boyd and Nancy), was born in 1998.

I continued to spend my time reading and enjoying a few favourite TV shows. I also very much enjoyed shopping. Jean had not been well, and although we still shopped together, most of my time shopping was with my dear friend Martha Coombs. Bill's time spent taking long, relaxing walks alone was still so important to him. He also spent much of his time reading and sometimes rereading some of the many books we had collected through the years.

Over the years, Bill and I were often invited to various schools for Remembrance Day assemblies. I always attended, and in the earlier years, so too did Bill. But as time went on, he chose to stay home. He never said why, but it wasn't hard to know the reason. Children seemed to enjoy my telling the many stories of the life of a war veteran, or what life was like in Britain during the war. I remember one assembly at Holy Redeemer School in Spaniard's Bay, when I was telling the story of all the children whose parents shipped them off to places like Scotland and North America. This was done so that they would be safe from the bombing in the bigger cities in England. In particular, I was trying to describe how thankful we should be for the lives we now have because of the efforts of the war veterans. The silence of the children and the emotion of the staff in that large gymnasium were palpable. For many years, I felt it my duty, when asked, to do these sorts of talks. It was a way to honour all those who served and especially for those, like my brother Sid, who were lost.

When Bill was in his early eighties, I started to recognize changes, although subtle, were happening to both his body as well as to his mind. At one point, he went for a walk up to Bishop's Cove, but when he turned around, he panicked. At that moment, he realized he didn't know which way was home. He did eventually find his way, but after that, he decided it was best not to walk to Bishop's Cove by himself again. One day soon after this, Bill and I went down to see Dr. Lonze Button, and he prescribed some medication to help Bill with remembering things a bit better. It seemed to help somewhat.

Some years previously, I wanted him to have a cellphone so that, if he was alone, he could call home. But Bill didn't want it. Since then, however, he did decide it might be a good idea to have a phone. We purchased one for him. Not long after that, he went down alongshore for a lot longer than he planned, so he decided to call me and let me know he was okay. He took out the cellphone and remembered how I had shown him to turn it on. But then, when he was getting ready to dial the number, he stopped. He had forgotten our telephone number at the house. The time for a cellphone appeared to have passed.

One afternoon in the early spring of 2005, our daughter-in-law Bernice visited us. We had a nice visit, and when she left, Bill asked, "Bernice, would you be able to give me a ride as far as the post office, please?"

"Of course, Mr. Lundrigan," Bernice answered.

When they got to the post office, Bernice said, "Mr. Lundrigan, I'll wait for you now and give you a ride back home."

With much protest, Bill insisted, "No, that's fine, Bernice, my dear. When I check the mail, I'll go for a little walk."

I believe he knew he couldn't go too far, but he told Bernice, "I will go up over Cries Hill, out Pot Brook, and then across the Green to the Meadow Road."

Bernice said, "Are you sure? I am happy to give you a ride back home."

Later, Bernice told me Bill's response was, "No, that's good, thank you. I wanted to have a little walk, but Edie worries since I lost my way coming back from Bishop's Cove. It's just a short walk, and I'll be fine, but don't tell Edie, will you?"

They both laughed, she drove on in the Mash, and as she went out of sight, Bill, hands in his pants pockets, back straight as a gun rod, was walking toward Cries Hill.

Besides my now well-recovered back surgery, Phil's health, and Bill's continuing memory decline, our lives were about to take another turn.

Jean had been sick as a child and had developed Crohn's disease as an adult. She seemed to be developing further complications through the years, and it was really beginning to impact her quality of life. And so, while we were all focused on how Phil and Bill were doing medically, suddenly Jean, whose kidneys had failed, started to have considerable grief with her dialysis treatments. She was forced (medically) to give up the process of peritoneal dialysis in favour of hemodialysis.

The autoimmune disease she'd had as a child seemed to leave her completely. As an adult, however, it appeared to become an increasingly negative influence on her health.

It was Easter Sunday, March 27, 2005. Jean had been spending time with Phil at an HIV retreat at the Lavrock Centre on the Salmonier Line. She was scheduled to do dialysis in St. John's that morning, so Phil took her in and waited for her. Jean had a difficult session on the dialysis machine, and for some reason, she had a lot of stomach discomfort. Phil brought her home to our house in Upper Island Cove for Sunday dinner. The pain in her stomach was getting worse. She didn't eat much and lay down on the bed for a while. Things didn't improve, so her only child, Trevor, came down and picked her up. Things only got worse with her stomach after she got home, so Trevor called the ambulance, which took her to Carbonear Hospital.

The pain increased further while she was at the emergency department. After a short while, Robert and Bernice came to visit with her. Around suppertime, they both overheard the ER doctor speaking on the phone, saying, "I believe she has pancreatitis, and with her renal disease, Carbonear Hospital is not the place for her to be treated. We think she should go to the Health Sciences Centre."

Not long after that, they put Jean in the ambulance and she went off to the Health Sciences Centre. Little did we realize it, but that was day one of eighty-eight consecutive days she would spend at the HSC. Her health continued to deteriorate, and before long she was in the intensive care unit. Jean had not been able to get well enough to speak much to Trevor and the family during all that time. When she did regain some strength for just a week or so, she communicated by writing her thoughts, questions, or requests.

She so wished that she could speak to her family. She was developing a greater sense that she was likely not going to get better, and she had much to say. It was not to be. Jean's condition worsened. The nurses were as kind as they were competent at their work, but her body was failing her. The rheumatic fever of her childhood and other medical issues over the years were too much for her small and frail body.

It was very difficult seeing Jean there, knowing that with each passing day her chance of survival was diminishing. Then on June 22, 2005, at fifty-eight years and with her family present, she quietly slipped away. Although this was very much about Jean's suffering, the pain I felt seeing my child suffer so much, and not being ready to leave this earth, was so very difficult. To see her go was devastating to all of us, especially to Trevor, who had already lost his dad years ago.

But by then, there was a certain relief that she had peace at last.

Admittedly, I don't believe Bill always understood what was happening. If he did understand, his mind by now was not allowing him to fully digest it. He would go in the intensive care unit to see Jean and often become upset, holding her hand while trying to hug and comfort her. Then, when we went outside to allow someone else to visit, he would laugh and chat with others as though nothing about what had just happened stayed in his mind.

Jean was buried on June 25, 2005, at St. Peter's Anglican Cemetery in Upper Island Cove.

During the ceremony, something most unusual occurred.

The day of the funeral was a very warm day, but the most prominent feature as we stood at the gravesite was that there was absolutely no wind. This was almost incredible for the top of the Long Hill in

Upper Island Cove, where the cemetery was located. It was almost never calm there. Jean's lifelong friend Rev. Howard Crane (who is the son of Bill's good and lifelong friend Joe Crane) was one of the officiants. Rev. Howard was in the process of offering the words of the committal when a quick but warm wisp of wind suddenly swirled and enveloped the area directly over and around the casket. It surprised most of those in attendance as they held onto their hymn books and service pamphlets.

For many Christians, wind is an important symbol and often associated with the Holy Spirit. It would not be unreasonable, then, for some people to interpret this sudden swirl of wind to symbolically represent some form of heavenly presence. It is an interpretation that I would certainly favour.

Front, L-R: Mavis, Willie, Edie, Jean. Standing, L-R: Sid, Boyd, Phil, Robert. Christmas 2004.

We missed Jean so very much. She had moved back to this area of the province after Lloyd died years ago, and we were in contact almost every day. So much was changing. Jean was now gone, and Phil was always on our minds because of his own health challenges. I also knew that Bill's health was going downhill very fast.

I wondered what the next few years would bring our way, as both physically and mentally, Bill had already shown much sign of decline.

As time passed, Bill began the inevitable but slow slide. It was not a graceful slide. While it had been happening for some time, few outside myself and the children could really see it. But by early 2006, it started to become more obvious. Things really started to unravel when, at the end of January, he needed to go into hospital for just an overnight stay for a minor medical procedure.

We had not had any snow that winter until Bill entered hospital. A storm came in and dumped a large amount of snow with high winds. It was impossible for anyone to get in to pick him up, so he ended up staying for two nights. On the second day, he was bored and thought, while he would be careful to see where he was going, he might go up the hallway for a short walk. He must have gone farther than he thought. He told me, "I looked around and wondered where I was and why I was there dressed in my pyjamas."

He found it all very upsetting. Eventually, someone noticed that he was roaming from door to door looking for something familiar.

A nurse who had been looking after him was kind enough to take him back to his room. He asked her to call Robert, and she did. He was upset when Robert answered the phone, since I think he knew his mind was in such an awful place. He wanted Robert to come to the hospital and bring him home right then. Because of the weather, however, Robert told his father he was unable to come that night. He promised he would come the next day, and sure enough, early the next morning, Robert and Bernice showed up for him. At this point, Bill was starting to need more and more care, and his days of walking were now in the past.

Of course, this was not his first bout with being in hospital. Several years prior to this, he had been admitted to Carbonear General

Hospital with an attack of pancreatitis. He was very ill with tremendous pain. He was experiencing all of this pain, and the doctor insisted he must stop drinking alcohol. I knew he had not drunk alcohol at all since he finished up his war service in January 1946. No matter how much he insisted he was a non-drinker, the doctor did not believe him. The doctor also questioned me on Bill's drinking habits.

As the days passed in hospital, Bill seemed to get worse, with pain that was almost unbearable. In order to relieve the pain, while still treating the cause of the problem, the doctor recognized the need for significant pain relief medication. It seemed that, at the point when the medication was administered, Bill's memory of what was happening evaporated. What replaced it seemed to be a desperately bad and never-ending nightmare—the old hag. He kept telling us that he was not in hospital but instead that he was being held prisoner in the old dilapidated Gospel Hall, which had been built in Bishop's Cove near the Bexley's Hill old Anglican Cemetery many years ago.

In the continuous hallucinatory state, it appeared he could not escape. What was worse was his perception that his whole family had turned their backs on him by denying that he was a prisoner. In his mind, it seemed that we tried to convince him he was in hospital. In this illness and possibly drug-induced state, Bill was convinced he was tied on by a rope fastened around his stomach, preventing him from escaping. He told each of us he needed us to cut the rope and was upset when not one of us would do so.

In Bill's mind, at that time, he could not make the connection with reality, nor could it be influenced by even his most trusted family members. He really felt he was imprisoned and, worse, alone in this struggle.

Finally, being on his own now, Bill felt he had no choice but to somehow break free of this place. He looked at this rope, but it was attached so tightly. If there was any chance of freeing himself, he had to detach the rope. So, at some point when no one was present, he pulled hard on the rope, and eventually it came free. At first he didn't see it, but after a while he noticed some blood on the floor. Now he realized someone was with him, trying to get him back in a bed. He felt he had to get past them. The reality, lost on Bill at that time, was that what he thought was a rope that he pulled to free himself was not a rope but a urine catheter that had been inserted to support his healing.

I don't believe he remembered much after that. He woke up in hospital with me sitting beside his bed. We talked for a while, but he was sleepy and couldn't stay awake long. After some time had passed, I was able to tell him that he had been very sick but the doctors said, after some rest, he would be fine. I also told Bill that the doctor had given him some medication that helped him sleep for a few days. When he gradually woke up, the pain had lessened quite a lot.

At that point, he had no memory of the last several days. The feeling that he was being held captive no longer existed. The nurses lovingly cared for him, and he began to piece together, from conversations with the medical staff, something about what had transpired over the period he had been in hospital. He was shaken to the core to learn what had happened to him.

He started to understand how he had insisted that he was a prisoner. Even worse than that, the doctor told him that he had to be put to sleep because he was unco-operative with both the nursing staff as well as with his family. Bill was incredibly distressed about behaving in such a way. Everyone continued to be supportive, but he was very saddened with the way he had unknowingly behaved.

I used to tell him he was very hard on himself. He never thought this feeling of regret would ever leave him, but of course, not too long after that, it did slip into the recesses of his mind. Before it did, though, he wrote a letter to his family about what happened. In the end, the contents of the letter will remain private, out of respect for the terror and torture that Bill felt then and for many years.

As Bill's situation continued in a downward direction, we were fortunate to have our eldest grandson, Craig, who was a registered nurse, come to help with Bill's care. Even though Bill didn't, or more aptly couldn't, recognize it, there was a lot that now he couldn't do for himself. Trying to help him was too much for me, given that I was still recovering from back surgery. In such a kind and caring manner, Craig was able to help Bill, including how to use a walker and go for a short walk on some days. Bill no longer felt well enough to walk anywhere near like he once did. Indeed, he seemed to have no interest in even trying. I believe he was slowly losing his ability to think clearly about things, and what made it very frustrating for him was it seemed he no longer had the ability to explain that to me or our children. But Craig knew, and I was thankful.

Then in June, and again in July 2006, Bill had to be admitted to Carbonear General Hospital because of issues with his stomach. They treated him with medication, but it didn't really do much to help. The doctors felt that a medication he was taking to help slow his memory loss was largely responsible for the issues with his stomach, so it was stopped. He felt somewhat better and went home with Craig and me, but his condition continued to deteriorate.

Bill's doctor told him there were not many options, but one thing they could try was a drug called Remicade. He told Bill this drug, for him at this time, considering his various health challenges, could be literally classified as a "kill or cure." Bill talked to his family about it and decided to use it. Unfortunately, the drug was not available at the hospital pharmacy. Members of the family searched high and low and, eventually, with the doctor's permission, were told it was available at Donovans Industrial Park. The race was on to acquire it, and one of the children went off to Donovans. Within three hours we had the drug and provided it to the physician.

With a couple of the children, I went to Bill and said, "Bill, we have great news. We have the medication, and the doctor has it now. He will come by to administer the first dose."

Bill just sat in the bed and placed one hand over his eyes and became upset.

I gave him a few minutes to collect himself and asked, "What's wrong, Bill? Is there something else going on?"

"No, Edie," he said. "I just can't take that medication. The doctor said it might very well kill me, and I can't do that to our grandchildren."

I always knew Bill was very compassionate, but this response was so profound that it momentarily threw all his family for a surprise. But then it started to sink in—by now, Bill knew the end was near, yet he had clearly chosen the welfare of others before himself. He would accept the consequences of not taking the medication, out of concern that taking it would cause so much emotional pain for his family, especially the younger ones. Even though he didn't take the medication, he was discharged from hospital and went on for a while before things really deteriorated.

While he was clearly unwell, as he approached the very late stages of his life, he still had that wit about him. Of course, I generally thought he didn't have a funny bone in his body. Others thought that Bill had a sharp "Island Cove" wit that had largely escaped me for all these years. Bill's jokes were very often situational in nature, or, as the saying goes, "You had to be there..."

For instance, Bill would often say to one of the children when they ate their dinner very fast, "You weren't long picking up your liver today, my son." This comment was made jokingly to compare the speed of eating your lunch with the speed at which a gull could swoop down and pick up one of its favourite dishes, a fish liver, floating on the water after someone cleaned some fish.

On one occasion, our daughter Mavis and her daughter were helping Bill stand but could not properly get him off the couch by themselves. I saw this and told Mavis I would come over to help. Bill heard what I said and whispered to Mavis, "Here come the big guns."

Mavis, Adrienne, and Bill got into a fit of laughter. I overheard the comment from Bill but pretended I didn't see anything funny about it and just sat right back down again.

I must admit, even on one of the last nights that he was able to stay in his own home, he could still see the humour in difficult times.

One night in late August, well after midnight, Bill was very unwell. I called Robert and Craig and asked if they would come down. Both of them showed up within a very short while and helped get Bill out of bed. He didn't say much, but we could see that he knew very well his time on this earth was getting near the end. He was wincing in pain and was in so much misery, he asked the boys to help him have a little walk around. While he was walking around the kitchen, with Robert and Craig holding him up, I looked out the kitchen window into the darkness. Bill had done the same so many nights over the years.

As I looked, I could see, unencumbered by fog, the lighthouse on Green Point. I said, "It's a great night out there tonight, Bill. I can see right over to the lighthouse."

Bill smiled while looking toward the boys and replied simply, "Yes, that's lovely, Edie, but we're not going over there tonight, are we?"

I believe he knew where he was going and in very short order. Within a few days, he ended up in hospital, never to return home to the sanctuary of our little house under the bank down in the Meadow. Never to use his "lookers" to scan for birds, seals, whales, or fishing boats. Never to take the long walks down alongshore, and never to see his children and grandchildren visit again. When he jokingly told me he wasn't going over there, what he really meant was that he had a sense that he was about to make his final trip. He wasn't wrong.

He was in hospital for a couple of days and told the family he wanted to go home, however his condition deteriorated so rapidly that he never spoke those words again.

One of the interesting things that occurred while he was in hospital for almost two months was that, seemingly due to his advanced dementia, he lost the ability to talk. Initially it seemed to us that he did not want to talk as much as usual, but really, it seemed his brain would not allow him to form the words. This continued until, finally, no words came at all. The only communication he could make was his response to someone touching him, which usually manifested itself in him pulling away or emitting a fairly loud and disapproving moan.

On one occasion in mid-October, Phil and I went to see him. As we got off the elevator on the seventh floor, we could hear who we felt certain was Bill in tremendous distress. Immediately, we proceeded to his room as fast as we could. When we arrived there, both of us were quite troubled to see that Bill's hands were being held down while he was being administered oxygen and medication through a mask over his nose and mouth. This action was immediately stopped by us.

When Bill arrived in hospital several weeks earlier, the attending physician gathered the family and told everyone that Bill was clearly in the final stage of his life and that his death could occur at any time. There was really nothing they could do to change the course of things, but they would do everything possible to make him comfortable.

As a family, we acknowledged that administering something like oxygen and medication may have been helpful to that comfort in normal circumstances. Given his reaction to having the mask over his face and of being held down, we felt this needed to stop. We recognized the terror he had faced during his war service, which had never left him. There could be no more such episodes, even if failure to provide such interventions hastened the moment of his passing. The doctor and the nursing staff were very supportive of that decision when so informed, and it never happened again.

30 — Robert

THE LAST POST

2006

I expect to pass through this world but once
Any good thing therefore that I can do
Or any kindness that I can show
To any fellow creature
Let me do it now
Let me not defer or neglect it
For I shall not pass this way again[8]

— Stephen Grellet, 1773–1855

This short poem was copied by my father, Willie, from one of the many books he read over the years. This passage was important enough to him that he took the time to type it out on a blank piece of paper, using his old typewriter that his daughter Mavis gave him years ago. I believe he felt it was a reflection of the way he tried to live his life. Through the way he lived, it seemed to me that he had a strong desire to be in touch with both the natural world as well as with himself.

---

8   Attributed to Stephen Grellet 1773–1855, French Quaker and Missionary.

As children, and later as adults, we always listened intently while he told the same stories of funny incidents during the war. We were all aware that, while giving us a brief window into his war experiences, he never shared any of the most horrifying circumstances of war. Deep inside, I think he hoped these stories helped his family to realize that, in life, doing well by others was the only thing that really mattered. It would be reasonable to say his life was not reflective of the typical churchgoing religious person, as that voice in Grellet's short poem implores us to be. But even with all his warts and human imperfections, he really tried to live a life caring for others before himself. And although he was not convinced he had been able to do that successfully, that realization never stopped him from continuing to try. That quality sometimes made him an outlier to others. Who could not have possibly understood what underpinned his beliefs or his actions? I also think he was well-aware of, understood, and accepted his lot in life.

But such is life, and it was his view that each of us must do our best to do right by others. For him, the sentiment was that we must do the right thing, even when the view was unclear, the sounds were muffled, and the path was rugged. I absolutely believe that his attempts to live a good life and help others had an impact. Providing support to others was, I believe, the very essence of his spirituality.

After many life challenges, he approached the end with the hope, and at least some confidence, that his war service may have had value. The six years that he was a member of the British Royal Navy were, I believe, the most difficult and yet the most wonderful years of his life. No matter what he did for the rest of his life, it invariably circled back to those years.

A few years ago, two high school students were doing a school project about war veterans. They wanted to interview Bill about his wartime experiences. He often felt too emotional to do these sorts of interviews, but for some reason, he was quite happy to do this one.

The interview was near the end when one of the young interviewers asked him the question, "Mr. Lundrigan, if you were granted the gift of time travel, knowing the horrors that awaited you, would you do it again?"

I was surprised and yet emotional when he answered without hesitation. He responded by saying, "I would definitely do it again. I met the love of my life in the middle of hell on earth, and I wouldn't change that for the world."

There are always mistakes and regrets in life, and like most people, I'm sure, he felt he had made his own share. As the curtain closed on his life here, I realized we must not let these define him.

In the Newfoundland of the early twentieth century, he grew up in a time and in a place devoid of a sense of the future, where the luxury of imagining was almost impossible, and the privilege of hope did not exist. Despite this, as a child he had a loving home with caring parents. His father and sister Mabel were taken away far too soon. He was not alone. While he had to face many obstacles and challenges, he would be the first to say, "So too did many others in my world. And many suffered more."

People could be forgiven for mistakenly thinking that he was living the life he always wanted, and for many years, that probably included Edie. But if he had ever considered what life he wanted to live, life for him morphed into something totally outside his control. The life he lived was not so much a want as it was the result of the hand he had been dealt. We realize now how much his early life experiences carved out the remainder of his life and, more importantly, impacted the lives of many of those he loved most.

Through the years, as children, we could see how he fought to stay strong. I am confident that, if his grandchildren and great-grandchildren could find it in their hearts to love him, only a fraction as much as he surely loved each one of them, he would have had a completely satisfying life. I know he loved Edie, as she did him, even though love was not something they talked about as openly as maybe they could have.

This has been an amazing journey of understanding for me. I feel that, as well as I thought I knew my parents, I have been able to come to understand them in a way and to an extent that, without this writing, I may never have been able.

My father, Willie, at eighty-five years of age, is in hospital now, in a non-expressive state. As our family members take turns sitting with him for many days, I often wonder and speculate what he would say, if he could.

If he could communicate, my understandings of who he really was have led me to believe it could likely be a variation of the following . . .

Here I am, in the final days of life. My body has started to fail me, and communication with others is very difficult, if not impossible. As time slows for me, finally, a sense of peace pushes away my darkness.

I always loved Upper Island Cove and living in the Meadow. Even when I left it to go to war, the homesickness was so intense. The people down in the Meadow and in all Upper Island Cove are good, solid people, and I have learned many lessons from them. We have always looked out for one another.

I will forever, even in death, love my dearest Edie. I have always been in awe of her strength, her courage, and her resolve. I know she made tremendous sacrifices. The determination she has shown over the years has been so powerful. Yet, sadly because of the darkness, my darkness, I was not always able to see it or acknowledge that preciousness in our journey together. She has been my love, my friend, and my anchor in a chorus of stormy seas. She has shown herself to be both a force of nature and a tonic for my battered soul.

I understand that my time is nearly done. My mind has drifted for longer than they realize, yet my path has never been clearer. My beloved Upper Island Cove, its people, and its character, which has lifted me up so often, is behind me now. Like many before me, I may even have made choices that placed my interests above the ones I love, yet their grace has saved a wretch like me. Please forgive me my trespasses.

My family has refused to leave me, these many days here. How do I deserve such complete devotion? The weakness flows through my body, yet my heart has never been so full. If only I could tell them to rest, tell them that I am okay, and tell them how much I have so dearly loved each of them. I wish I could tell them that although I know well that the end is near, I do not fear it. I am truly at peace, yet I am unable to speak of this joy . . .

It is only as I reflect through these last embers of my life that I recognize how the fear, the nightmares, the fight for survival of others, and of myself, defined my refusal to be defeated. And all of this has all led to this moment of pure ecstasy.

I can only hope that my people see me in the spirit that I tried to live my life. As I prepare to leave this earth, I also hope my family recognizes that, even in the most challenging of times, although I have struggled, I have never given in.

I have never surrendered. I have been bent but never broken.

Yes, my head has been bloody yet remained, always, unbowed.

The hour is nigh. The time has run its course.

As my heart finally rests, I take my leave from the sweetness of this life . . .

But it is with gratitude that I will finally escape from the damnation of this war that, to now, has shadowed my every waking hour and has robbed the nights. My final thoughts must be of my family, and my final message to Edie:

ROBERT W. LUNDRIGAN

my dearest
the sky is clear
the shelters are empty
children are laughing

it will be okay now
the bugler plays
the flag rests

there will be peace and
we shall sleep
down in the meadow

31 — Edie

LIFE AFTER BILL

2006–2016

"I am overcome with joy and thankfulness. Through this selfless gift of Bernice, my son's life will be restored..."
— Edie Lundrigan

What now, Bill?
The winter after Bill passed, I spent living in our home alone. Except largely for going to bed, being alone was not altogether that different for me. Spending that winter entirely by myself had helped me realize that I didn't want to live there completely alone.

Our children are doing well, except Phil, who continues to face challenges, and Robert, who expects to start dialysis soon. Bill and I had spoken of Phil many times and wanted him to be settled. Bill is gone now, and I have decided that Phil should live in the house that Bill and I built, in the Meadow, where our children grew up. I considered going into a retirement living centre, but each of my children and their partners offered the opportunity for me to come and live with each of them. I was very appreciative of this but did not want to be any sort of intrusion.

In the spring of 2007, and after a lot of thought, I decided to move to Spaniard's Bay with our son Robert and daughter-in-law Bernice. My only request in relocating was that I not be required to live in a basement apartment. No one needed to ask why. They knew the answer from conversations over the years. My family realized that if I were to live in a below-ground apartment, it would only be a constant reminder of the war years and the troubling memories of the many harrowing nights in the Anderson air-raid shelter. There, we would wait anxiously for the direct hit of a bomb, many of which the Luftwaffe poured from the sky. Never again could I bring myself to spend time in any underground facility.

The next several years of my life were going very well. I missed Bill and Jean, but I tuck away in private any thoughts of the sadness of their absence. All my children regularly visit me, and I visit them from time to time. I also spend most Christmas Eves in Upper Island Cove with Phil because he is alone. I know, especially after his diagnosis of HIV in 1994, I spent a lot of time "fussing" over him. It could be anything from worrying about him travelling to me making sure he had enough food on his plate at one of our family get-togethers.

After Bill passed away, Phil nominated him for the nationally established Minister of Veterans Affairs Commendation Award. Phil wrote the Department of Veterans Affairs Canada, outlining the nature of Bill's volunteer efforts over many years. A short time later, he received word that his father had been approved for the volunteer recognition, posthumously.

The Minister of Veterans Affairs Commendation Award was described by Veterans Affairs as,

> "*Since serving in uniform, many of Canada's veterans have continued to provide outstanding service to their country, the community, and to fellow Veterans. To formally recognize these contributions, the Governor General has authorized the creation of the Minister of Veterans Affairs Commendation.*"

Left: Minister of Veterans Affairs Commendation
Right: Willie's war service and Legion volunteer medals

On September 17, 2007, accompanied by Phil, I flew to Halifax to be presented with the Minister of Veterans Affairs Commendation on behalf of Bill. This consisted of a bronze bar, which was to be worn with the veteran's military service medals, a lapel pin, and a citation which stated,

> "*Mr. Lundrigan was a Second World War Veteran who served with the Royal Navy from 1940–1946. After surviving a torpedo attack in November of 1940, he went on to take part in D-Day on June 6, 1944. Mr. Lundrigan was a member of the Royal Canadian Legion since 1958. Together with other members of his community, he cut wood and helped build Branch 22 in Upper Island Cove. He served the Legion in many capacities, including Branch President. He continued to be an active member of Cpl. Matthew Brazil Chapter, Branch #9 in Spaniard's Bay. He regularly participated in annual Remembrance Day ceremonies in the local schools, including Holy Redeemer, where his name and photograph have been inscribed on*

their 'Wall of Honour.' During the 'Year of the Veteran,' Mr. Lundrigan concluded the assembly by symbolically presenting the students with the White Ensign, a flag from one of his warships. A well-known community leader, Mr. Lundrigan was also a member of the George Cross Island Association and the Naval Association. Through his active involvement, he was an outstanding role model for veterans, students, teachers, and his fellow citizens of Upper Island Cove."

This was quite an honour for Bill, and I am glad that Phil played a role in the award process.

I have much to be thankful for, and I was so especially delighted when, in the spring of 2009, after Robert had been on dialysis for a year and a half, something very special was about to happen.

Robert began dialysis and had not been doing well. No one was more aware of this than Bernice. She had made it known several years ago that she wished to be tested to see if she could be an organ donor for Robert. She was turned down but refused to let it go. She tried again and was turned down. Again, she pleaded her case, and this time she was listened to. The team at the renal transplant clinic agreed to send both her file and Robert's to Ottawa for review. In March 2009, they received word that the match was good and the surgery would go ahead in April. Here is my note from the surgery day and the days that followed . . .

"It is April 23, 2009, the day of the surgery. I am sitting by the phone today waiting for a call letting us know how the surgery is going. None of us are unmindful that this is major surgery for both Robert and Bernice, and I am praying that all goes well.

The call comes, and the power of this beautiful news of the successful transplant process immediately causes emotion to so completely wash over me!"

In the days following, I write,

"Bernice, I will be forever grateful, and I will never forget what you have done for my son.

The surgery and the recovery have gone exceedingly well for both Robert and Bernice, and within a month they will be both back home in Newfoundland.

The days pass and, in Ottawa, Robert and Bernice are getting stronger. They will be staying for about a month after the surgery."

May 22, 2009,

"Today is the day Robert and Bernice fly home. We are all excited to see them. Jokingly, Robert says he is glad to be able to go to the bathroom."

Since the surgery, now a month ago, Robert appears to be on the road to a full and healthy life, and Bernice also seems to be doing remarkably well.

Our family and I are all grateful to Robert's dear wife, Bernice, who has fought and succeeded in being permitted to give Robert one of her kidneys. This is an example of love that anyone could hardly imagine. I am overcome with joy and thankfulness. Through this selfless and altruistic gift of Bernice, my son will be able to live a better-quality life.

I have felt for some time that establishing and following routines are important. A regular daily schedule has always served me well. After I moved to Spaniard's Bay, I spent every morning from 9:30 to 10:30 a.m., as well as 9:00 to 10:00 p.m., visiting with Bernice and Robert. So regular were these visits, they both used to say, they could set the clock by them. I'm sure Robert and Bernice knew I was coming out from the apartment long before I arrived because of the rolling, droning sound of the tires of my walker on the hard floor. I went to bed at 11:00 p.m.—not 10:45 p.m., and not 11:15 p.m.

As the years went by, I realized I was beginning to slip into a new phase of my life. I came here to this lovely apartment to keep my independence but not have to be responsible for everything needed to maintain a home. I realized, before I came, that Robert was getting closer to dialysis each day, and it was never my intent for him or Bernice to provide for my personal care. I also wondered what it would be like to be able to chat with other people. It was lovely here in my apartment, but Robert and Bernice were still relatively young and were living their lives, not without their own struggles, with Robert's health. It was time for me to consider the next steps in my journey.

An example of how my needs were changing was what happened one night in the fall of 2014, when Bernice and Robert had an event in St. John's. Robert told me they wouldn't be late, so I said that was fine. At about 8:00 p.m., however, I heard a beeping noise that really bothered me. I called Robert, and he listened to the sound over the phone.

He told me not to worry about it since it was just a reminder that the battery in the smoke detector needed replacing. But I couldn't stop worrying. A few minutes later, I called Mavis to come and see what was going on. Mavis felt as Robert did, that it was just a reminder to change the battery in the smoke detector. I was still not convinced, so I asked Mavis to call Robert again and tell him that I needed him to come home.

Within an hour, Robert and Bernice were home from the event in St. John's. When Robert replaced the battery in the smoke detector, all went back to normal. I was relieved, but now I felt quite badly that he and Bernice had to leave the event they were attending to come home on the whim of this old lady. After that, I spent more time thinking that I didn't want Robert and Bernice to go out because something else might happen. At the same time, I realized this was not reasonable and that they had given up a lot by having me here. Simply put, they deserved to be able to enjoy their time, especially now that Robert was no longer on dialysis.

Finally, in February 2016, I told Robert and Bernice that I wanted to visit a couple of retirement homes to see how I felt about possibly moving to one. They both appreciated what I was doing but insisted I stay here in the apartment. They suggested that if I wanted to try living in a retirement home, I go there in the summer, only for the period while they were on vacation. We agreed that might be a good thing, now that I was clearly not comfortable to be alone much anymore. I visited two retirement homes and decided to make arrangements to go to the Bay Roberts Retirement Centre for a six-week period in the summer.

The arrangements were made, and I was scheduled to go there on June 11, 2016. Then something happened that I could not understand. I woke up one morning and realized something was different about how I felt. I was a bit slower getting ready to go out to see Robert and Bernice. When I sat down and began to speak, the words didn't want to come out in the right order. Right away, Robert and Bernice suspected a stroke and arranged for me to see a doctor immediately. I did, and my family doctor reported that I did have a stroke, but there was no long-term damage.

One thing that became clear was that, as a result of that event, I had lost my ability to read. It was amazing. I felt well and could still talk, although maybe with a slight difference. I could think clearly, however the ability to read seemed to have been impacted quite a bit. I spent the rest of the spring with the help of Robert and Bernice trying to relearn how to read. It never came back fully, but it did improve a little.

While I was planning for the next stage of my life, Mavis was planning as well. She and her first husband had separated in 2011. In May 2016, joined by some family and friends in the Dominican Republic, she married Wesley Mitchell.

Apart from the stroke I'd had in February 2016, all went well, and in June 2016, as scheduled, I moved to the retirement centre and was very much enjoying being there. At first it was a little difficult to find my way to and from the dining room, but I eventually got used to it. I made friends there, especially with a Mrs. Mercer from Bay Roberts, who was much younger than me. She was such a kind and caring person.

I quickly became comfortable with the staff and residents and made the decision to stay there on a permanent basis. At that point, I thought, moving here is something maybe I should have considered earlier. Things were going along quite smoothly, but it wasn't long before I began to experience some more health issues. I found myself talking a lot—so much that it seemed I couldn't stop talking. As time went on, this worsened. I began saying something I intended to talk about, but the words I said seemed to be replaced by others that clearly did not make sense to the listener. My family and the staff were very supportive, but I knew they could not understand what I was attempting to say.

Then by early fall, I was lying in bed one morning and couldn't get up. This occurred twice, and the second time, the staff called Robert. When he came to my bedside, even though my speech had been so garbled, I said very clearly, "Robert, I can't get up!" Robert and a staff member helped me sit up, but I was unable to sit independently. Robert called the ambulance, which transported me directly to the emergency room at the Carbonear General Hospital.

As it turned out, after a long day at the hospital emergency room, where Sid and Robert, along with Bernice and other family members, took turns sitting with me, the medical staff determined I'd had a second stroke, accompanied with a significant bleed. Ultimately, though, the worst news was that I had developed brain cancer. At my age of ninety-three, this was terminal. I accepted this news with as much grace and dignity as I could muster for someone who was not yet ready to die.

32 — Edie

CAN I FINALLY FORGIVE?

2012–2016

In 1950, we built our house right next to the home of Agnes and Rudolph, who were roughly our age and with whom we became great friends. Bill, of course, had known them previously, and over the years the four of us and our children had been great neighbours and friends.

It seemed like our two families had children in roughly the same sequence, such that most of the children in one family had a friend in the other family who was approximately the same age. Throughout the years, all the children, in both families, frequently went back and forth to each other's houses.

The youngest of the neighbouring children, Karen Mercer, was similar in age and spent time playing with our youngest, Boyd. Long after those childhood friendships, Karen continued a close relationship with our family, especially Bill and me. I am reminded of a time when, as a child of about four or five, she had a bicycle accident that resulted in her sustaining a bad cut.

When anything in the local area occurred, such as an accident, the call usually went out, "Go get Edie." This was the case when I was asked to accompany Karen and her worried parents to the local medical centre. She had a significant cut on her head, and while talking with her, to help keep her calm, I also kept a steady pressure on the cut. When the doctor saw the wound, he decided to put her "to sleep," to close the gash with eleven stitches.

When Karen became an adult, she continued to stay in touch with us, and especially with me after Bill's passing. It was not unusual for me to receive a letter from or talk with Karen. I certainly had a lot of love and respect for this young woman.

Karen always remembered the incident when she cut her head and I accompanied her to the doctor. She told me her early memory of our relationship was after I returned from England, from my second trip back to visit family and to enjoy the Queen's Silver Jubilee, in 1977. When I returned to Newfoundland, I brought Karen back a little necklace with an attached pendant and a piece of peppermint candy, which was wrapped in the colours of the Union Jack.

We kept in touch, and one day when I was out in the garden attending my flowers, Karen, who by now was in high school, came out in their neighbouring back garden.

I asked her, "Karen, how are things in school?"

"Good, really. I have been studying about World War II and just saw the older film called *Bridge on the River Kwai* in the school auditorium," she answered.

I think Karen was surprised when I said, "Oh my, what a coincidence. My brother Sid was a prisoner of war there. Tragically, he died there as a result of horrible treatment at the hands of his Japanese captors."

Karen wanted to know more, so I shared with her how Sid had been captured during the Japanese invasion of Singapore and the whole story of his incarceration and treatment. We had a number of these discussions, which seemed to touch Karen deeply. In time, Karen left home for post-secondary school after finishing high school at Ascension Collegiate, but we stayed in touch.

Over twenty years later, Karen, now a nurse, who was married to an American army officer, Sean Blundon, was living in places practically all over the world. At one point, Karen found out that they would be transferred to Kuala Lumpur, Malaysia. Realizing they were going to be close to my brother Sid's final resting place, Karen had purchased a bouquet of red, white, and blue silk flowers, which she took with her to Malaysia in 2003. Karen was determined to visit Sid's gravesite for me. In the summer of 2004, accompanied by her husband and their three young daughters, she travelled to Thailand and visited "the bridge on the River Kwai" to learn more about my brother and the circumstances there during World War II. They visited the Commonwealth War Cemetery in Kanchanaburi, Thailand, where we believed Sid was buried. There, they began reading the burial markers, when someone yelled out and asked who they were looking for. Karen told the man who they were looking for, only to receive the response, "He's not here," and the person inquiring began to walk away. They followed him to a small office on the cemetery grounds, and he began a search in his records to locate Sid. This gentleman, who it turns out was the cemetery curator, did help them find out that my brother was buried not there but rather in Thanbyuzayat, Burma (now Myanmar).

The curator informed Karen that many British servicemen, including my brother, who had died within seventy kilometres of the Thai–Burma border during the building of the railroad, had been exhumed and reburied on the Burmese side of the border. The curator said he had documentation he believed had been smuggled out of camp by various members of Sid's regiment. He promised to send copies if he located them. About three weeks later, the material was sent to Karen. It outlined the horrific conditions in which the POWs lived and were forced to work, and in which many, including my brother Sid, died. Karen sent me a copy of this information. She and her family also attempted to travel to Burma in 2004, but because of local violence and instability, the trip had to be cancelled.

After her husband had been assigned to several other locations,

Karen and family eventually moved again to the Southeast Pacific area. They first went to Singapore, and then in 2012 to Malaysia. With the same bouquet of silk flowers in hand, Karen vowed that she was not leaving the area without placing the flowers on Sid's grave. And so, in July of 2015, Karen and Sean travelled to Rangoon, Burma (now Yangon, Myanmar). Even though that area of the world had been embroiled in civil strife for many years, Karen was true to her word.

With flowers, flags, and a flask in their possession, they began a seven-hour road trip to Thanbyuzayat, and the next morning on to the Commonwealth War Cemetery. Karen told me how they arrived mid-morning to a well-groomed row upon row of grave markers with a single large Cross, mid-centre to the multiple rows.

With the help of a guide and a translator, they found Sid's grave marker, within a few minutes, resting among another 3,000-plus servicemen from Britain, New Zealand, Australia, and other countries. I was glad that Karen described it as a "solemn and peaceful resting place for many forgotten, brave, young men and their souls."

After all these years, finally someone, so dearly close to me, had actually seen the bronze placard with raised lettering that showed the regiment number, emblem, and Sid's identifier. Karen and Sean were able to place a piece of blank paper over the grave marker and lightly, with a plain pencil, etch Sid's name and everything associated with his final resting place into the paper.

They placed a fairly large Union Jack flag at Sid's grave, and some smaller flags around graves nearby. Karen, with great care, placed the silk flowers, and Sean honoured my brother by having a "drink to his service and sacrifice."

Later, Karen assembled a photo/memory album, with side notes explaining the journey, enclosed the raised paper in a protector, and sent it to me for my birthday.

When I received the package from her, I was speechless. I found the pictures so very powerful. Opening this package about my brother's gravesite left me with a stronger emotional reaction than I could have ever imagined, so many years later.

I saw the picture of my brother's grave marker, and I ran my fingers over the picture and closed my eyes. My heart swelled, and tears ran freely. I imagined my Karen, so gently running her fingers over my brother's grave marker, as she knelt before it in the lush green grass before it a world away. Could I have possibly felt more connection to Sid even if I were there myself?

I don't think I was ever able to make complete peace with the people responsible for my brother's horrific death. But through the love, kindness, and generosity of spirit, my faithful and generous friend from next door helped me to be more at peace with Sid's death than at any time since I knew he had died seven decades ago.

I could never have imagined such a beautiful birthday gift. For the first time in years, my emotions poured out, releasing a burden that had always been present. It would be hard to imagine a better way to have honoured my dear brother and bring closure for me. I wished I could have told Mum and Dad.

Bill and his family have all passed on now, and so too have my two neighbours, Agnes and Rudolph. But I have a beautiful friendship still with my neighbours' youngest daughter, Karen. Both before and since the passing of her parents, she and her husband, Sean, and family have regularly returned for summer vacations at her parents' house next door.

Karen and I continued our relationship and visited together throughout the rest of my life. I was so proud of what my selfless young neighbour had achieved to help me move away from the years of hurt and bitterness and toward a greater sense of peace.

The best way for me to describe my feelings about what Karen had done is to say that, when we found out that Sid died and how he died, I felt a bitterness which has stayed with me all these years. How could I ever know then that, a whole world and a whole lifetime away, I would have a friend with such a beautiful soul who, by visiting my brother's gravesite, would give me such a level of comfort? I will always be grateful to her for this journey through time.

Conclusion — Robert

FOREVER ENGLAND

2016

If I should die, think only this of me:
That there's some corner of a foreign field
That is for ever England . . .
    — "The Soldier" by Rupert Brooke

Willie and Edie were born into two separate and very different worlds, and yet as a couple they worked through and overcame these differences and lovingly raised a family of six. Though challenged, together they provided their children with emotional stability, even in the darkest of times.

As I reflect on their lives, it seems their biggest objective was always that they do right by their children, grandchildren, and great-grandchildren. At some level, their story is about providing hope for people challenged by circumstance and adversity. My hope is that, through this story, others may find the courage, and most of all the support systems, to guide and protect them on that personal journey.

Edie was often seen by others as a staunch citizen of Britain and a person who embodied the "stiff upper lip" associated with British people generally. Make no mistake about it, she was always resolute when it came to protecting, advocating, and building a life for her family. But most of all, Edie dedicated her life to Willie, or Bill, of course, as only she called him. This was a life, at least from 1949, built from nothing but a small, tattered suitcase that she dragged from West Thurrock, England, to the bottom of Lundrigan's Lane, when she, Bill, and their two children found their way to meet Aunt Sis on that dreary April evening.

Throughout the years, Edie became the one depended on for handling local emergency situations, without ever being impeded by or even showing strong emotion herself. From her perspective, such unchecked emotion could interfere with the quick and objective decision-making required in these situations. It was only in her private notes that there could be found any evidence of the pain she felt personally while attending the needs of her husband and her family. Edie had a rather unique ability to separate and lock away her emotional response in various circumstances. It wasn't that she did not feel these emotions—rather, it was a matter of how and when she allowed them to surface. People in the community appeared to appreciate her calmness under pressure.

Willie was not able to hide or conceal his emotions. It seems that the experiences, especially during the over 2,100 days of service in Europe, that helped mould him, in the end betrayed him. Unlike Edie, he was not the one to be relied on in an emergency. He was not the parent who could always find the comforting words when someone needed them. He was not the one to be able to walk tall and proud at the Remembrance Day ceremonies. Yet he did everything possible to support his family and his community in ways that Edie never could. He was the person who spent much of his life supporting a variety of community organizations. And he was the one who seemed to seek out every person who was sick or just shut in or had some other need.

In Edie's case, there were times, when she attended a funeral or any emotionally difficult situation, where she rarely wept or showed strong emotion. She confided there were times she wished she could cry and "get it out," as she would say. Bill, however, sometimes wished the opposite and very much wanted to keep his emotions in check.

How much these differences resulted from genetic predispositions or from environmental influences is hard to say. We know that during the first half of the twentieth century, Britain and its people had been directly challenged by two World Wars. The very survival of this nation required a practical and useful response by individual citizens. There was no time for emotion to cloud judgment or interfere with the need for a timely and reasoned response. In Britain, being seen to be able to control emotions appears to have been very much a cultural expectation. That is the way Edie often characterized it, yet such an expectation was not part of Willie's early life.

Edie was very much a staunch defender of all things British. She was determined to be everything one could imagine the consummate British loyalist could ever be, for her Queen and country. She was born into somewhat of a modestly privileged life, compared to life here in Newfoundland at that time, yet she left it all for love.

Although Willie was a caring husband and father, Edie found herself being the one who her family turned to in order to keep everything together, even in the most difficult of times. Others might not have been able to navigate the difficult years better than circumstances forced her to do. And despite the strong connection to her family and her country, she did it without ever a consideration of leaving Newfoundland, Bill, or her Newfoundland family, to return to England.

Indeed, the powerful sense of separation from both her family, as well as from her way of life in England, was indelibly embedded in her mind. Yet her personal loyalty to Willie and her family could never permit her personal needs to take precedence over the life they had built together.

Several years ago, I met a woman who, although (or maybe because) she was so different than Edie, allowed a true understanding of Edie.

This lady appears to have lived a comfortable life and maybe even a financially privileged one. On one occasion, the issue of living in a small Newfoundland outport community was raised. This lady, obviously feeling very comfortable with her lot in life, in the small city of St. John's, made the comment that she could not allow herself to live "out in the bay."

That comment, figuratively, brought Edie's life in focus. Edie had already lived a level of some considerable comfort in a large urban setting in England during the 1930s. This, of course, was long before the "city lady" had even been born. The conditions of comfort, bordering on privilege, that were Edie's life could not have been imagined in Newfoundland during that time. Not likely even by those of the local Water Street merchant class. Subsequently, out of the strong sense of duty to her country and to her family, Edie and others like her had already faced high lev-

Bill (Willie) and Edie Lundrigan, circa 1994

els of danger during World War II. She then willingly moved to a part of the world where everything about this new Canadian province was probably less developed than what she and they had previously experienced. And she did so without ever flinching. I couldn't help but feel a strong sense of pride for her having chosen to leave a life of comfort for the hardship of early post-confederation Newfoundland.

I could muster only pity for the "city lady."

In the last part of her life, with her dearest husband and eldest daughter, Jean, having passed, and the children now, including Phil, living independent lives, Edie was preparing for her next journey.

Edie was living a quiet life. Before he passed, Willie and Edie celebrated sixty-one years of marriage. Looking back on those years, all but four of them in Newfoundland, it had been quite a journey. When asked would she do it again, she replied, "Yes, I would! I would do it, even with all the ups and downs, because without this journey, I would not have had Bill and we would not have the family that we have."

From growing up in the small village of West Thurrock, England, Edie lived an improbable life. Maybe this path she had travelled was always meant for her. It had certainly been a time of learning, and she had such strength to overcome waves of adversity and yet became a stronger person because of it.

Edie once commented, "I suppose everyone has a desire to feel that, when the end comes, they have lived a life of value, a life worth living."

There is little doubt that, alone, but also together with her Bill, she made her contribution to our world. Although that contribution may be seen by some as but a footnote in the pages of history, we can be certain it has benefited quite a number, including her now large and enduring family of twenty-three grandchildren and great-grandchildren.

Edie lived most of her life down in the Meadow in Upper Island Cove. She did not regret leaving England, but it pulled at her heartstrings even in her later years. Most of her English family had passed on, and after Lil passed in 2000, it is only Edie who was left. Life had changed, and in the country into which she was born, there was little of familiarity left to put her back there. Yet, in many ways, it always was home. Sweet memories of England seemed such an absorbing part of who she was.

In the early 1980s, she decided to become a citizen of Canada. After all, her children, and, by now, a large contingent of grandchildren, were Canadian citizens. Even Willie, to his ultimate protest and displeasure toward Canada, was indeed by default a Canadian citizen. Edie was initially proud of becoming a citizen of Canada, but as time passed, she regretted having given up her British citizenship to do so. In some ways she felt a sense of betrayal to her country of birth and of love.

Sadly, however, it would only be after she had passed that her family realized, quite by accident, that she had not given up her British citizenship. It turns out that Canada and Britain have a mutual agreement whereby, having become a citizen of Canada, she still retained her British citizenship.

At her request, the words "Forever England" had already been inscribed on her headstone. That headstone was put in place for their daughter Jean, Willie, and Edie when Jean died in June 2005. For some years since then, probably as a symbolic gesture of her love for and loyalty to Britain, she implored her family to swear that, after her death, the inscription "War Bride" should be carved on her headstone. She never knew that the headstone inscription "Forever England" was not only a symbolic gesture but a statement of fact, since her status as a British citizen had never changed.

Just like Willie before her, who died on November 10, ten years earlier, this fateful month of remembrance was approaching again. It would soon be time to rest. In her later years, Edie often reflected on her life, some of which I have attempted to paraphrase below.

As my life comes to an end, just like Bill before me, my journey will soon be over. Like him, the weakness in my body has prevented me from expressing the words I want to say to my dear family. I am unable to tell them how I have loved each of them from the moment I first saw them. I want to tell them how proud I am of the lives they have lived and the families they have raised.

I very much want to remind each of them to never forget their English heritage. I dearly want to make sure the "War Bride" inscription is placed on my headstone.

But then, they well know these things, and just as I lived, I should not now be asking for too much. I have had much time to tell my family all that is important for them and for me. Even if now my voice lies silent, my heart and my spirit are full, full of a good life, with a wonderful family to carry on a heritage and strength of character that, I believe, is such a part of who we are.

I truly thank my God for my unconquerable soul, yet I am aware of my mortality.

I am not afraid as I prepare for my final journey. I am anxious now, through passing, to find a sense of peace, and to especially find forgiveness, for a people, which has so long eluded me.

> *In the twinkle of an eye*
> *through time and space*
> *I have journeyed far*
> *England at my back*
> *as my family takes the lead*
> *ten years have gone, but*
> *we are bound together Bill,*
> *In November.*

At the age of ninety-three, after being in hospital for about three weeks, Edie simply fell off to sleep. Her family took turns keeping vigil and sharing that quiet but precious time with her in her palliative care room. Carbonear General Hospital is located near the ocean, overlooking Conception Bay. From many parts of the triangular-shaped building, you can look out over the bay, past the horizon, where lies the vast Atlantic Ocean as far as England itself.

That image would not have been lost on Edie, nor was it on her family who shared the last days there with her.

On November 1, 2016, the sun had just broken that eastern horizon. In the presence of her eldest son and dear brother's namesake, Sidney John, and his wife, Ivy, Edie silently breathed no more. With dignity and grace, she had slipped from this life to begin a new journey, unencumbered by the burdens so carried in this earthly life.

"Philip's Place"

That little bungalow, built by Willie and Edie, still sits proudly overlooking the ocean. Edie and Willie's son Phil continued to live at the family home, down in the Meadow, in Upper Island Cove. He as much as, if not more than, Edie and Willie before him, cherished that little bungalow as a living shrine to his parents and to the strength of the family's Newfoundland, Irish, and British roots. There wasn't a day when the Union Jack did not proudly fly from his flagpole. He held fast to the memories but also every morsel and trinket that previously belonged to his parents.

As many of his family and friends would know, Phil was a talented writer, but unfortunately his multiple illnesses and health challenges robbed and ultimately silenced his ability to be focused and engage in that craft. Each day, as I had been writing the initial draft of this manuscript, I called Phil, or he called me, and we talked extensively of the contents of this piece of writing. He was ecstatic that one of his siblings was writing this story of well-lived and full lives of our parents. Of course, in true Phil fashion, he made many suggestions for changes and/or other content or focus that had not been included. I incorporated many of his suggestions.

On May 9, 2022, Phil celebrated his sixty-second birthday. All his siblings, as well as many friends, visited him that day or connected through social media and shared in his celebration. But just five days later, around noon on Saturday, May 14, 2022, Phil's body failed to answer the call. He quietly passed away, finally being freed of his many physical struggles.

True to his wishes, on a beautifully calm and sunny Saturday morning in early July 2022, his ashes were spread over his father, Willie's, favourite fishing shoal of Crab Ledge. The next day, we held a memorial service in our back garden, which was attended by family and friends. Since then, the house that Edie and Willie built, and which was Phil's for the last fifteen years of his life, has been sold. The new owner has shown much respect to Phil by giving his new home the name "Philip's Place."

Phil left us with a touching note thanking us for supporting him and reminding us of the love of our parents.

"As a family, go forward together and love each other as our parents steadfastly loved each of us. I love all of you."

— Philip A. Lundrigan

Thank you for reading.

LOVE
&WAR

Acknowledgements

First and foremost, I give my humble thanks and endearing love to the primary characters in this writing, my dear parents, Edith and William Lundrigan. I am humbled to have been a child of your union.

For her unending support, as well as for her patience and skill in editing this document, my sincere thanks to my wife and partner, Bernice.

None of this would be possible without the almost constant love, support, and input of my siblings, Boyd Lundrigan, Philip Lundrigan (deceased during this writing process), Mavis Lundrigan Mitchell, and Sid Lundrigan.

For his encouragement and guidance for me to start and continue this project, I thank my long-time friend and author, Patrick J. Collins. Many thanks as well to Jack Harrington, Douglas Lundrigan, Melvin Mercer, Ida Linehan Young, and WritersNL for their thoughtful advice. I would also like to thank my publisher, Flanker Press.

And with such gratitude, I wish to thank many of my cousins, neighbours, and family friends, with very special mention to a dear family friend, Karen (Mercer) Blundon, for her contribution to the chapter "Can I Ever Forgive?"

PHOTO BY DARLENE STAMP

Robert W. Lundrigan was born and raised in the beautiful community of Upper Island Cove. There, the kindness of the people and the richness of the social fabric supported him in striving to be the best version of himself. He graduated from Memorial University and began his career working with the Newfoundland and Labrador Housing Corporation for three years. He then became an educator for the next twenty-nine years. After retiring from teaching, Robert spent the next fourteen years as a business and political consultant. He continues to write and enjoys his time with his wife, Bernice, their two adult children, and their families. Robert also loves spending early summer mornings in their small fishing boat.

Robert and Bernice have made the lovely community of Spaniard's Bay their home since 1980.

LOVE & WAR

Index

Andrews, Stephanie (Lundrigan) 198

Baggs, Rosanah (Lundrigan) 5, 124
Baggs, Walter 5, 11, 76, 124
Bakewell, Fred 112, 113
Bakewell, Lil (England) 22, 95, 96, 112, 165, 178, 201, 204, 218, 219, 258
Bishop, Ernest 185
Blundon, Karen (Mercer) 247-251
Blundon, Sean 249-251
Bowring, Tony 183
Butt, Mabel (Lundrigan) 8, 13-15, 133, 167, 193, 235
Button, Lonze 221

Chalker, James Ronald "Jim" 141
Chamberlain, Arthur Neville 20
Churchill, Winston Leonard Spencer 23, 24, 54, 83
Clarke, Joe 44
Clarke, Robert John 171
Clark, Mark 78
Coombs, Dick 30, 31, 41, 76
Coombs, Dorothy 160
Coombs, Harold 139, 154
Coombs, Martha 221
Coombs, Phoebe 139
Cox, Jack 219
Crane, Howard 225
Crane, Joe 6, 7, 12, 19, 147-150, 225
Crane, Mary Emma 160, 161
Crane, Nath 139, 154
Crane, Nellie 139, 178
Crosbie, John Chalker 207
Crowley, Angus 44

Dowling, Jack 29
Dowling, Jemima (Smith) 29
Drover, Arch 125, 137, 166, 202
Drover, George 30, 31, 76
Drover, Mary Margaret 157
Drover, Myra (Lundrigan) 8, 9,

11, 14, 29, 41, 137, 166, 167, 201
Drover, Theresa 186

Efford, Ruben John 203
England, Alfred Jr. "Alf" 22, 26, 27, 62, 94, 106, 179, 217
England, Alfred Sr. "Alf" 23, 24, 27, 63, 107, 178
England, Annie Louisa (Steel) 23, 27, 63
England, David 49
England, George 25
England, Harry 22, 62, 94, 106, 179, 217
England, Ruth (Chiddicks) 25
England, Sidney John Thomas "Sid" 22, 62-65, 94, 95, 99, 106-109, 217, 221, 248-251, 260
England, Wally 23
Eveleigh, Jean (Lundrigan) 108, 113, 119, 122, 124, 127, 131, 133, 134, 142-144, 157, 160, 164, 165, 168, 171, 173, 174, 178, 180, 182, 193, 196-198, 200, 205, 209, 217, 221, 223-226, 240, 257, 258
Eveleigh, Lloyd 174, 196, 197, 225
Eveleigh, Trevor 193, 196-198, 223, 224

Flynn, Paddy 27
Froude, Albert 44

Gosse, Harold 145
Greeley, Irene 187
Greeley, Leander 187
Greene, Robert 44
Gullage, Fred 44
Gushue, Patrick 44

Humphries, Dot 46
Hussey, Willie 173

Jones, Nath 154
Jones, William 150

Keeping, Heber 61
Kerr, Jack 90

Lester, Walt 58
Lundrigan, Andrew 220
Lundrigan, Angela 220
Lundrigan, Bernice (Roberts) 181, 193, 196-198, 209, 213, 222, 223, 226, 239, 240, 242-246
Lundrigan, Bertha 165, 166, 174, 175, 180
Lundrigan, Boyd 157, 160, 173, 174, 176, 180, 181, 188, 195, 204, 220, 225, 247
Lundrigan, Cavell 101, 142, 187,

208
Lundrigan, Clifford 188, 189
Lundrigan, Collin 196
Lundrigan, Craig 190, 196, 231
Lundrigan, Edward 5, 8, 11, 76, 77, 100, 101, 151, 217
Lundrigan, Edwin 101
Lundrigan, Elizabeth (Smith) "Aunt Sis" 124-129, 138, 176, 254
Lundrigan, Ian 2, 8, 9, 127, 135, 167, 174, 175, 180
Lundrigan, Ivy (Porter) 190, 196, 260
Lundrigan, Jennifer 196, 198
Lundrigan, Jessie 174, 175, 180
Lundrigan, John Howard 187
Lundrigan, Josiah "Joe" 101, 125, 154, 187, 189, 208
Lundrigan, Keith 196
Lundrigan, Maggie (Coaker) 157
Lundrigan, Mark 2, 16
Lundrigan, Mary (John's wife) 193
Lundrigan, Mary (John's daughter) 193
Lundrigan, Nancy (Jones) 204, 220
Lundrigan, Philip A. "Phil" 156, 157, 160, 168, 176, 180-182, 184, 188, 206, 209-211, 218, 219, 222, 223, 225, 226, 232, 239-242, 257, 260-262
Lundrigan, Ray 2, 8, 9, 11, 17, 18, 127, 135, 158, 159, 165-167, 170, 174, 180
Lundrigan, Sidney John "Sid" 108, 119, 122, 124, 126, 133, 134, 142-144, 151, 157, 160, 168, 171, 174, 180, 182, 188-191, 194, 196, 246, 260
Lynch, George "Deaney" 135
Lynch, Warren "Deaney" 151

McLeod, Roy 44
Mercer, Agnes 140, 166, 174, 202, 247, 251
Mercer, Betty 208
Mercer, David 140
Mercer, Dick 139
Mercer, Elijah "Lije" 7
Mercer, Fred 28, 171
Mercer, George 208
Mercer, Gordon 171
Mercer, Greg 200, 202
Mercer, Harris 144, 146
Mercer, Hayward 154, 193
Mercer, Jim "Jim Hann" 75
Mercer, Jim "Jimmy Dood" 15, 19, 150
Mercer, Nathan 50, 52, 53, 55, 56
Mercer, Ralph 150
Mercer, Roslyn 160

Mercer, Rudolph 140, 150, 166, 174, 202, 247, 251
Mitchell, Mavis (Lundrigan) 157, 160, 168, 176, 181-185, 188, 196, 200, 204, 225, 230, 231, 233, 244, 245
Mitchell, Wesley 245
Moore, Bertram Leslie 43
Moores, Frank Duff 187
Morris, Percy 44
Mouland, William 44
Mountbatten, Albert Victor Nicholas Louis 69
Murphy, Hank 187
Murrin, Ray 126

Nash, Leonard 44
Neil, Ed 187

Osbourne, Wilbur 6, 7, 12, 13
Ottenheimer, Gerald Ryan "Gerry" 187

Paddock, James H. 44
Parsons, Churchill 39, 40, 44
Parsons, Kay 139
Parsons, Mary 193
Power, John 44
Pynn, Clarence 60

Reid, Les 138, 154, 165, 166
Reid, Lydia (Lundrigan) 8, 9, 11, 29, 41, 138, 165-167
Roche, Francis J. 44
Rogers, Max 150
Roosevelt, Franklin Delano 54
Rowsell, Fred 201, 202

Sharpe, Sus 157
Sheppard, George 44
Sheppard, Lewis 145
Sheppard, William 150
Simms, Ernest 60
Smallwood, Joseph Roberts "Joey" 141, 187
Smith, E. E. 34
Smith, Flo 35
Smith, Mary 35
Smith, Theodore 144
Smith, Will Duncan 142-144
Squires, Adrienne 220, 231
Squires, Christopher 205
Squires, Kevin 196, 220

Wall, Jan 91-93
Whelan, James 44
Wynter, William 44

Young, Bertha 15, 142
Young, Haig 187
Young, John 15
Young, Will "Budget" 19